Voices of the HOLOCAUST

10/00

Voices of the HOLOCAUST

VOLUME 1

Antisemitism
Escalation
Holocaust

LORIE JENKINS
McELROY

DETROIT • NEW YORK • LONDON

REF
940.5318

VOI

Voices of the
HOLOCAUST

Lorie Jenkins McElroy, Editor

Staff

Elizabeth Des Chenes, *U·X·L Senior Developmental Editor*
Carol DeKane Nagel, *U·X·L Managing Editor*
Thomas L. Romig, *U·X·L Publisher*

Margaret Chamberlain, *Permissions Specialist*
Shalice Shah, *Permissions Associate*

Shanna P. Heilveil, *Production Assistant*
Evi Seoud, *Production Manager*
Mary Beth Trimper, *Production Director*

Tracey Rowens, *Art Director*
Cynthia Baldwin, *Product Design Manager*
Linda Mahoney, *Typesetting*

Library of Congress Cataloging-in-Publication Data

Voices of the Holocaust/Lorie Jenkins McElroy, editor
    p. cm.
    Includes bibliographical references and index.
    Contents: v. 1. Antisemitism, escalation, holocaust—2. Resisters, liberation, understanding.
    Summary: Presents six theme-based original documents, such as speeches, letters, and book excerpts, from 1020 to approx. 1950, which examine the Holocaust.
    ISBN 0-7876-1746-6 (set: alk. paper). — ISBN 0-7876-1747-4 (v. 1: alk. paper).— ISBN 0-7876-1748-2 (v. 2: alk. paper)
    1. Holocaust, Jewish (1939-1945)—Juvenile literature. 2. Righteous Gentiles in the Holocaust—Juvenile literature. 3. Anti-Nazi movement—Juvenile literature. 4. World War, 1939-1945—Jews—Rescue
    Juvenile literature. [1. Holocaust, Jewish (1939-1945). 2. Righteous Gentiles in the Holocaust. 3. Anti-Nazi movement. 4. World War, 1939-1945—Jews—Rescue.]
    I. McElroy, Lorie Jenkins.
    D804.34.V66. 1998
    940. 53' 18—dc21
                                                        97-33195
                                                        CIP AC

Printed in the United States of America
10 9 8 7 6 5 4 3 2

contents

Bold type indicates volume numbers
Regular type indicates page numbers

volume 1

antisemitism 1: 1

escalation

holocaust

volume 2

resisters 2: 253

liberation 2: 348

reader's guide

V oices of the Holocaust presents 34 excerpted documents written by people whose lives were forever changed by the events of the Holocaust. The autobiographical essays, diary entries, newspaper articles, court transcripts, letters, and reminiscences in these two volumes reflect the experiences of oppressors, resisters, liberators, witnesseses, and survivors. Some entries, such as the selections from Adolf Hitler's memoir *Mein Kampf* or Albert Speer's *Inside the Third Reich,* explore the development and inner workings of the Nazi regime. Other excerpts, including Janina David's *A Square of Sky,* Gonda Redlich's *Terezin Diary,* and Kim Malthe-Bruun's *Heroic Heart,* reflect the horrors faced by ordinary citizens during the Holocaust years. The search for justice and understanding is the focus of documents such as *Eichmann in Jerusalem* by Hannah Arendt, *Maus* by Art Spiegelman, and "Why I Write" by Elie Wiesel.

Format

Both *Voices of the Holocaust* volumes are divided into three chapters. Each of the six chapters focus on a specific theme: Antisemitism, Escalation, Holocaust, Resisters, Liberation, and Understanding. Every chapter opens with an historical overview, followed by four to seven document excerpts.

Each excerpt is divided into six sections:

- **Introductory material** places the document and its author in an historical context

- **Things to Remember** offers readers important background information about the featured text

- **Excerpt** presents the document in its original spelling and format

- **What happened next...** discusses the impact of the document on both the speaker and his or her audience

- **Did you know...** provides interesting facts about each document and its author

- **For Further Reading** presents sources for more information on documents and speakers

Additional Features

Many of the *Voices of the Holocaust* entries contain a short boxed biography on the speaker. In addition, call-out boxes within entries examine related events and issues, while black-and-white illustrations help illuminate the text. Each excerpt is accompanied by a glossary running alongside the primary document that defines terms, people, and ideas. Both volumes contain a timeline of important events and cumulative index.

Comments and Suggestions

We welcome your comments and suggestions for documents to feature in future editions of *Voices of the Holocaust.* Please write: Editor, *Voices of the Holocaust,* U·X·L, 835 Penobscot Bldg., Detroit, Michigan, 48226-4094; call toll free: 1-800-347-4253; or fax: 313-961-6347.

acknowledgments

S pecial thanks are due for the invaluable comments and suggestions provided by the Holocaust Reference Library advisors:

Dr. William J. Shulman, President, Association of Holocaust Organizations, and Director, Holocaust Resource Center & Archives in New York; Linda Hurwitz, Director, The Holocaust Center in Pittsburgh, Pennsylvania; Max Weitz, Director, Holocaust Resource Center of Minneapolis, Minnesota; Jonathan Betz-Zall, Children's Librarian, Sno-Isle Regional Library System, Edmonds, Washington; and Debra Lyman Gniewek, Library Services Coordinator, Office of Information Technology, School District of Philadelphia, Pennsylvania.

The editor extends added thanks to Ina Gallon for her careful and thoughtful research and material selection, and to Don Sauvigne for his assistance throughout the project. Acknowledgment also goes to the staff of the United States Holocaust Memorial Museum in Washington, D.C., for its help with photographs and research material.

HOLOCAUST timeline

1899 Houston Stewart Chamberlain publishes *The Foundations of the Nineteenth Century,* a book that uses racialism to explain European history.

1903 Russian antisemites circulate *The Protocols of the Elders of Zion,* a forgery that describes the master plan of an alleged Jewish conspiracy to dominate the world.

1923 Alfred Rosenberg reissues an official Nazi party version of *The Protocols.*

1925 Adolf Hitler describes his racial beliefs concerning the superiority of German people and the inferiority of Jews in his memoir *Mein Kampf* ("My Struggle").

1933 Adolf Hitler becomes Chancellor of Germany and appoints Joseph Goebbels as Reich Minister of Public Enlightenment and Propaganda.

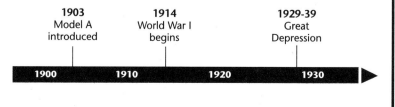

1903
Model A
introduced

1914
World War I
begins

1929-39
Great
Depression

1900   1910   1920   1930

1933 Inge Deutshkron, a young Jewish girl living in Berlin, witnesses a nation-wide boycott against Jewish-owned businesses.

1933 The Nazis conduct book burnings and impose censorship throughout Germany.

1935 The Nazi government orders Franziska Schwartz, a deaf German teenager, to appear at a health center for sterilization.

1935 Wilhelm Frick drafts the Nuremberg Laws, which deny German citizenship rights to Jews and prohibit marriage and sexual relationships between Jews and non-Jews.

1936 Participation in Hitler Youth becomes mandatory. All ten-year-old boys are required to register at government offices for group membership.

1938 *New York Times* reporter Otto D. Toliscus gives an account of the two-day campaign of violence against Jews known as "Kristallnacht."

1939 Several hundred Jews attempt to emigrate from Germany on board the steamship *St. Louis,* but are forced to return to Europe.

1939 Wilhelmine Haferkamp and other fertile German women receive the Mother's Cross, a medal honoring their child-bearing accomplishments.

1939 In accordance with the principles of the Jehovah Witness faith, young Elisabeth Kusserow refuses to salute the Nazi flag and is sent to reform school for six years.

1939 Adolf Hitler appoints Hans Frank Governor-General of certain sections of Poland that later become the "resettlement" areas for Jews and others deemed unfit for Reich citizenship.

1933
Japan quits
League of
Nations

1936
Spanish Civil
War begins

1939
Germany
invades
Poland

| 1933 | 1935 | 1937 | 1939 |

1939 Reinhardt Heydrich issues a directive to Nazi task forces ordering the "resettlement" of Jewish Poles to urban centers near railroad lines.

1940 Writing in his diary, Chaim A. Kaplan records his observations about the formation of a Jewish ghetto in the Polish city of Warsaw.

1940 The Warsaw ghetto becomes "closed," sealing Janina David and her parents off from surrounding neighborhoods.

1940 The Nazis imprison Christian Reger for defying the state-sponsored religion known as the German Faith Movement.

1941 Rudolph Höss, Commandant of the Auschwitz concentration camp, oversees the first experiments using poisonous gas for the extermination of large masses of human beings.

1941 Avraham Tory, a Lithuanian Jew, survives a Nazi-ordered "action" that removes nearly 10,000 people from the Kovno ghetto, about half of whom are children.

1941 Gonda Redlich arrives at the ghetto in Theresienstadt, Czechoslovakia, which the Nazis portray as a "model Jewish settlement."

1942 A small group of high-ranking Nazi party and government officials meet to discuss the "Final Solution," a code name for their plan to eliminate all European Jews.

1942 Anne Frank and her family move into a secret annex built on the top stories of a house in Amsterdam.

1942 Etty Hillesum assists new arrivals at the Westerbork transit camp where Dutch Jews are held before deportation to death camps in Poland.

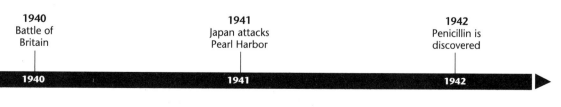

1940
Battle of Britain

1941
Japan attacks Pearl Harbor

1942
Penicillin is discovered

1940   1941   1942

1942 Hirsch Grunstein and his brother go into hiding in Belgium to escape the Nazis. The boys stay with a couple who volunteers to give them shelter.

1942 Wladyslaw Bartoszewski, a Catholic Polish resister, helps form a Jewish relief committee called Zegota.

1943 Hans and Sophie Scholl are arrested on a Munich university campus for distributing pamphlets for the White Rose resistance group.

1943 After abandoning his university studies to fight fascism, a young Jewish Italian man named Primo Levi is captured by the Nazis and sent to Auschwitz.

1944 Corrie Ten Boom and her family are imprisoned by the Gestapo for their involvement in an underground operation to aid Jews in Holland.

1944 Hannah Senesh, a Jew living in Palestine, parachutes behind enemy lines as part of a British-sponsored rescue mission to reach Jews and other resisters.

1944 A young Swedish businessman named Raoul Wallenberg arrives in Hungary to help save the surviving Jews trapped in Budapest.

1944 Oskar Schindler seeks permission from the Nazis to spare Jewish prisoners from death by employing them at a munitions factory in Czechoslovakia.

1944 Kim Malthe-Bruun joins the Danish resistance movement and is arrested by the Gestapo.

1945 American reporter Edward R. Murrow broadcasts his impressions of the Buchenwald concentration camp shortly after its liberation.

1945 British forces liberate French prisoner Fania Fénelon from the Bergen-Belson concentration camp in northern Germany.

1943
Warsaw
ghetto
uprising

1944
Battle of
Leyte Gulf

1945
World War II
ends

| 1943 | 1944 | 1945 | 1946 |

1945 Heinrich Himmler, the senior Nazi official responsible for overseeing the mass murder of six million European Jews, is captured by the Allies and commits suicide.

1945 Robert H. Jackson gives the opening address for America before the International Military Tribunal at Nuremberg.

1947 Survivor Simon Wiesenthal forms the Jewish Historical Documentation Center in Austria to track down Nazi war criminals.

1957 After emigrating to the United States, Gerda Weissmann Klein writes a memoir called *All But My Life*.

1960 Elie Wiesel publishes *Night,* an autobiographical account of his experiences during the Holocaust.

1961 Hannah Arendt attends the trial of Adolf Eichmann, a notorious Nazi criminal who fled to Argentina after the war.

1970 After serving 20 years in prison, former Nazi Albert Speer publishes his autobiography *Inside the Third Reich.*

1992 Art Spiegelman wins a Pulizer Prize for *Maus,* a cartoon-style novel about the author's experiences as a child of Holocaust survivors.

1993 The United States Holocaust Memorial Museum opens in Washington, D.C.

1997 Riva Shefer, a 75-year-old Latvian Jew who survived a Nazi labor camp, becomes the first recipient of money from a $200 million Swiss fund established to aid Holocaust survivors.

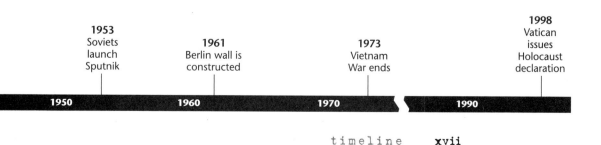

1953 Soviets launch Sputnik

1961 Berlin wall is constructed

1973 Vietnam War ends

1998 Vatican issues Holocaust declaration

1950   1960   1970   1990

credits

The editors wish to thank the copyright holders of the excerpted documents included in this volume and the permissions managers of many book and magazine publishing companies for assisting us in securing reproduction rights. What follows is a list of the copyright holders who have granted us permission to reproduce material for *Voices of the Holocaust*. Every effort has been made to trace copyright, but if omissions have been made, please contact the publisher.

Arendt, Hannah. From *Eichmann in Jerusalem: A Report on Banality of Evil.* Penguin Books, 1994. Copyright © by Hannah Arendt, 1963, 1964. Copyright renewed by Lotte Kohler, 1991, 1992. All rights reserved. Reproduced by permission.

Bartoszewski, Wladyslaw. From The *Warshaw Ghetto: A Christian's Testimony.* Translated by Stephen G. Cappellari. Beacon Press, 1987. © 1987 Beacon Press. Reproduced by permission.

David, Janina. From *A Square of Sky: Recollections of My Childhood.* W. W. Norton & Company, Inc, 1964. Copyright © 1964 by Janina David. Renewed 1982. Reproduced by permission.

Deutschkren, Inge. From *Outcast: A Jewish Girl in Wartime Berlin*. Translated by Jean Steinberg. Fromm International Publishing Corporation, 1989. Translation copyright © 1989 Fromm International Publishing Corporation. Reproduced by permission.

Fénelon, Fania with Marcelle Routier. From *Playing for Time*. Atheneum, 1977. English translation copyright © 1977 by Michael Joseph Ltd and Atheneum Publishers. All rights reserved. Reproduced by permission of Michael Joseph, Ltd. In the U.S. by Atheneum, a division of Simon & Schuster, Inc.

Frank, Anne. From *The Diary of A Young Girl: The Definitive Edition*. Edited by Otto H. Frank & Mirjam Pressler, translated by Susan Massotty. Bantam Books, 1995. English translation copyright © 1995 by Doubleday, a division of Bantam Doubleday Dell Publishing Group, Inc. Reproduced by permission of Bantam Books, a division of Bantam Doubleday Dell Publishing Group, Inc.

Friedman, Ina R. From *The Other Victims: FirstPerson Stories of Non-Jews Persecuted by the Nazis*. Houghton Mifflin Company, 1990. Copyright © 1990 by Ina R. Friedman. All rights reserved. Reproduced by permission.

Friedman, Saul S. From *The Terezin Diary of Gonda Redlich*. Translated by Laurence Kutler. The University Press of Kentucky, 1992. Copyright © 1992 by The University Press of Kentucky. Reproduced by permission of The University Press of Kentucky.

Greene, Bette. From *Summer of My German Soldier*. The Dial Press, 1973. Copyright © 1973 by Bette Greene. All rights reserved. Reproduced by permission.

Haferkamp, Wilhelmine. From "Motherhood Times Ten, and Food to Spare," in *Frauen: German Women Recall the Third Reich*, by Alison Owings. Rutgers University Press, 1993. Copyright © 1993 by Alison Owings. All rights reserved. Reproduced by permission.

Hillesum, Etty. From *An Interrupted Life—The Diaries, 1941-1943 and Letters from Westerbork*. Translated by Arnold J. Pomerans. Pantheon Books, 1986. Copyright © 1986 by Random House, Inc. Reproduced by permission.

Höss, Rudolph. From *Death Dealer: The Memoirs of the SS Kommandant at Auschwitz*. Edited by Steven Paskuly, translated by Andrew Pollinger. Prometheus Books, 1992. Copyright © 1992 by Steven Paskuly. All rights reserved. Reproduced by permission.

Jens, Inge. From *At the Heart of the White Rose: Letters and Diaries of Hans and Sophie Scholl.* Edited by Inge Jens, translated by J. Maxwell Brownjohn. Harper & Row, Publishers, 1987. © 1987 HarperCollins Publishers, Inc. Reproduced by permission of Harpercollins Publishers, Inc.

Kaplan, Chaim A. From *Scroll of Agony: The Warsaw Diary of Chaim A. Kaplan.* Translated and edited by Abraham I. Katsh. Collier Books, 1973. Copyright © 1963, 1973 by Abraham I. Katsh. All rights reserved. Reproduced by Hamish Hamilton Ltd. In the U.S. reproduced by permission of Macmillan Publishing Company, a division of Simon & Schuster, Inc.

Keneally, Thomas. From *Schindler's List.* Touchstone Book, 1982. Copyright © 1982 by Serpentine Publishing Co. Pty, Ltd. Reproduced by permission.

Klein, Gerda Weissmann. *From All But My Life.* Hill and Wang, 1995. Copyright © 1957, 1995 by Gerda Weissmann Klein. Reproduced by permission of Hill and Wang, a division of Farrar, Straus and Giroux, Inc.

Levi, Primo. From *Survival in Auschwitz: The Nazi Assault on Humanity.* Translated by Stuart Woolf. Collier Books, 1993. Reproduced by permission.

Malthe-Bruun, Kim. From *Heroic Heart.* Edited by Vibeke Malthe-Bruun, translated by Gerry Bothmer. Random House, 1955. Copyright, 1955, renewed 1983 by Random House, Inc. All rights reserved. Reproduced by permission.

Murrow, Edward R. From *In Search of Light: The Broadcasts of Edward R Murrow, 1938-1961.* Alfred A. Knopf, 1967. © Copyright 1967 by the Estate of Edward R. Murrow. Reproduced by permission.

New York Times, November 11, 1938. Copyright © 1938, renewed 1966 by The New York Times Company. Reproduced by permission.

Rosenberg, Maxine B. From *Hiding to Survive: Stories of Jewish Children Rescued from the Holocaust.* Clarion Books,

1994. Copyright © 1994 Maxine B. Rosenberg. Reproduced by permission.

Senesh, Hannah. From *Hannah Senesh: Her Life & Diary.* Schocken Books, 1972. Copyright © Nigel Marsh, 1971. Reproduced by permission.

Speer, Albert. From *Inside the Third Reich.* Translated by Richard and Clara Winston. Galahad Books, 1995. Copyright © 1970 by the Macmillan Company. All rights reserved. Reproduced by permission George Weidenfeld & Nicolson Limited. In the U.S. reproduced by permission of Macmillan Publishing Company, a divison of Simon & Schuster, Inc.

Spiegelman, Art. From *Maus II: A Survivor's Tale: And Here My Troubles Began.* Pantheon Books, 1991. Copyright © 1986, 1989, 1990 1991 by Art Spiegelman. All rights reserved. Reproduced by Pantheon Books, a division of Random House, Inc.

Tory, Avraham. From *Surviving the Holocaust.* Edited by Martin Gilbert, translated by Jerzy Michalowicz. Cambridge, MA: Harvard University Press, 1990. Copyright © 1990 by the President and Fellows of Harvard College. Reproduced by permission.

Wallenberg, Raoul. From *Letters and Dispatches, 1924-1944.* Translated by Kjersti Board. Arcade Publishing, 1995. Translation copyright © 1995 by Arcade Publishing, Inc. Reproduced by permission.

Wiesel, Elie. From *From the Kingdom of Memory: Reminiscences.* Schocken Books, 1995. Copyight © 1990 by Elirion Associates, Inc. Reproduced by permission.

Wiesenthal, Simon. From *The Murderers among Us.* McGraw-Hill Company, 1967. Copyright © 1967 by Opera Mundi, Paris. Reproduced by permission of the author.

The photographs appearing in *Voices of the Holocaust* were received from the following sources:

On the cover: Elie Wiesel (**Courtesy of Archive Photos. Reproduced by permission.**).

United States Holocaust Memorial Museum (USHMM) Photo Archives. Reproduced by permission: 3, 4, 20, 27, 35, 40, 47, 49, 50, 76, 79, 83, 95, 99, 109, 140, 146,

Voices of the HOLOCAUST

antisemitism

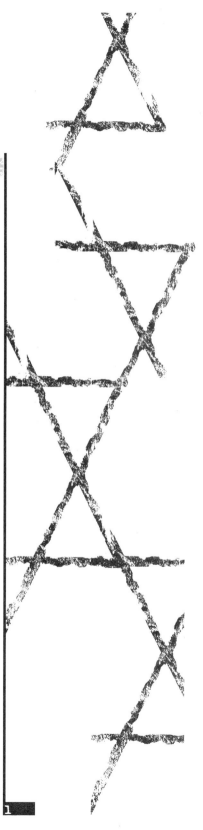

Antisemitism, or hatred of people of the Jewish faith, is believed to have begun throughout Europe during the Middle Ages. The cycle of anti-Jewish sentiment that intensified in Germany after World War I (1914-1918) originated in the eastern and central countries of Europe, where large Jewish minorities lived. Jews were thought to be responsible for spreading ideas about communism, Marxism, democracy, and other controversial political ideologies—ideologies that advocated "rule by the people" and caused Russian imperial (royal) rule to topple. In Russia, antisemitism took a violent turn when organized mobs began attacking Jews. In 1903 the secret czarist police circulated a forged document called *Protocols of the Elders of Zion* to justify their murderous riots. The *Protocols* allegedly contain the minutes of a secret meeting of Jewish leaders who were planning to take over the world.

Members of the nationalistic movement in Germany quickly used the *Protocols* forgery in the antisemitic campaign raging within their own country. Defeat in World War I had devastated the morale of German citizens. Rampant unemployment, economic insecurity, and a chaotic political situation combined to create a climate where many Germans felt they were victims of negative outside influences. Although Jews represented less than one percent of the German population, angry nationalist groups blamed them for the troubles and instability facing Germany in the 1920s and 1930s. Many nationalists also believed in racialism, or racial doctrine. First introduced by scholars in the mid-1800s, racialism proposed that all races are *not* created equal. Although this philosophy existed in many countries, the idea of a "master race" thrived particularly well in Germany.

One nationalist party, the National Socialist German Workers' party (or the Nazi party), grew increasingly in size and popularity. According to **Nazi racial doctrine**, Germans were descendants of a master race—the "Aryan" race. Nazi racialists viewed all history as a struggle between the supreme Aryan race and the corrupting influences of inferior races. The Nazis mistakenly viewed Jews as members of a distinctive, substandard race and considered them to be the most dangerous threat to the survival of the German nation.

Racialism played a critical role in the Nazi regime led by **Adolf Hitler**, who ruled Germany from 1933 to 1945. Hitler describes his philosophies in his semiautobiographical book *Mein Kampf* (*My Struggle*). Written in 1923, *Mein Kampf* became the bible of the growing Nazi party. According to Hitler, the resurrection of the German nation could only be achieved by understanding—and solving—"the Jewish problem." As the popularity of the Nazi party grew in the late 1920s and early 1930s, people around the world read Hitler's book. While many of his followers took his ideas seriously, others dismissed his ravings as too outrageous to cause serious concern.

As soon as Hitler became chancellor of Germany on January 30, 1933, he moved quickly to dismantle the democratic processes taking place within the German nation. Once he had created a dictatorship (government by a single, and often unjust, ruler), he focused his attention on instituting anti-Jewish measures. **Inge Deutschkron** gives her account of living in Berlin (the German capital) as a ten-year-old Jewish girl

Deutsche, verteidigt Euch
gegen die jüdische
Greuelpropaganda,
kauft
nur bei Deutschen!

Germans defend
yourselves against jewish
atrocity propaganda
buy only at German shops!

when Hitler came to power. She vividly recalls how her father barely escaped arrest for his political activities in the Social Democratic party, which opposed the Nazi party. Deutsch-kron also gives a firsthand report of the boycott against Jewish businesses on April 1, 1933. This boycott was the first Nazi-organized, nationwide anti-Jewish action.

One month after the boycott, Hitler staged a dramatic demonstration of **Nazi censorship** by conducting a massive book burning campaign. Parades of Nazi members and storm troopers marched through German cities and towns by torch-light. They raided libraries and bookstores, removing contro-

*A page from an antisemitic German children's book called **Der Giftpilz** (**The Poisonous Mushroom**).*

versial books on political and social philosophies that clashed with the Nazi way of thinking. The banned books were then thrown into raging bonfires, creating a spectacle that caught the world's attention.

After the terror-filled years of 1933 and 1934, many German Jews mistakenly hoped the **Nuremberg Laws** would help reestablish a degree of stability. These laws denied German citizenship to people of "non-German blood." Marriage and sexual relations between Jews and non-Jews were forbidden. A supplemental, or added, decree defined a Jew as anyone who had three or four Jewish grandparents. For the first time in modern history, a state defined its citizenship based on race. As the efforts to eliminate Jews from Germany grew more extreme after 1938, the definition of who was to be considered Jewish continued to entangle Nazi policymakers.

Frau Wilhelmine Haferkamp was twenty-two years old and pregnant with her fourth child when Hitler came to power in 1933. Consistent with Nazi aspirations, the Hafer-kamps had many more children during the 12 years of the Third Reich (as rule by the Nazi government was called). To achieve his goal of building a so-called "superrace" of Aryans, Hitler banned birth control and abortion and offered financial aid to worthy, racially pure Aryan families. Frau Haferkamp tells how she risked her own safety and that of her family by giving food to Nazi prisoners who worked near her home.

Haferkamp also discusses how the Nazi party pressured Germans to enroll their children in special youth programs such as **Hitler Youth**. Hitler believed the children of Germany represented the greatest potential for the future of the Third Reich. He created a broad-based organization dedicated to teaching Nazi beliefs and creating intense party loyalty among all the young people of Germany. By training young men and boys to become Nazis, the Hitler Youth organization played an important role in World War II (1939-1945). Throughout the war, the organization provided a steady supply of highly dedicated Nazis who were willing to fight fearlessly and ferociously for the German dream of Aryan domination.

Protocols of the Elders of Zion

First published in the
Russian newspaper *Znamya*
("The Banner")

August 26-September 7, 1903

Defeat in World War I (1914-1918) devastated the morale of German citizens. (World War I grew out of a struggle for power and territory in Europe. The German effort to expand their empire split European nations into two camps: Austria, Germany, Turkey, Italy, and Bulgaria fought against the combined powers—also called the Allied powers—of Serbia, Russia, France, and Britain, as well as the United States.) Mourning the end of imperial rule (rule by an emperor), Germans resented the democratic Weimar Republic (the German government established after World War I), which had been imposed upon them by the Treaty of Versailles. (The Treaty of Versailles was the peace treaty Germany had been forced to sign after losing World War I. Its terms were quite harsh and included the strict limitation of German armed forces; the loss of significant amounts of German territory; an admission that Germany was responsible for starting the war; and payments or reparations over many years to the Allied forces, especially to France, for the enormous destruction caused by the war.)

The newly formed republic faced serious challenges from two opposing political movements within Germany: (1) communist influences (based on a political and economic theory that advocates the formation of a classless society through the communal, or group, ownership of all property) and (2) a zealous nationalistic movement called *voelkisch*, meaning "of the people." (Extreme nationalists had a twisted notion of patriotism and felt that loyalty to Germany should be placed above all else.) Economic problems further complicated the political turmoil in postwar Germany. The punitive (or punishing) reparations and naval blockades imposed on Germany disrupted commerce significantly. Severe inflation and the 1929 New York stock market crash brought further trouble to an already struggling economy.

Rampant unemployment, economic insecurity, and the chaotic political situation combined to create a climate where many Germans felt they were victims of negative outside influences. Increasingly violent nationalist groups believed that the introduction of foreign ideas such as democracy (government by the people) from the West and communism from the East had contaminated their beloved country. Angry nationalists blamed Jewish people in particular for the troubles and instability facing Germany in the 1920s and 1930s.

The first signs of antisemitism (hatred or prejudice against Jews) showed up throughout Europe during the Middle Ages. The wave of antisemitism that intensified in Germany after World War I (1914-1918) originated in eastern and central Europe, where large Jewish minorities lived. In Russia, antisemitism took a deadly turn when organized mobs began attacking local Jews. These violent riots and massacres, called *pogroms,* occurred in Russia between 1881 and 1920.

As early as 1903, Russian antisemites circulated a forged document called the *Protocols of the Elders of Zion* to justify the pogroms. The *Protocols* pamphlet reads like a factual first-hand report of a secret meeting of Jewish elders who are planning to take over the world. The instigators of the pogroms relied upon this forged document to legitimize, or support, the escalating violence that brutally killed 100,000 Jews in Russia between 1918 and 1920. When antisemitic army officers fled to Germany after the Russian Revolution, they brought the controversial and hateful *Protocols* with them. (The 1917 Russian Revolution ended the monarchy, or royal rule, in Russia and resulted in the formation of the communist Soviet Union.)

Members of the nationalistic movement in Germany quickly moved to use the *Protocols* forgery in the antisemitic campaign raging within their own country. Many nationalistic groups advocated antisemitism and retold history as a struggle between the Aryan race (a term used to refer to Germans) and Jews. Although Jews represented less than one per-

Nazi Racial Doctrine

The other founders of the Nazi party (the National Socialist German Workers' party) believed devoutly in the idea of a superior race. According to party philosophy, the history of all civilizations reveals a struggle between the supreme Aryan, or German, race and the corrupting influences of other, inferior races. Party members felt the Jewish people represented the most dangerous threat to the survival of the German nation, and viewed Jews as a negative force in history, destined to destroy and disrupt Aryan progress.

In the mid-1850s, French writer Arthur Comte de Gobineau published one of the most influential books ever written on the topic of racial-ism. His four-volume work, called *Essays on the Inequality of Human Races,* contains controversial theories of race superiority and the importance of racial purity. Many Germans used Gobineau's ideas to give credibility to "antisemitism," a loosely organized movement opposed to Jews. In 1879 German racialist Wilhelm Marr coined the phrase "antisemitism," which means prejudice against Jews. Marr established the Anti-Semitic League as the first political organization devoted to the promotion of hatred toward Jews.

Houston Stewart Chamberlain, an Englishman who became a German citizen, wrote another popular the-

cent of the German population, many people blamed the Jews for the nation's defeat in World War I and the failing economy that followed. In truth, thousands of Jewish men had served in the German army during the war, and many had received military honors.

German Jews tended to live in cities such as Hamburg and Berlin and were concentrated in certain professions and occupations associated with urban society. As economic difficulties persisted in Germany, the perception arose that all Jews were wealthy and in fact benefited financially at the expense of non-Jews. The *Protocols* provided the type of evidence many Germans needed to become convinced of the

(Continued from previous page)

ory of racial doctrine. Published in Munich, Germany, in 1899, *The Foundations of the Nineteenth Century* attempts to trace all of Europe's history according to race ideology. Chamberlain credits the Teutons, an ancient Germanic race, as being a creative, regenerative force in history; conversely, he labels the Jews as an alien, disruptive influence.

The ideas of Gobineau and Chamberlain led to the development of eugenics (pronounced you-JEH-nix), a pseudoscience (pronounced SUE-doe-science; meaning theories that are wrongly regarded as scientific) devoted to controlled race breeding. While eugenics received a small degree of support in both the United States and Europe in the 1920s and 1930s, the Nazis actually incorporated its ideals into their own national, social, and political policies.

Proponents of racial doctrine established "scientific" criteria to identify members of the true Aryan race. In classrooms throughout Germany, Nazi teachers were required to measure and record physical attributes of their students such as skull size, hair color, and eye color. This commitment to preserve the "master race" led the Nazis to deport and eventually exterminate those they felt represented a risk to the purity of German blood.

supposedly evil nature and influence of Jews. The sense of mysticism and secrecy surrounding the *Protocols* only contributed to the impression of the pamphlet's authenticity.

The *voelkisch,* or nationalist movement, provided the ideological roots of the Nazi party, which formed in 1920. The Nazis (the term "Nazi" is the abbreviation for the National Socialist German Workers' party) exploited the *Protocols* throughout their regime. (They held power from 1933 to 1945.) While the infamous forgery first appeared in Germany in 1918, an influential Nazi leader, Alfred Rosenberg, reissued an official party version of the *Protocols,* along with commentaries, in 1923.

Things to Remember While Reading the *Protocols*:

- Keep in mind that the *Protocols* were meant to be first-hand reports of a secret meeting held among Jewish elders. The speaker is supposed to be a member of a secret Jewish organization whose goal is world domination. The word "protocol" refers to the minutes or reports of a conference or congress.

- Written in 24 sections, the *Protocols* describe the master plan of an alleged Jewish conspiracy to take control of the world. The following excerpts describe some methods Jews would allegedly use to destroy existing governments.

- An English newspaper pronounced the *Protocols* a forgery in 1921, as did a Swiss court in 1935. In fact, the anonymous author plagiarized, or copied, most of the *Protocols* from a French political essay directed against Napoleon III and published in 1864. The forger adapted the original philosophical discussions about despotism (an abusive, unfair, or oppressive ruling power) to sound as if they are the opinions and plans of Jewish leaders.

- The Nazis consistently relied on the *Protocols* as proof of a worldwide Jewish conspiracy to dominate the world. Notice the Twelfth Protocol describes how the Jews are planning to take control of the press as a means to mislead and ultimately rule society. Ironically, the Nazis applied this very technique of controlling public opinion by outlawing all nonparty publications in 1933. In many ways, the *Protocols* served as a guidebook for how the Nazis eventually tried to conquer and rule the world.

Protocols of the Elders of Zion

First Protocol

People with corrupt instincts are more numerous than those of noble instinct. Therefore in governing the world the best results are obtained by means of violence and **intimidation**, *and not by academic discussions. Every man aims at power; everyone would like*

Intimidation: Bullying, frightening, or otherwise compelling with threats.

to become a **dictator** if he could do so, and rare indeed are the men who would not be disposed to sacrifice the welfare of others in order to attain their own personal aims. What restrained the wild beasts of prey which we call men? What has ruled them up to now? In the first stages of social life they submitted to brute and blind force, then to law, which in reality is the same force, only masked. From this I am led to deduct that by the law of nature, right lies in might. Political freedom is not a fact, but an idea.

Third Protocol

Today I can assure you that we are ... within a few strides of our goal. There remains only a short distance and the cycle of the **Symbolic Serpent**—that badge of our people—will be complete. When this circle is locked, all the States of Europe will be enclosed in it, as it were, by unbreakable chains....

Under our **auspices** the **populace exterminated the aristocracy** which had supported and guarded the people for its own benefit, which benefit is inseparable from the welfare of the populace. Nowadays, having destroyed the privileges of the aristocracy, the people fall under the **yoke** of **cunning profiteers and upstarts**.

We intend to appear as though we were the liberators of the labouring [laboring] man, come to free him from this **oppression**, when we shall suggest to him to join the ranks of our armies of **Socialists**, **Anarchists**, and **Communists**. The **latter** we always **patronize**, pretending to help them out of **fraternal principle** and the general interest of humanity **evoked** by our socialistic **masonry**. The aristocracy, who ... shared the [fruits of the] labour [labor] of the working classes, [wanted the workers to be] well-fed, healthy and strong. We are interested in the opposite, i.e. in the **degeneration** of the **Gentiles**. Our strength lies in keeping the working man in perpetual want and **impotence**; because, by so doing, we retain him subject to our will and, in his own surroundings, he will never find either power or energy to stand up against us....

Dictator: Leader of a government in which absolute—and often unfair and oppressive—power is held by a single person.

Symbolic Serpent: A representation of the organized Jewish efforts to take control of the world.

Auspices: Support.

Populace exterminated the aristocracy: The common people destroyed the privileged or "noble" class.

Yoke: A device placed around the head of an animal or a person; a yoke symbolizes bondage.

Cunning profiteers and upstarts: People who use cleverness or trickery to achieve self-serving aims.

Oppression: Unjust or cruel use of power.

Socialists: Supporters of a political and economic system based on government control of the production and distribution of goods.

Anarchists: People who rebel against authority or ruling power.

Communists: Advocates of a political and economic theory that strives for the formation of a classless society through the communal, or group, ownership of all property.

Latter: The last of two or more things mentioned.

Patronize: Assuming an air of superiority and then "lowering" oneself to deal with an inferior.

Fraternal principle: Brotherly concerns; common beliefs.

Evoked: Called forth, brought out, or brought to mind.

Masonry: Relating to Freemasons, an international fraternal society (a society of "brothers," men joined by a common interest or bond).

Degeneration: Declining; sinking.

Gentiles: People who are not Jewish.

Impotence: Lack of power or strength.

Castes: Social classification based on birth or heredity.

*The Gentiles are no longer capable of thinking without our aid in matters of science. That is why they do not realize the vital necessity of certain things, which we will make a point of keeping against the moment when our hour arrives.... In schools the only true and most important of all sciences must be taught, that is, the science of the life of man and social conditions, both of which require a division of labour [labor] and therefore the classification of people in **castes** and classes....*

*We persuaded the Gentiles that **liberalism** would bring them to a kingdom of reason. Our **despotism** will be of this nature, for it will be in a position to put down all rebellions and by just severity to exterminate every liberal idea from all institutions.*

*When the populace noticed that it was being given all sorts of rights in the name of liberty, it imagined itself to be the master, and tried to assume power. Of course, like every other blind man, the mass came up against innumerable obstacles. Then, as it did not wish to return to the **former régime**, it laid its power at our feet.... We have led the nations from one disappointment to another, so that they should even **renounce** us in favour [favor] of the King-Despot of the blood of **Zion**, whom we are preparing for the world....*

Sixth Protocol

*Soon we will start organizing great monopolies—reservoirs of **colossal** wealth, in which even the large fortunes of the Gentiles will be involved to such an extent that they will sink together with the credit of their government the day after a political crisis takes place....*

*We must use every possible kind of means to develop the popularity of our Supergovernment, holding it up as a protection and **recompenser** of all who willingly submit to us.*

The aristocracy of the Gentiles, as a political power, is no more—therefore we need not consider it any more from that point of view. But as landowners, they are still dangerous to us, because their independent existence is ensured through their resources. Therefore, it is essential for us, at all costs, to deprive the aristocracy of their lands. To this purpose the best method is to force up rates and taxes.... At the same time we must give all possible protection to trade and commerce, and especially to **speculation,** *the principle role of which is to act as a* **counterpoise** *to industry. Without speculation industry will enlarge private* **capitals**....

Twelfth Protocol

Literature and journalism are the two most important educational powers; for this reason our government will buy up the greater number of periodicals. By these means we shall neutralize the bad influence of the private press and obtain an enormous influence over the human mind. If we were to allow ten private periodicals we should ourselves start thirty, and so forth.

But the public must not have the slightest suspicion of these measures, therefore all periodicals published by us will seem to be of contradictory views and opinions, thus inspiring confidence and presenting an attractive appearance to our unsuspecting enemies, who will thus fall into our trap and will be disarmed.... These newspapers, like the Indian god **Vishnu,** *will be possessed of hundreds of hands, each of which will be feeling the pulse of varying public opinion....*

If any chatterers are going to imagine that they are repeating the opinion of their party newspaper, they will in reality be repeating our own opinion, or the opinion which we desire. Thinking that they are following the **organ** *of this party, they will in reality be following the flag which we will fly for them....*

Already there exists in French journalism a system of masonic understanding for giving **countersigns.** *All organs of the*

Liberalism: Favoring a broad-minded approach to government, with emphasis on individual rights and support of change (as in the policies of government) when necessary.

Despotism: A political system in which the ruler exercises absolute power.

Former régime: Previous system of government.

Renounce: In this case, to turn away from or deny.

Zion: A term used broadly to refer to the Jewish people, the Jewish homeland, or an ideal nation.

Colossal: Enormous.

Recompenser: One who repays for damages.

Speculation: Engaging in risky business transactions in the hope of obtaining a sizeable gain.

Counterpoise: An influence that counteracts another.

Capitals: The value of accumulated goods.

Vishnu: In statues and artwork, this Indian god is represented as having several arms and hands.

*press are tied by mutual professional secrets in the manner of the ancient **oracles**. Not one of its members will betray his knowledge of the secret, if such a secret has not been ordered to be made public. No single publisher will have the courage to betray the secret entrusted to him, the reason being that not one of them is admitted into the literary world without bearing the marks of some shady act in his past life. He would only have to show the least sign of disobedience and the mark would be immediately revealed. Whilst [while] these marks remain known only to a few, the **prestige** of the journalist attracts public opinion throughout the country. The people follow and admire him.*

*Our plans must extend chiefly to the **provinces**. It is essential for us to create such ideas and inspire such opinions there....*

Epilogue

*According to the records of secret Jewish Zionism, **Solomon** and other Jewish learned men already, in 929 B.C., thought out a scheme in theory for a peaceful conquest of the whole universe by Zion.*

*As history developed, this scheme was worked out in detail and completed by men, who were subsequently initiated in this question. These learned men decided by peaceful means to conquer the world for Zion with the slyness of the symbolic serpent, whose head was to represent **the initiated** into the plans of the Jewish administration, and the body of the serpent to represent the Jewish people—the administration was always kept secret, even from the Jewish nation itself. As this serpent penetrated into the hearts of the nations which it encountered, it got under and devoured all the non-Jewish power of these states. It is foretold that the snake has to finish its work, strictly adhering to the designed path, until the course which it has to run is closed by the return of its head to Zion and until by this means, the snake has completed its round of Europe and has encircled it—and until, **by dint of** enchaining Europe, it has encompassed the whole world. This it is to accom-*

Organ: Periodical; newspaper.

Countersigns: Secret signals or passwords.

Oracles: A person through whom a god is believed to speak.

Prestige: Degree of influence or social standing.

Provinces: Outlying territories.

Solomon: An ancient king of Israel known for his wisdom.

The initiated: People who are knowledgeable about or experienced in something.

By dint of: Because of.

antisemitism

plish by using every endeavor to subdue the other countries by an economical conquest.

The return of the head of the serpent to Zion can only be accomplished after the power of all the **Sovereigns** of Europe has been laid low, that is to say, when by means of economic crises and wholesale destruction effected everywhere there shall have been brought about a spiritual demoralization and a moral corruption, chiefly with the assistance of Jewish women masquerading as French, Italians, etc. These are the surest spreaders of **licentiousness** into the lives of the leading men at the heads of nations....

A sketch of the symbolic serpent is shown as follows: Its first stage in Europe was in *429 B.C. in Greece, where, in the time of Pericles, the serpent first started eating into the power of that country. The second stage was in Rome in the time of Augustus about 69 B.C. [more likely 29 B.C.] The third in Madrid in the time of Charles V, A.D. 1552. The fourth in Paris about 1700, in the time of Louis XVI. [This should be Louis XIV.] The fifth in London from 1814 onwards (after the downfall of* **Napoléon**). *The sixth in Berlin in 1871 after the* **Franco-Prussian war**. *The seventh in* **St. Petersburg**, *over which is drawn the head of the serpent under the date of 1881.*

All these states which the serpent **traversed** have had the foundations of their constitutions shaken, Germany, with its apparent power, forming no exception to the rule. In economic conditions England and Germany are spared, but only till the conquest of Russia is accomplished by the serpent, on which at present all its efforts are concentrated. The further course of the serpent is not shown on this map, but arrows indicate its next movement towards Moscow, Kieff, and Odessa.

It is now well known to us to what extent the latter cities form the centres [centers] of the **militant** Jewish race. Constantinople is shown as the last stage of the serpent's course before it reaches Jerusalem.

Sovereigns: Leaders of monarchies.

Licentiousness: Lack of moral discipline.

Napoléon: Reference to Napoléon Bonaparte, the emperor of France from 1804 to 1815.

Franco-Prussian war: 1870-1871; Prussia was a powerful German state in the nineteenth century. The Franco (or French) and Prussian war took place during a particularly turbulent time in European history and resulted in a stunning defeat for the French.

St. Petersburg: Capital of Russian empire from 1712 to 1917.

Traversed: Crossed.

Militant: Aggressive; willing to fight for a cause.

Only a short distance still remains before the serpent will be able to complete its course by uniting its head to its tail...

Signed by the representatives of Zion,
of the 33rd degree.
(Cohn, pp. 285-97)

What happened next...

Hitler and the Nazi party made antisemitism the central part of their philosophy and official government policy. The *Protocols* helped the Nazis exploit the myth of a Jewish world-conspiracy—a conspiracy to first gain power and then institute a reign of terror against non-Jews. Anyone who challenged Nazi policy or defended the Jewish cause risked being labeled a part of this alleged conspiracy. The literary hoax of the *Protocols* profoundly influenced twentieth-century history by ultimately helping to justify genocide, or the systematic murder, of the Jewish people. Six million Jewish men, women, and children—representing two-thirds of all European Jews—died at the hands of the Nazis. This campaign to annihilate, or eliminate, the Jews is known as the Holocaust.

Did you know...

- Various antisemitic individuals and groups around the world translated and published the *Protocols of the Elders of Zion.* After World War I, the *Protocols* were available in every European language, plus Japanese, Chinese, and Arabic. At one time, only the Bible—the all-time international bestseller—exceeded the *Protocols* in circulation.

- In 1920, Henry Ford published the *Protocols* both in his newspaper the *Dearborn Independent* and in a book titled *The International Jew.* The prestige of Ford's name gave tremendous credibility to the *Protocols* within the United States and around the world. *The International Jew* sold over half a million copies in the United States, was translated into 16 languages, and became an official part of Nazi propaganda.

Alfred Rosenberg (1893-1946)

Alfred Rosenberg was born in Reval (now Tallinn), Estonia. He had a degree in engineering and also studied architecture. After participating in the 1917 Russian Revolution, he fled to Paris and then immigrated to Munich, where he became a German citizen in 1920. A close associate of Adolf Hitler and among the most educated of the Nazis, Rosenberg was regarded as the ideological leader of the party and one of its founders.

Beginning in 1921, Rosenberg served as publisher of the party's monthly magazine, *The World Struggle*. When the Nazis took control of the German government in 1933, Hitler appointed Rosenberg to head the Party Foreign Affairs Department. In 1934 Rosenberg became responsible for training all Nazi members in party doctrine.

Besides reissuing the German version of the *Protocols of the Elders of Zion*, Rosenberg himself wrote a famous antisemitic book. Regarded as a bible of the Nazi party, *The Myth of the Twentieth Century* quickly became a bestseller when it was first published in 1930. Rosenberg's book gave pseudo-scientific (pronounced SUE-doe-scientific; meaning theories that are wrongly regarded as scientific) support to the Nazi myth about the need for the Aryan race to struggle for "blood purity." This goal was to be achieved by avoiding contamination by (or having children with) "lesser" races, notably the Jews. Rosenberg's influence helped brand Jews as political opponents of the Germans and established antisemitism as an essential part of Nazi ideology. Sales of *The Myth* reached more than one million copies by 1944, second in circulation only to Hitler's book *Mein Kampf*. Both books were required reading in schools during the Nazi regime.

- Due to a lawsuit and mounting criticism, Ford publicly retracted his accusations of a Jewish conspiracy. In 1927, he denied responsibility for what had been published in *The International Jew* and attempted to withdraw the book from circulation. Unfortunately the damage had already occurred, for Ford's book did more to make the *Protocols* famous than any other publication. Hitler greatly admired Ford and his antisemitic writings and kept a photograph of Ford on his desk for several years.

For Further Reading

Bachrach, Susan D. *Tell Them We Remember: The Story of the Holocaust.* Boston: Little, Brown, and Company, 1994.

Cohn, Norman. *Warrant for Genocide: The Myth of the Jewish World Conspiracy and the Protocols of the Elders of Zion.* London: Serif, 1967. Reprinted, 1996.

Patterson, Charles. *Antisemitism: The Road to the Holocaust and Beyond.* New York: Walker, 1989.

Adolf Hitler

Excerpt from
Mein Kampf ("My Struggle")

Published in 1925

The book *Mein Kampf* by Adolf Hitler (published in English as *My Struggle*) reveals the philosophies of one of the most influential and dangerous people of the twentieth century. Written in 1923 during the early stages of Hitler's political career, *Mein Kampf* became the bible of the growing Nazi party (taken from the full name of the National Socialist German Workers' party). In this rambling, poorly written, semi-autobiographical work, Hitler presents himself as a political savior to the German people, who were still recovering from the disastrous defeat of World War I (1914-1918).

According to the ideology embraced by Hitler and the Nazis, race played a central role in every aspect of human existence. The Nazi party believed that Germans—as members of the "Aryan" race—were destined to rule all other races. Furthermore, noted the Nazis, the German race had grown weak over the centuries due to the mixing of their superior blood with the blood of inferior races. In particular, Jewish people were said to pose the most sinister threat to the purity and strength of the Aryan race. According to Hitler, Jews were actually members of a separate race, not just followers of a distinctive religion. The social, political, and economic resurrection of Germany could only be achieved by understanding "the racial problem and hence the Jewish problem," he stated. The divinely inspired (meaning directed by God) task of the German people, according to Hitler, was to preserve "the most valuable stocks" (the strongest and the brightest Germans) and to remove corrupting influences, such as the despised Jews.

Antisemitism (hatred of Jews) intensified in Germany as Hitler and many others blamed the Jews for their humiliating

defeat in World War I. Jews were viewed as being responsible for the spread of Marxism (the belief that a revolution by the working class would eventually lead to a classless society), democracy (government by the people), and other liberal (supportive of change) political ideologies that helped topple imperial (or royal) rule in Germany. Hitler thought Jews were attempting to dominate German citizens through the newly established democratic Weimar Republic, the government that was formed in Germany after its loss in the war and its signing of the Treaty of Versailles. Like other antisemites of his time, Hitler also believed in the myth of a Jewish conspiracy to dominate the world as described in a widely circulated pamphlet titled *Protocols of the Elders of Zion*.

Hitler entered politics after World War I in opposition to the Weimar regime (government in power). In 1920 he helped form the National Socialist German Workers' party ("Nazi" party, for short). The party members fervently believed in antisemitism, nationalism (placing Germany above all else), and the racialist belief of Aryan supremacy. Under Hitler's leadership, the Nazis unsuccessfully attempted to overthrow the government on November 8, 1923. Since this failed coup attempt occurred in a Berlin beer hall, it is now known as the Beer Hall Putsch. ("Putsch" is German for "unsuccessful rebellion.") Hitler was jailed for nearly a year, during which time he dictated *Mein Kampf* to a fellow Nazi. For several years the government banned the Nazi party and forbade Hitler from speaking publicly.

The Nazi party started to regain strength in the late 1920s. As the popularity of the party spread, people throughout Germany and the world began to read *Mein Kampf*. While many of Hitler's followers took his ideas seriously, opponents dismissed them as being too wild and preposterous to cause worry. Few foreign leaders believed *Mein Kampf* to be an actual plan for the destruction of the Jews. But after Hitler declared himself the "führer," or leader, of Germany in 1934, *Mein Kampf* became required reading in schools throughout the Third Reich (the name given to the Nazi-controlled government in Germany. The word "reich," pronounced RIKE, means "empire" or "kingdom.") The Nazis also required couples to have a copy of Hitler's book in order to be married.

The publication of *Mein Kampf* proved an enormous financial success for Hitler. His famous book was translated into 11 languages and sold more than 5.2 million copies by 1939, making Hitler a millionaire. The following passage from *Mein Kampf* shows that Hitler felt it was his destiny—and that of all Germans—to defend Aryan racial purity.

Things to Remember While Reading *Mein Kampf*:

- Hitler's confessional autobiography contains numerous grammatical errors, disjointed (unconnected) thoughts, and awkward expressions. His writing reflects the limited education he received before dropping out of school at the age of sixteen. However, Hitler had great talents as an orator, or public speaker. The content of *Mein Kampf* is better understood if imagined as a speech.

- *Mein Kampf* serves as Hitler's account of how he developed his racial philosophy. He attributes his transformation into a devout antisemite to events that occurred while he was living in Vienna, Austria. One day while strolling through the city, he claims that he noticed an eastern European Jew wearing a black caftan (a full-length garment). Hitler asked himself if this man could be a German and thus began his self-guided study of race and history.

- Hitler believes fervently that Jews are members of an inferior race conspiring to dominate the world. He holds them responsible for the development of Marxism, democracy, and all other liberal political philosophies—the very philosophies he feels are responsible for the ruin of Germany.

- In the passage cited below, Hitler uses the term the "Jewish question" to refer to the problem presented by the presence of Jews in society. As the supreme leader of Germany, Hitler initiated numerous anti-Jewish measures that eliminated the rights of Jews as citizens. After Germany invaded several countries and became enmeshed in World War II (1939-1945), the Nazis planned for the complete elimination of European Jewry through mass extermination. This plan was code-named the "Final Solution."

- To preserve the racial purity of Germany, Hitler recommends that the government enact laws regulating human reproductive rights. Physically or mentally disabled people should be sterilized to prevent them from passing their inferior genes on to future generations.

Mein Kampf (My Struggle)

I gradually became aware that the **Social Democratic** press was directed predominantly by Jews; yet I did not attribute any special significance to this circumstance, since conditions were exactly the same in the other papers. Yet one fact seemed **conspicuous:** there was not one paper with Jews working on it which could have been regarded as truly national, according to my education and way of thinking.

I swallowed my disgust and tried to read this type of **Marxist** press production, but my revulsion became so unlimited in so doing that I **endeavored** to become more closely acquainted with the men who manufactured these **compendiums** of **knavery.**

From the publisher down, they were all Jews.

I took all the Social Democratic pamphlets I could lay hands on and sought the names of their authors: Jews. I noted the names of the leaders; by far the greatest part were likewise members of the 'chosen people,' whether they were representatives in the Reichsrat or trade-union secretaries, the heads of organizations or street agitators. It was always the same gruesome picture. The names of the Austerlitzes, Davids, Adlers, Ellenbogens, etc., will remain forever graven in my memory. One thing had grown clear to me: the party with whose petty representatives I had been carrying on the most violent struggle for months was, as to leadership, almost exclusively in the hands of a foreign people; for, to my deep and joyful satisfaction, I had at last come to the conclusion that the Jew was no German.

Social Democrats: Political party of the Marxist movement in Germany.

Conspicuous: Noticeable; obvious.

Marxist: Political beliefs professed by Karl Marx, who advocated empowerment of workers and the formation of a classless society.

Endeavored: Attempted.

Compendiums: Collections.

Knavery: Dishonest or mischievous act.

German citizens salute Hitler at the opening of the 11th Olympiad. The Olympic Games were held in Berlin during August 1936.

Seducer: A person who leads others astray, convincing them to be disobedient or disloyal.

Sojourn: Visit or travel.

Only now did I become thoroughly acquainted with the **seducer** of our people.

A single year of my **sojourn** in Vienna has **sufficed to imbue me with the conviction** that no worker could be so stubborn that he would not in the end **succumb** to better knowledge and better explanations. Slowly I had become an expert in their own **doctrine** and used it as a weapon in the struggle for my own profound conviction.

Success almost always favored my side.

The great masses could be saved, if only with the gravest sacrifice in time and patience.

But a Jew could never be parted from his opinions.

antisemitism

At that time I was still childish enough to try to make the madness of their doctrine clear to them; in my little circle I talked my tongue sore and my throat hoarse, thinking I would inevitably succeed in convincing them how ruinous their Marxist madness was; but what I accomplished was often the opposite. It seemed as though their increased understanding of the destructive effects of Social Democratic theories and their results only reinforced their determination.

The more I argued with them, the better I came to know their **dialectic**. *First they counted on the stupidity of their* **adversary**, *and then, when there was no other way out, they themselves simply played stupid. If all this didn't help, they pretended not to understand, or, if challenged, they changed the subject in a hurry, quoted* **platitudes** *which, if you accepted them, they immediately related to entirely different matters, and then, if again attacked, gave ground and pretended not to know exactly what you were talking about. Whenever you tried to attack one of these* **apostles**, *your hand closed on a jelly-like slime which divided up and poured through your fingers, but in the next moment collected again. But if you really struck one of these fellows so telling a blow that, observed by the audience, he couldn't help but agree, and if you believed that this had taken you at least one step forward, your amazement was great the next day. The Jew had not the slightest recollection of the day before, he rattled off his same old nonsense as though nothing at all had happened, and, if* **indignantly** *challenged,* **affected** *amazement; he couldn't remember a thing, except that he had proved the correctness of his* **assertions** *the previous day.*

Sometimes I stood there thunderstruck.

I didn't know what to be more amazed at: the **agility of their tongues** *or their* **virtuosity at lying**.

Gradually I began to hate them.

Sufficed to imbue me with the conviction: Convinced me ("me" being Hitler).

Succumb: Surrender; yield.

Doctrine: Principles; beliefs.

Dialectic: Political discourse or discussion to investigate an idea.

Adversary: Opponent.

Platitudes: Dull remarks.

Apostles: Followers sent on a mission.

Indignantly: Characterized by anger at injustice.

Affected: Put on; faked; pretended.

Assertions: Declarations.

Agility of their tongues: Ability to speak with ease.

Virtuosity at lying: Great skill at deceiving others.

*All this had but one good side: that in proportion as the real leaders or at least the **disseminators** of Social Democracy came within my vision, my love for my people inevitably grew. For who, in view of the **diabolical craftiness** of these seducers, could damn the luckless victims? How hard it was, even for me, to get the better of this race of dialectical liars! And how **futile** was such success in dealing with people who twist the truth in your mouth, who without so much as a blush **disavow** the word they have just spoken, and in the very next minute take credit for it after all.*

No. The better acquainted I became with the Jew, the more forgiving I inevitably became toward the worker....

Inspired by the experience of daily life, I now began to track down the sources of the Marxist doctrine. Its effects had become clear to me in individual cases; each day its success was apparent to my attentive eyes, and, with some exercise of my imagination, I was able to picture the consequences. The only remaining question was whether the result of their action in its ultimate form had existed in the mind's eye of the creators, or whether they themselves were the victims of an error.

I felt that both were possible.

*In the one case it was the duty of every thinking man to force himself to the forefront of the **ill-starred** movement, thus perhaps **averting catastrophe**; in the other, however, the original founders of this plague of the nations must have been **veritable** devils; for only in the brain of a monster—not that of a man—could the plan of an organization assume form and meaning, whose activity must ultimately result in the collapse of human civilization and the consequent devastation of the world.*

In this case the only remaining hope was struggle, struggle with all the weapons which the human spirit, reason, and will can devise, regardless on which side of the scale Fate should lay its blessing.

Disseminators: Those who spread ideas.

Diabolical craftiness: Devilish skill or cleverness.

Futile: Serving no purpose.

Disavow: Deny responsibility for.

Ill-starred: Unlucky.

Averting catastrophe: Avoiding tragedy or ruin.

Veritable: True.

Thus I began to make myself familiar with the founders of this doctrine, in order to study the foundations of the movement. If I reached my goal more quickly than at first I had perhaps ventured to believe, it was thanks to my newly acquired, though at that time not very profound, knowledge of the **Jewish question**. This alone enabled me to draw a practical comparison between the reality and the **theoretical flim-flam** of the founding fathers of Social Democracy, since it taught me to understand the language of the Jewish people, who speak in order to conceal or at least to veil their thoughts; their real aim is not therefore to be found in the lines themselves, but slumbers well concealed between them.

For me this was the time of the greatest spiritual upheaval I have ever had to go through.

Adolf Hitler and Heinrich Himmler review SS troops during a Reich Party Day ceremony in September 1938.

Jewish question: A phrase created by antisemites (people opposed to Jews) to refer to the "problem" created by the existence of Jews in society.

Theoretical flim-flam: Deceptive nonsense.

*I had ceased to be a weak-kneed **cosmopolitan** and become an anti-Semite....*

*When over long periods of human history I scrutinized the activity of the Jewish people, suddenly there rose up in me the fearful question whether **inscrutable Destiny**, perhaps for reasons unknown to us poor mortals, did not with **eternal and immutable resolve**, desire the final victory of **this little nation.***

Was it possible that the earth had been promised as a reward to this people which lives only for this earth?

Have we an objective right to struggle for our self-preservation...?

As I delved more deeply into the teachings of Marxism and thus in tranquil clarity submitted the deeds of the Jewish people to contemplation, Fate itself gave me its answer.

*The Jewish doctrine of Marxism rejects the aristocratic principle of Nature and replaces the eternal privilege of power and strength by the mass of numbers and their dead weight. Thus it denies the value of personality in man, **contests** the significance of nationality and race, and thereby withdraws from humanity the premise of its existence and its culture. As a foundation of the universe, this doctrine would bring about the end of any order intellectually conceivable to man. And as, in this greatest of all recognizable organisms, the result of an application of such a law could only be **chaos**, on earth it could only be destruction for the inhabitants of this planet.*

*If, with the help of his Marxist creed, the Jew is victorious over the other peoples of the world, his crown will be the funeral wreath of humanity and this planet will, as it did thousands of years ago, move through the **ether devoid of** men.*

Cosmopolitan: Man of the world.

Inscrutable Destiny: Mysterious and irresistible power; forces of fate that cannot be understood.

Eternal and immutable resolve: Never-ending and unchanging determination.

This little nation: The Jewish nation.

Contests: Challenges.

Chaos: Utter confusion.

Ether: Regions beyond earth; heavens.

Devoid of: Without.

Inexorably avenges: Constantly pursues punishment for.

Infringement: Violation.

*Eternal Nature **inexorably avenges** the **infringement** of her commands.*

Hence today I believe that I am acting in accordance with the will of the Almighty Creator: by defending myself against the Jew, I am fighting for the work of the Lord.... There is only one holiest human right, and this right is at the same time the holiest obligation ...: to see to it that the blood is preserved pure and, by preserving the best humanity, to create the possibility of a nobler development of these beings....

*The **folkish** state must make up for what everyone else today has neglected in this field. It must set race in the center of all life. It must take care to keep it pure. It must declare the child to be the most precious treasure of the people. It must see to it that only the healthy **beget** children; that there is only one disgrace: despite one's own sickness and deficiencies, to bring children into the world, and one highest honor: to renounce doing so. And conversely it must be considered **reprehensible**: to withhold healthy children from the nation. Here the state must act as the guardian of a **millennial** future in the face of which the wishes and the selfishness of the individual must appear as nothing and submit. It must put the most modern medical means in the service of this knowledge. It must declare unfit for **propagation** all who are in any way visibly sick or who have inherited a disease and can therefore pass it on, and put this into actual practice. Conversely, it must take care that the fertility of the healthy woman is not limited by the financial irresponsibility of a state regime which turns the blessing of children into a curse for the parents....*

*Those who are physically and mentally unhealthy and unworthy must not perpetuate their suffering in the body of their children. In this the folkish state must perform the most gigantic educational task. And some day this will seem to be a greater deed than the most victorious wars of our present **bourgeois** era....*

Folkish: Of the people.

Beget: Produce.

Reprehensible: Worthy of the most severe disapproval.

Millennial: Spanning one thousand years.

Propagation: Natural reproduction; breeding.

Bourgeois: Conformity to middle-class conventions.

Procreate: Reproduce.

Degenerate: Degraded or lowered in some way.

*A prevention of the faculty and opportunity to **procreate** on the part of the physically **degenerate** and mentally sick, over a period of only six hundred years, would not only free humanity from an immeasurable misfortune, but would lead to a recovery which today seems scarcely conceivable. If the fertility of the healthiest bearers of the nationality is thus consciously and systematically promoted, the result will be a race which at least will have eliminated the germs of our present physical and hence spiritual decay.*

For once a people and a state have started on this path, attention will automatically be directed on increasing the racially most valuable nucleus of the people and its fertility, in order ultimately to let the entire nationality partake of the blessing of a highly bred racial stock. (Hitler, pp. 61-65, 402-5)

What happened next...

Basing their ideology on intense racialism, antisemitism, and German nationalism, the Nazis came to power in 1933 promising the revival of a broken country. Hitler was fanatically devoted to the principles of Aryan supremacy. These feelings led him to initiate devastating anti-Jewish measures. Through a process that evolved from exclusion (restricting Jewish rights) to expulsion (forcing Jews to leave Germany) and finally to annihilation (mass killings of Jews), the Nazi government eliminated Jews from public life in Germany. Hitler's determination for Aryan domination sparked a war that engulfed the entire world. In his quest to expand the *Lebensraum,* or living space, of the Aryan race, he launched the invasion of numerous surrounding countries in Europe and brutally murdered millions of people who belonged to supposedly inferior races.

By 1941 the Nazis had several million Jews incarcerated (imprisoned) in the Polish ghettos (isolated sections of a city). The party's main goal was to remove Jews from all German-occupied countries, and they set out to achieve this

Adolf Hitler (1889-1945)

Adolf Hitler was born in the small village of Braunau, Austria. He had a stormy relationship with his elderly father, who worked as a customs inspector. Young Adolf's mother, however, is said to have doted on him and favored him over her other children.

At his father's insistence, Hitler enrolled in a school for technical training but dropped out at the age of sixteen. He eventually moved to Vienna, Austria, to pursue his interest in painting but was rejected for admission to the prestigious Vienna Academy of Fine Arts. Struggling to support himself by painting postcards, Hitler began to give political lectures in crowded cafés. He angrily rejected Marxism and democracy while promoting the causes of German nationalism and antisemitism. The humbling experiences of Vienna hardened Hitler, who finally moved to the land he worshiped—Germany.

Hitler gave up his Austrian citizenship to serve in the German army in World War I. He proved himself to be a courageous soldier, receiving two medals for his war service. He was temporarily blinded and severely wounded by a gas attack one month before the war ended in November 1918. While working as a political spy for the beaten German army, Hitler discovered and joined the German Workers' party, which grew to become the Nazi party.

In the years following World War I, Hitler left the army and devoted his energy to the building of the Nazi party. He rose to party leadership and participated in a failed attempt to overthrow the German government in 1923. While serving a prison sentence for the aborted coup (failed overthrow), Hitler laid down his political philosophy in *Mein Kampf*. He spent the next decade planning a complete Nazi takeover of the German government. Appointed chancellor in 1933 and *führer*, or leader, in 1934, Hitler ruled Germany until the end of World War II. Rather than be captured by the Allies (the forces that fought against Germany in World War II), he reportedly committed suicide in his underground bunker (a fortified chamber) in Berlin on April 30, 1945.

goal by organizing the complete evacuation and extermination of European Jewry. This plan was code-named the "Final Solution."

Nearly six million Jews died in what is now known as the Holocaust. Hitler's campaign for Aryan world domination resulted in a death toll of more than 35 million people. The unbelievably brutal manner in which Nazis treated Jews—and all the people of invaded countries—reflects Hitler's true intentions concerning his quest for racial superiority and purity. He reveals these intentions in *Mein Kampf*.

Did you know...

- Hitler originally titled his semiautobiographical book *Four and a Half Years of Struggle against Lies, Stupidity, and Cowardice*. At his publisher's insistence, Hitler shortened the title to *My Struggle* (or *Mein Kampf*).

- When the Nazis seized power in Germany in 1933, Jews represented less than one percent of the total German population of 65 million.

- During the 1880s, Heinrich Muller, a scholar specializing in the history of languages, popularized the term "Aryan" as a name of a particular language group. Muller became outraged when racialists began to use "Aryan" to refer to a race. The Nazis perpetuated this inaccuracy by continuing to refer to German people as members of the "Aryan race."

- When the term "antisemitism" originated, people believed all Jews descended from a race called Semites. In fact, Semites are a branch of the Caucasian (white) race, which includes Jews, Arabs, and others from the Mediterranean area.

For Further Reading

Hitler, Adolf. *Mein Kampf*. Translated by Ralph Manheim. Sentry Edition. Boston: Houghton Mifflin, 1943.

Orgel, Doris. *The Devil in Vienna*. New York: Dial Books for Young Readers, 1978.

Shirer, William. *The Rise and Fall of Adolf Hitler*. New York: Random House, 1984.

Inge Deutschkron

Excerpt from *Outcast: A Jewish Girl in Wartime Berlin*

First published in 1978; English translation published in 1989

As soon as Hitler became German chancellor on January 30, 1933, he moved quickly to dismantle (break apart) the democratic processes (government by the people) in Germany. Days after being sworn in, he banned public meetings and assemblies that were deemed "dangerous" to national security, a move that greatly aided the Nazis in controlling the upcoming elections. By enforcing this decree, they silenced their political opponents, including the communists (advocates of a political and economic theory that strives for the formation of a classless society through the communal, or group, ownership of all property), Social Democrats, and Catholics. A fire destroyed the *Reichstag* (parliament) building a month later, and the Nazis immediately blamed the incident on the communists. (Disagreement still exists today about Nazi involvement in the fire.) Fear of a violent uprising paralyzed Germany, and the Nazis seized the opportunity to tighten their reigns on the control of information within the country.

On February 28, 1933, Hitler issued an emergency decree that suspended freedom of speech and the press. These actions effectively eliminated non-Nazi access to newspapers and radio. The results of the last free election, held on March 5, enabled the Nazis to control government power by forming a coalition (a union or alliance designed to take joint action) with other nationalist parties. (Nationalism is a sense of loyalty or devotion to a nation—in this case, it represents glorification of German pride, culture, and interests above all others.)

The Nazis escalated their suppression of political opposition before turning their attention to the Jews. On March 24,

Nazi Censorship

On the night of May 10, 1933, a month after the boycott of Jewish businesses, the Nazis conducted a massive book burning. Under the ominous light of torch fires, party members marched in parades, singing party songs and lighting bonfires throughout Germany. They raided libraries, universities, and bookstores and burned works they felt should not be read by Germans.

The Nazi demonstrators removed books by Jews such as noted physicist Albert Einstein and the father of psychoanalysis, Sigmund Freud, as well as the works of foreign authors—American writers Ernest Hemingway and Jack London included. Helen Keller's books were also burned, since the Nazis disapproved of educating people with disabilities. (Keller was deaf and blind.) After learning of the book burning, Keller remarked, "Tyranny cannot defeat the power of ideas."

The Nazi party exercised complete control over the ideas that could and would reach the German public. Under the direction of Joseph Goebbels, the Reich Minister for Public Enlightenment and Propaganda, the party oversaw all forms of communication, including newspapers, magazines, books, public meetings, art, music, and radio. In addition to removing certain books from schools, the Nazis issued newly written textbooks to instill party beliefs in students. One such book, *The Poisonous Mushroom,* taught children to distrust and hate all Jews.

1933, the party passed the Enabling Act, which ended the powers of *Reichstag* and created a dictatorship (a form of government in which absolute power is held by a single, and often oppressive or unjust, ruler) by transferring all legislative power to Hitler. Within months, all non-Nazi political parties, trade unions, and organizations were banned. Using the terrorist tactics of the SA or storm troopers (members of a private and brutal Nazi army), the Nazis arrested political opponents and held them without trial. In fact, the political enemies of the Third Reich became the first occupants of the Nazi con-

A storm trooper stands in front of the Tietz department store. The sign reads "Germans defend yourselves; don't buy from Jews!"

centration camps. (The Third Reich is the name given to the Nazi-controlled government in Germany; the word *reich*, pronounced RIKE, means "empire" or "kingdom.")

Next, the Nazis turned their attention to other people they considered enemies of the state—German Jews. According to Nazi racial doctrine, Jews threatened the purity of the German or "Aryan" race. The government announced a nationwide boycott of Jewish businesses on April 1, the first planned anti-Jewish action. The Nazis justified the boycott as a way of striking back against Jewish criticism of the party and its philosophy. Nazi storm troopers painted graffiti on Jewish shops in cities throughout Germany and pasted signs on windows that read: "Don't Buy from Jews" and "The Jews Are Our Misfortune." Members of the storm troopers and the SS (*Schutzstaffel,* the elite police unit of the Nazi party) stood menacingly at the doors of Jewish-owned shops to keep patrons from entering. Violence erupted in many cities, and, according to Nazi instructions, the police made no attempt to control it.

Inge Deutschkron was a ten-year-old Jewish child living in Berlin when Hitler came to power in 1933. In the following document, Deutschkron describes her observations of these early days of terror and confusion as the Nazis took over Germany. Her descriptions reveal the common feelings of most Jewish Germans at that time—denial and disbelief. Assuming that Nazi rule would be short-lived, many people underestimated the brutality and power of the regime.

Things to Remember While Reading *Outcast*:

- During the Nazi era, political events such as rallies and marches were frequently marked by violence. Deutschkron witnessed such violence firsthand—she saw a parade marcher mortally wounded and watched as protestors threw stones at her family's home.

- Deutschkron's family first experienced persecution due to their political activities, not their religion. As a leader in the Social Democratic party, her father was in danger of being arrested and sent to a concentration camp such as Dachau. The Nazis relied on storm troopers to terrorize and suppress opponents of Nazism.

- Notice that Deutschkron and her family want to believe the violence they experience will pass. Little did she know that her fearfulness regarding her father's night away from home would become her daily reality in the years to come.

Outcast: A Jewish Girl in Wartime Berlin

"*You're Jewish," my mother said to me. "You must let the world know that that doesn't mean you're not every bit as good as they."*

What did it mean, being Jewish? I didn't ask. What interested me was what was going on outside in our corner of Berlin, on our quiet street. I liked looking out of the window of our apartment on Hufelandstrasse. It may have been nothing more than a sleepy little corner, yet for a ten-year-old there was much to see. I could watch the other children play. I was not allowed to play outside; my parents thought it wasn't safe. I, of course, didn't agree. I knew all the children by name, but I wasn't allowed to play with them. All I could do was watch. It hurt....

*I knew that my parents were **Socialists**, and like most children growing up in a loving family I identified with my parents. My father held some sort of office in the Social Democratic Party, and devoted much of his free time—as a teacher he had more than most—to party work. I took it for granted that all aspects of life were supposed to constitute a conscious, uncompromising **affirmation** of socialism, whether by being active in the People's Welfare Organization or shopping at the **co-op**.*

Not only did I share my parents' belief, but it also filled me with self-confidence and pride. It may seem odd, but my fondest childhood memories are not of vacations or other childish pleasures but of sitting with adults in some smoke-filled backroom of a Berlin pub helping fold leaflets. And I was also proud to have my parents take me along on one of their "symbolic" walks, at which Social Democrats "accidentally" bumped into each other and greeted each other loudly with the slogan "Freedom." The May Day demonstrations gave me a taste of the shared feeling of commitment and unity of politically engaged people.

Socialists: Supporters of a political theory that grew out of communistic principles; socialism proposes equal distribution of economic power.

Affirmation: Dedication.

Co-op: Short for "cooperative"; a business owned by and operated for the benefit of the people it services.

Nazi students and SA members unload materials for a book burning. The banner on the back of the truck reads "German students march against the un-German spirit."

Communists: Followers of a political doctrine that originated in Russia and advocated a classless society.

Of course I was not completely unaware of the gathering political storm clouds; no one involved in the political battles of the early thirties could fail to notice them. In my mind's eye I can still see all those different demonstrators: the **Communists** with their red flags and their bands; the men of the Social Democratic defense organization, with whom I identified; the militarily precise brown columns of the **SA**, which frightened me. There are **indelible** memories—of a Communist, mortally wounded in a clash with **Nazis**, struggling to get back on his feet, of accounts of **pitched** street battles between political **adversaries**, including between Communists and Socialists.

Who the Nazis were, what they were doing and what they wanted, I learned from my father. Hitler means terror, **dictatorship**, war, he used to tell me. He campaigned tirelessly in the last *free election before Hitler's takeover. "Berlin will stay **Red**," he pro-claimed in meeting after meeting, indoors and out. He did not let up even when our next-door neighbor was wounded by a bullet meant for him.*

Even though I was not familiar with all the details and did not quite understand everything, I sensed the general tension. When stones were thrown at an electioneering banner we had strung along our balcony, I knew intuitively that I too was involved in the battle.

*On that evening, March 31, 1933, I looked out the window, but not at the children at play. I had trouble concentrating. I felt **apprehensive**; an indefinable sense of danger was in the air. I knew that the Nazis, as their first public anti-Jewish measure, were planning a boycott of Jewish businesses on April 1. I kept looking in the direction of the corner pub, which I couldn't see from my window. It was a known Nazi hangout. I listened for my father's footsteps; he should have been home long ago. Mother too was uneasy. She kept going to the door to peer down the staircase. She came into my room, pushed me away from the window, and, more harshly than she probably meant to, told me to go and play domi-noes with Lotte, our helper, while she herself remained at the win-dow staring out into the dark.*

I sat down with Lotte and listlessly began our game. Sud-denly the bell rang. My mother appeared in the doorway. Lotte didn't move. At that moment our fear took concrete shape, filling the room. With great self-control, my mother asked Lotte to answer the door. As soon as my mother heard the familiar voice of one of our political friends she ran to the door and pulled him into one of the other rooms. All I was able to hear before they disappeared were the words: "Your husband must get out of town immediately."

Our visitor left, and my mother also got ready to go out. I was terrified, but I didn't say a word. I felt she wasn't even aware of my presence. Outwardly calm, she told me she was going out to look

SA: Abbreviation for *Sturmabteilung,* German for "storm troopers."

Indelible: Unable to be removed or erased; lasting.

Nazis: Abbreviation for National Socialist German Workers' party.

Pitched: In this case, "pitched" means intense.

Adversaries: Opponents.

Dictatorship: A form of government in which absolute—and often unfair and oppressive—power is held by a single person.

Red: Meaning "of communism."

Apprehensive: Fearful.

The cover of *Der Giftpilz* (*"The Poisonous Mushroom"*), an antisemitic children's book.

for Father, who probably was still tied up with exams at school, and that she'd be back soon. Without another word she was out the door. Lotte nodded silently. She wasn't much older than I, probably around eighteen, and I don't know which of us was more scared. We tried to resume our game, but it was no use. We kept listening for familiar steps that didn't come.

I don't remember how long we sat like that, only that Mother didn't return until quite late. Again, she appeared very calm as she *told us that Father would spend the night with friends. She didn't tell us why, and I knew that it was better not to ask. Without further protest I went to bed, but from my room I could hear her telling Lotte that Dr. Ostrowski had been arrested and also Mr. Weber, that no one knew what was going to happen next, that it might be a good idea for us to pack some bags and spend the next night somewhere else.*

Two men who were friends of the family had been arrested, and apparently my father was also in danger. "The Nazis keep pointing at your apartment," our visitor had told Mother. Everybody in the neighborhood knew our politics.

"Arrests"—it was a word I had begun to see and hear a lot, but until that evening it had been an **abstraction**. *Now it became frightening reality. At that time the Nazi actions still were directed primarily against their political opponents. The Jews had not yet become prime targets. The overwhelming majority of Berlin Jews was not politically involved. My father's few Jewish friends from his college days neither understood nor sympathized with his politics; some even said that Hitler was the only one who would be able to bring order into the political* **chaos** *of the* **Weimar Republic**. *As for the arrests of those days, they were simply "excesses."*

The night passed without incident. The next day my father came back. There was nothing unusual about him; he appeared to be in good spirits. Apparently the father of one of his students, out of gratitude that his daughter had passed her baccalaureate, offered to put him up for the night when he heard of his predicament. His host was a nonpolitical Jewish doctor, and Father made us laugh with his story of sleeping in the doctor's office amid the medical instruments and a skeleton that cast weird shadows. It was all still strange, unreal. None of us could dream that the day would come when we'd be deeply grateful for such a shelter.

Outside they were marching with the "steady firm steps" of the **Horst Wessel** *song. They tore the black, red, and gold banner*

Abstraction: Not connected to or made real by association with a particular instance.

Chaos: Utter confusion.

Weimar Republic: Democratic government imposed upon Germany at the end of World War II.

Horst Wessel: Popular song of the Nazi party named after a murdered storm trooper.

Inge Deutschkron (c. 1923—)

After World War II ended in 1945, Inge Deutschkron began making plans with her mother to rejoin her father in England. They raised the money they needed for their trip by selling American cigarettes on the German black market (an illegal system of trading). Once in England, Deutschkron studied languages at London University and then left to work on behalf of socialist organizations in Asia. (Socialism is a political and economic system based on government control of the production and distribution of goods. Socialists champion the removal of private property in a quest to attain a classless society.)

After living in Burma, Nepal, and Israel, Deutschkron took a job as a German correspondent for the Israeli newspaper *Maariv*. She became an Israeli citizen in 1966 and has worked as an editor at *Maariv* in Tel Aviv since 1972. Thirty years passed before she felt she could write about her experiences as a young Jewish girl growing up in wartime Berlin. First published in 1978, Deutschkron's *Outcast* was translated into English and published in the States in 1989.

of the Weimar Republic in shreds and carried **placards** with slogans like "Germans, don't buy from Jews. World Jewry wants to destroy Germany. Germans, defend yourselves." All this I could see from the window of our apartment. We didn't go out that day...

We left our home on the evening of April 1 as **unobtrusively** as possible, practically stealing away. After the noise of that day, all those drums, fifes, and marches, the quiet of the evening was almost **tangible**. Not many people were out on the street. A few Jewish shops bore the traces of what had happened: a **Star of David** painted on one store front, broken windows in another. That was all. It is not unlikely that in view of the now peaceful atmosphere my parents were asking themselves whether they

Placards: Posters.

Unobtrusively: Not noticeably or aggressively.

Tangible: Capable of being perceived or realized.

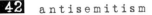

might not have been able to stay in our apartment, whether what we had been witnessing was nothing more than a bad dream that would pass as suddenly as it had come.

What we heard in Spandau also sounded reassuring. True, SA guards had posted themselves in front of Uncles Hannes' shop. One of them even excused himself: "It's just one of those measures..." Customers were not molested. The mood that evening was very strange. Hope resurfaced that in the end everything would turn out all right.

We stayed in Spandau for a few days, and then returned to our apartment. But it no longer seemed like our old home to me; it had lost its reassuring aura of security. I kept listening for strange footsteps **presaging imminent** *danger. My parents did not seem quite as worried. Some of our friends who'd been arrested by the* **Gestapo** *were released. I overheard only fragments of their accounts: "I had to run along a long corridor, and when I didn't follow their commands fast enough, they beat me until I lost consciousness...." Others refused to talk about their experience, and still others never came back. They were sent to concentration camps; very few of them survived. The initials "KZ" [Konzentrationslager] had not yet acquired their ominous overtone. Names were whispered: "Oranienburg," "Dachau." (Deutschkron, pp. 1-12)*

Star of David: A six-pointed figure used to symbolize Judaism.

Presaging: Warning or prediction about the future.

Imminent: Ready to happen.

Gestapo: In German, *Geheime Staatspolizei;* Secret State Police.

KZ: German term for concentration camps.

Dachau: One of the first concentration camps.

What happened next...

One week after the boycott, the Reich passed the first anti-Jewish law of the Nazi regime. Enacted on April 7, 1933, the Law for the Restoration of the Professional Civil Service forced Jews and other "non-Aryans" from civil service (government management) positions. Additional decrees forbade non-Aryan lawyers from practicing law. Eventually non-Aryan professors, judges, and doctors were also unable to practice their professions. Throughout the 1930s, the Nazis continued to pass legislation designed to strip Jews of their rights and force them onto the fringes of society.

Like many other Jewish professionals and civil servants living in Germany, Deutschkron's father was fired from his job as a teacher. He managed to escape to England after realizing that he would soon be arrested, leaving Deutschkron and her mother behind in Berlin. At that time, the Deutschkron family, like countless other Jewish families, was hopeful that Hitler's rule would not last long.

Together mother and daughter experienced the progressive stages of antisemitic terror. First the Nazis required them to wear yellow cloth stars sewn to their garments at all times. Once World War II began in 1939, escape became impossible for Inge and her mother. The Gestapo, the secret state police of the Nazi regime, rounded up all Jews living in Berlin to prepare them for deportation (banishment; being sent out of the country). In order to escape the concentration camps, they pretended to be non-Jewish Germans. Living in constant danger and fear, the Deutschkrons were dependent on the kindness of others who risked their lives to help protect them. At the close of the war, they managed to secure refugee status. (A refugee is a person who flees to a foreign country to avoid persecution.) Deutschkron then traveled to England with her mother to be reunited with her father.

Did you know...

- After the failed attempt by the Nazis to overthrow the Weimar Republic in 1923, Hitler realized the importance of gaining power through legal means. The Nazis won enough seats in the *Reichstag* (parliament) to secure Hitler's place as chancellor in January 1933.

- One of the most notorious concentration camps—Dachau—first housed known political opponents of the Nazi party, including communists and socialists. The Nazis established Dachau on March 20, 1933, just two months after Hitler became chancellor.

- One hundred years before the Nazis started their campaign of burning books (books that they felt threatened the party's ideals), the poet Heinrich Heine, a German Jew, wrote about the practice of book burning. His observations turned out to be eerily prophetic: "Where one burns books," he remarked, "one will, in the end, burn people."

For Further Reading

Deutschkron, Inge. *Outcast: A Jewish Girl in Wartime Berlin.* Originally published in German, 1978. Reprinted, New York: Fromm International Publishing Corporation, 1989.

Forman, James. *Nazism.* New York: Franklin Watts, 1978.

Richter, Hans P. *Friedrich.* Translated by E. Kroll. New York: Holt, Rinehart and Winston, 1970. Reprinted, Puffin, 1987.

The Nuremberg Laws and the Implementing Decree

Issued by the Reichstag Party Congress

September 15 and November 14, 1935

A dolf Hitler was obsessed with ideas about race when he was appointed to the office of German chancellor on January 30, 1933. For years, he had written articles and given speeches that expressed his belief in racial purity and the superiority of Germany and its people. Hitler saw Germans as members of an Aryan (or German) "master race." The history of civilization, he believed, reflected the struggle between creative Aryan forces and substandard non-Aryan influences. In the view of Hitler and the Nazis, Jews were members of a completely different, non-Aryan race (the Semitic race), not simply members of a distinct religion and culture. Once the Nazis took control of the German government, their racial beliefs became a part of official policy.

Hitler obtained dictatorial control over the German government and people within two months of becoming chancellor. In addition to outlawing political opposition, the Nazis also instituted government-condoned (supported or sanctioned) violence to silence their critics. On March 20, 1933, the Nazis opened the first concentration camp—Dachau—to retain communists, socialists, trade unionists (workers who join together for a common purpose, usually to increase their political power), and other political dissidents (opponents) who "continue to agitate and to cause unrest." (Communists are advocates of a political and economic theory that strives for the formation of a classless society through the communal, or group, ownership of all property. Socialism is a political and economic system based on government control of the production and distribution of goods. Socialists champion the removal of private property in a quest to attain a classless society.)

By seizing control of the press and radio, the Nazis were able to spread racialist and nationalist propaganda throughout Germany without any challenges. As they continued strengthening their legal position of power, the Nazis simultaneously escalated anti-Jewish—or antisemitic—government measures, carefully testing the reactions within Germany and abroad.

From the beginning of his rule as chancellor, Hitler relied on his private army, the storm troopers (*Sturmabteilung* or SA), to frighten and terrorize Jews living in Germany. During the first few months of his rule, violence and administrative actions forced hundreds of Jews from their positions as judges, lawyers, journalists, and professors. Roving bands of storm troopers randomly vandalized synagogues and broke windows of Jewish-owned stores and businesses. After months of informally organized and frequently violent anti-Jewish attacks, the Nazi government officially ordered a day-long national boycott (ban; to stop

On March 25, 1933, in New York City, thousands of communists listened as one of their leaders condemned the Hitler regime.

doing business with) of Jewish businesses to begin the morning of April 1, 1933. Angered at the international protest against the Nazi government's anti-Jewish activities, Hitler is believed to have ordered the boycott as revenge. He accused "international Jewry" (Jews worldwide) of spreading "atrocity propaganda" against Germans (wicked and revolting ideas that damaged Germany's reputation). The official boycott was his way of silencing further criticism both domestically and overseas.

A week after the boycott, the Reich government enacted the first anti-Jewish legislation (official law). It called for the dismissal of Jews and other non-Aryans from civil service (government) jobs. In order to minimize objections, Hitler allowed exemptions for Jewish civil servants who had fought in World War I or those who had lost their fathers or sons in the war. Nonetheless, thousands of Jewish workers, including schoolteachers, were fired from their jobs. Other decrees sought to reduce what many Germans perceived as an unfair proportion of Jews in certain professions and positions. Laws prohibited (restricted) non-Aryan lawyers and non-Aryan doctors from practicing their professions in Germany. In addition, only a limited number of Jewish students were admitted to colleges and universities. Jews were also banned from participating in cultural activities and from owning land.

After the death of German president Paul von Hindenburg on August 2, 1934, Hitler declared himself *führer* ("leader"), ensuring his complete control over Germany. He established two principles for all Germans to follow: rule by the führership and devotion to achieving race domination. Having mandated or ordered the sterilization of people with hereditary diseases to preserve German racial purity, Hitler felt it was time to address the "blood and race" problem created by the presence of Jews. In the fall of 1935, he requested his minister of the interior, Wilhelm Frick, to draft measures that would protect Germans from Jewish "impurity."

Hitler decided he wanted to announce the new race laws concerning Jewish citizenship and blood relationships at the annual Nazi party rally in Nuremberg on September 15, 1935. Frick ordered members of his staff to gather in

Nuremberg; there, they worked frantically to draft the antisemitic laws. According to historians, the decision to create these laws occurred so hastily that Frick's assistants forgot to bring enough paper with them and had to jot down their ideas on menu cards instead.

Because they were presented at the September party ceremony in Nuremberg, the laws regarding Jewish citizenship and race came to be known as the Nuremberg Laws. Consistent with the existing Nazi program of depriving Jews of their rights, the Nuremberg Laws denied German citizenship to people of "non-German blood." Marriage and sexual relations between Jews and non-Jews were also forbidden. The Nazis emphasized that these decrees merely formalized the unofficial discriminatory measures that had existed prior to 1935.

Since the Nuremberg Laws did not define a Jew as a person with certain religious beliefs, considerable confusion

The Nazi government announced a boycott of Jewish businesses on April 1, 1933. In this photo, an SA member distributes boycott pamphlets to German pedestrians.

1333

Reichsgesetzblatt

Teil I

| 1935 | Ausgegeben zu Berlin, den 14. November 1935 | Nr. 125 |

Erste Verordnung zum Reichsbürgergesetz.
Vom 14. November 1935.

Auf Grund des § 3 des Reichsbürgergesetzes vom 15. September 1935 (Reichsgesetzbl. I S. 1146) wird folgendes verordnet:

§ 1

(1) Bis zum Erlaß weiterer Vorschriften über den Reichsbürgerbrief gelten vorläufig als Reichsbürger die Staatsangehörigen deutschen oder artverwandten Blutes, die beim Inkrafttreten des Reichsbürgergesetzes das Reichstagswahlrecht besessen haben, oder denen der Reichsminister des Innern im Einvernehmen mit dem Stellvertreter des Führers das vorläufige Reichsbürgerrecht verleiht.

(2) Der Reichsminister des Innern kann im Einvernehmen mit dem Stellvertreter des Führers das vorläufige Reichsbürgerrecht entziehen.

§ 2

(1) Die Vorschriften des § 1 gelten auch für die staatsangehörigen jüdischen Mischlinge.

(2) Jüdischer Mischling ist, wer von einem oder zwei der Rasse nach volljüdischen Großelternteilen abstammt, sofern er nicht nach § 5 Abs. 2 als Jude gilt. Als volljüdisch gilt ein Großelternteil ohne weiteres, wenn er der jüdischen Religionsgemeinschaft angehört hat.

§ 3

Nur der Reichsbürger kann als Träger der vollen politischen Rechte das Stimmrecht in politischen Angelegenheiten ausüben und ein öffentliches Amt bekleiden. Der Reichsminister des Innern oder die von ihm ermächtigte Stelle kann für die Übergangszeit Ausnahmen für die Zulassung zu öffentlichen Ämtern gestatten. Die Angelegenheiten der Religionsgesellschaften werden nicht berührt.

§ 4

(1) Ein Jude kann nicht Reichsbürger sein. Ihm steht ein Stimmrecht in politischen Angelegenheiten nicht zu; er kann ein öffentliches Amt nicht bekleiden.

(2) Jüdische Beamte treten mit Ablauf des 31. Dezember 1935 in den Ruhestand. Wenn diese Beamten im Weltkrieg an der Front für das Deutsche Reich oder für seine Verbündeten gekämpft haben, erhalten sie bis zur Erreichung der Altersgrenze als Ruhegehalt die vollen zuletzt bezogenen ruhegehaltsfähigen Dienstbezüge; sie steigen jedoch nicht in Dienstaltersstufen auf. Nach Erreichung der Altersgrenze wird ihr Ruhegehalt nach den letzten ruhegehaltsfähigen Dienstbezügen neu berechnet.

(3) Die Angelegenheiten der Religionsgesellschaften werden nicht berührt.

Reichsgesetzbl. 1935 I

344

arose over how to classify Jews, especially people of mixed Jewish blood (called *Mischlinge*). A supplemental (added) decree passed on November 14, 1935, defined a Jew as anyone who had three or four Jewish grandparents. The decree also stipulated that a person would be considered a Jew if he had two Jewish parents and either belonged to the Jewish community or was married to a Jewish person. As the efforts to eliminate Jews from Germany grew more extreme after 1938, the subject of the *Mischlinge* continued to pose a problem for Nazi policymakers.

Things to Remember While Reading the Nuremberg Laws:

- The Reich Citizenship Law stripped Jews of their German citizenship and created a distinction between "citizens" and "subjects." According to these new definitions, a citizen of the German Reich was someone of German blood. Since Jews were considered to represent a race separate from Germans, they could only be subjects—never citizens.

- The Law for the Protection of German Blood and German Honor prohibited marriages and sexual relationships between Germans and Jews. Notice the term "Jew" is used instead of "non-Aryan" to designate the intended target of the legislation.

- Section 3 of the Law for the Protection of German Blood prohibits the employment of "German" females (under age 45) in Jewish households. The Nazis objected to the use of Aryans as servants to supposedly inferior non-Aryans such as Jews.

- According to Section 4 of the Law for the Protection of German Blood, Jews were prohibited from hoisting (raising) the newly recognized flag of the German Reich but were allowed to honor "Jewish" colors.

- Unlike the Nuremberg Laws, the First Regulation to the Reich Citizenship Law uses religion as way of defining Jewishness. The racialist doctrine of the Nazi party viewed Jews as members of a distinctive race, not simply members of a religion or community. However, in order to implement their anti-Jewish measures, the Nazis resorted to using religious practice as a way to identify who was a Jew.

- To separate full-blooded Jews from the *Mischlinge,* the Nazi administration employed "family researchers." However, many families lacked sufficient records and evidence of their full ancestral background. As a result, final decisions about race classifications were frequently based on random, biased court rulings.

The Reich Citizenship Law of 15 Sept 1935

The **Reichstag** has adopted unanimously, the following law, which is herewith **promulgated:**

Article 1

(1) A subject of the State is a person, who belongs to the protective union of the German **Reich**, and who, therefore, has particular obligations towards the Reich.

(2) The status of the subject is **acquired** in **accordance** with the **provisions** of the Reich- and State Law of Citizenship.

Article 2

(1) A citizen of the Reich is only that subject, who is of German or **kindred** blood and who, through his conduct, shows that he is both desirous and fit to serve faithfully the German people and Reich.

(2) The right to citizenship is acquired by the granting of Reich citizenship papers.

(3) Only the citizen of the Reich enjoys full political rights in accordance with the provisions of the Laws.

Article 3

The Reich Minister of the Interior **in conjunction with** the Deputy of the **Fuehrer** will issue the necessary legal and administrative **decrees** for the carrying out and **supplementing** of this law.

[Nuremberg], 15 Sept 1935 at the Reichsparteitag of Liberty
The Fuehrer and Reichs Chancellor
Adolf Hitler
The Reichs Minister of the Interior
Frick

Reichstag: Germany's parliament.

Promulgated: To make known by open declaration.

Reich: German word for empire.

Acquired: Gotten or possessed as one's own.

Accordance: Agreement.

Provisions: Under the conditions set forth in the law in question.

Kindred: A group of related individuals.

In conjunction with: Acting with.

Fuehrer: Also spelled "führer"; means "leader" in German.

Decrees: An order, usually having the force of law.

Supplementing: Adding to.

Law for the Protection of German Blood and German Honor of 15 September 1935

*Thoroughly convinced by the knowledge that the purity of German blood is essential for the further existence of the German people and **inturned** by the **inflexible** will to safe-guard the German nation for the entire future, the Reich Parliament (Reichstag) has resolved upon the following law unanimously which is promulgated herewith:*

Section 1

(1) *Marriages between Jews and **nationals** of German or kindred blood are forbidden. Marriages concluded **in defiance of** this law are **void**, even if, for the purpose of evading this law, they are concluded abroad.*

(2) ***Proceedings** for **annulment** may be initiated only by the Public **Prosecutor**.*

Section 2

***Relations** outside marriage between Jews and nationals of German or kindred blood are forbidden.*

Section 3

Jews will not be permitted to employ female nationals of German or kindred blood in their household.

Section 4

(1) *Jews are forbidden to **hoist** the Reichs and national flag and to present the colors of the Reich.*

(2) *On the other hand they are permitted to present the Jewish colors. The exercise of this authority is protected by the State.*

Section 5

(1) *Who acts **contrary** to the **prohibition** of section 1 will be punished with hard labor.*

Inturned: Probably a misspelling of "interned," meaning bound or confined by.

Inflexible: Rigid; incapable of being changed.

Nationals: Citizens.

In defiance of: Despite; challenging or disagreeing.

Void: Not legally valid.

Proceedings: Action taken.

Annulment: To make legally void or nonexistent.

Prosecutor: An attorney who conducts court business on behalf of the government.

Relations: In this case, sexual relations.

Hoist: Raise or fly.

Contrary: Being opposite to or in conflict with.

Prohibition: Forbidding by authority; an order to prevent someone from doing something.

A photomontage that includes the front page of the Badische Presse with the headline "The Nuremburg Laws." The accompanying identification card belongs to a German Jewess.

(2)	The man who acts contrary to the prohibition of section 2 will be punished with imprisonment or with hard labor.

(3)	Who acts contrary to the provisions of sections 3 or 4 will be punished with imprisonment up to a year and with a fine or with one of these penalties.

Section 6

The Reich Minister of the Interior in agreement with the Deputy of the Fuehrer and the Reich Minister of Justice will issue the legal *and administrative regulations which are required for the **implementation** and supplementation of this law.*

Section 7

The law will become effective on the day after the promulgation, section 3 however only on ... 1 January 1936.

[Nuremberg], the 15 September 1935 at the Reich Party Rally of freedom.

The Fuehrer and Reich Chancellor
Adolf Hitler
The Reich Minister of Interior
Frick
The Reich Minister of Justice
Dr. Gurtner
The Deputy of the Fuehrer
R. Hess
Reich Minister without portfolio

First Regulation to the Reich Citizenship Law of 14 Nov. 1935

Article 1

(1) *Until further issue of regulations regarding citizenship papers, all subjects of German or kindred blood, who possessed the right to vote in the Reichstag elections, at the time the Citizenship Law came into effect, shall, for the time being, possess the rights of Reich citizens. The same shall be true of those whom the Reich Minister of the Interior, in conjunction with the Deputy of the Fuehrer, has given the **preliminary** citizenship.*

(2) *The Reich Minister of the Interior, in conjunction with the Deputy of the Fuehrer, can withdraw the preliminary citizenship.*

Implementation: Carrying out.

Preliminary: Something temporary that comes before something more permanent.

Article 2

(1) The regulations in Article 1 are also valid for Reichs subjects of mixed, Jewish blood.

(2) An individual of mixed Jewish blood, is one who descended from one or two grandparents who were racially full Jews, insofar as does not count as a Jew according to Article 5, paragraph 2. One grandparent shall be considered as full-blooded Jew if he or she belonged to the Jewish religious community.

Article 3

Only the Reich citizen, as bearer of full political rights, exercises the right to vote in political affairs, and can hold a public office. The Reich Minister of the Interior, or any agency empowered by him, can make exceptions during the transition period, with regard to occupying public offices. The affairs of religious organizations will not be touched upon.

Article 4

(1) A Jew cannot be a citizen of the Reich. He has no right to vote in political affairs; he cannot occupy a public office.

(2) Jewish officials will retire as of 31 December 1935. If these officials served at the front in the World War, either for Germany or **her allies**, they will receive in full, until they reach the age limit, the pension to which they were entitled according to last received wages; they will, however, not advance in seniority....

(3) The affairs of religious organizations will not be touched upon.

(4) The conditions of service of teachers in Jewish public schools remain unchanged, until new regulations of the Jewish school systems are issued.

Her allies: In this case, the countries that fought with Germany in World War I, namely Austria, Turkey, and Bulgaria.

Article 5

(1) A Jew is anyone who descended from at least three grand-parents who were racially full Jews. Article 2, par. 2, second sentence will apply.

(2) A Jew is also one who descended from two full Jewish parents, if:

    (a) he belonged to the Jewish religious community at the time this law was issued or who joined the community later.

    (b) he was married to a Jewish person, at the time the law was issued, or married one subsequently.

    (c) he is the offspring from a marriage with a Jew, in the sense of Section 1, which was contracted after the Law for the Protection of German Blood and German Honor became effective....

    (d) he is the offspring of an extramarital relationship, with a Jew, according to Section 1, and will be born out of wedlock after July 31, 1936.

Article 6

(1) As far as demands are concerned for the pureness of blood as laid down in Reichs law or in orders of the N.S.D.A.P. and its **echelons**—not covered in Article 5—they will not be touched upon.

(2) Any other demands on pureness of blood, not covered in Article 5, can only be made with permission from the Reich Minister of the Interior and the Deputy of the Fuehrer....

Article 7

The Fuehrer and Reichs Chancellor can grant exemptions from the regulations laid down in the law.

Echelons: Levels within an organization.

Axis: Germany and her allies in World War II.

Berlin, 14 November 1935
The Fuehrer and Reichs Chancellor
Adolf Hitler
The Reich Minister of the Interior
Frick
The Deputy of the Fuehrer
R. Hess
—Reich Minister without Portfolio

(As translated from the Reichsgesetzblatt by the Office of U.S. Chief of Counsel for the Prosecution of Axis Criminality in Mendelsohn, pp. 22-32)

What happened next...

Many Jews believed that the Nuremberg Laws would help reestablish a degree of stability in Germany. Even though they had lost their political rights, Jews hoped that the official decrees would reduce violent and random attacks against their synagogues (Jewish places of worship), businesses, and homes. In fact, many Jews who had immigrated to other countries during the terror-filled years of 1933 and 1934 returned to Germany after 1935.

Fearing international criticism, Hitler also relaxed many antisemitic measures in preparation for the 1936 Olympic Games, scheduled to be held in Berlin. To create a false impression for foreign visitors, the Nazis removed from public places throughout the city many signs that read: "Jews Unwelcome." While German Jewish athletes were not allowed to participate in the Olympics, the führer did have to contend with the outstanding performance of ten black American athletes, including track sensation Jessie Owens, who won four gold medals. Consistent with Nazi racialist beliefs, Hitler considered blacks to be inferior to Aryans. He showed his displeasure at Owens's win by leaving the Olympic stadium before the athlete received one of his medals. Once the Olympic Games ended, Hitler and the Nazis resumed their hostile actions to persecute German Jews.

Wilhelm Frick (1877-1946)

Wilhelm Frick was one of the driving forces behind the institution of the Nuremberg Laws. After receiving his doctorate in law from Heidelberg, Frick worked as an official in the Munich police department from 1904 to 1924. A long-standing sympathizer of the Nazi cause, he met Hitler early on, when the aspiring Nazi leader first applied for permits to hold political meetings. Serving as Hitler's right-hand man inside the Munich police department, Frick was able to help free Hitler after an arrest.

For his participation in the 1923 Munich Beer Hall Putsch, an early Nazi uprising, Frick was arrested and sentenced to prison. After his sentence was suspended (set aside) in 1924, he resumed his duties at the police head-quarters and was elected as one of the first Nazi party delegates to the Reichstag.

Frick was also the first Nazi to hold an important provincial (local government) post, becoming minister of the interior in Thuringia in 1930. While serving this post, he fired anti-Nazi police officers, released criminals involved in the murder of two prominent German Jews, banned jazz music and the antiwar film *All Quiet on the Western Front,* and introduced special nationalistic prayers for schools (prayers that placed the well-being of Germany above all else).

When the Nazis came to power in 1933, Hitler appointed Frick Germany's minister of the interior, an important position that he held until 1943. Frick's main role in the Nazi party was to help Hitler gain power legally and establish a totalitarian police state (firm, centralized control of all citizens). In addition to drafting the Nuremberg Laws on Citizenship, Frick used his legal background to craft laws that abolished (did away with) non-Nazi political parties, trade unions, and all provincial legislatures.

Frick also failed to impose any legal limitations on the powers of the Gestapo or the SS. At the Nuremberg trial held after World War II, he refused to testify and was found guilty of crimes against peace, war crimes, and crimes against humanity. Frick was hanged at Nuremberg on October 16, 1946.

Over the course of their 12-year reign, the Nazis enacted some 400 laws and decrees regarding Jews living under the jurisdiction of the Third Reich. In fact, the Nazis published 13 supplementary (added) orders to the Reich Citizenship Law (one of the two laws referred to as the Nuremberg Laws), including the last one passed on July 1, 1943.

Under the Nuremberg Laws, race became the legal basis for national citizenship for the first time in modern history. The Nuremberg Laws also paved the way for further anti-Jewish regulations. In 1938, the Nazis instituted the "Aryanization" of Jewish businesses, which meant Jews were forced to sell their stores and shops to Germans at hugely discounted prices. The complex web of anti-Jewish decrees isolated Jews from other Germans and set them outside of any protective governing jurisdiction (meaning they had no legal representation). Completely at the mercy of their persecutors, German Jews increasingly lost the political, legal, and social rights that bound them to society.

Nuremberg, a charming medieval city, became the favorite showplace of the Nazi party and the setting for spectacular party rallies. After the Nazis entered World War II, the sound of Allied bombing replaced the sound of marching feet and nationalist songs that once filled the crooked, cobblestone streets. (The combined forces of Great Britain, the United States, the Soviet Union, France, and China were known as the Allied Powers during World War II.) Nuremberg suffered severe damage from air and land bombing raids that occurred during the war. After Germany's defeat in 1945, the Allies chose Nuremberg as the site for the public trial of 22 Nazi leaders.

Did you know...

- The Nuremberg Laws set strict rules on citizenship by defining what it was to be German—and, most importantly, what it was to be Jewish. Citizenship was denied to individuals of Jewish ancestry. In order to clarify cases of mixed "blood" or heritage—cases in which less than three grandparents were Aryan, or German—the Nazis issued elaborate diagrams of "acceptable" family trees.

- Even after the Nuremberg Laws were adopted, many Jews did not leave Germany because they loved their country and considered themselves German. Many believed that the reign of Hitler and his antisemitic ideas would be short-lived. Eventually, government restrictions made escape from Germany very difficult for Jews.

- Film director Leni Riefenstahl captured the spectacular 1934 Nazi party rally at Nuremberg in her documentary masterpiece *Triumph of the Will,* which remains one of the most famous pieces of Nazi propaganda (a vehicle that spreads the Nazi message).

- Unlike his close and loyal friend Wilhelm Frick, Adolf Hitler escaped the Nuremberg Trials after World War II by shooting himself in his underground bunker (fortified chamber) in Berlin on April 30, 1945.

For Further Reading

Bachrach, Susan D. *Tell Them We Remember: The Story of the Holocaust.* Boston: Little, Brown, and Company, 1994.

Chaikin, Miriam. *Nightmare in History: The Holocaust, 1933-1945.* New York: Clarion Books, 1987.

The Holocaust: Selected Documents in 18 Volumes. Edited by John Mendelsohn. New York: Garland Publishing, 1982.

Koehn, Ilse. *Mischlinge, Second Degree.* New York: Greenwillow Books, 1977.

Frau Wilhelmine Haferkamp

Interview in *Frauen,
Motherhood Times Ten,
and Food to Spare*

Conducted by Alison Owings, 1987

They didn't go to war and, in most cases, they weren't active members of the Nazi party (taken from the full name of the National Socialist German Workers' party). But the women who lived in Nazi Germany (1933-1945) served as firsthand witnesses, observing the Third Reich in action. (The Third Reich is the name given to the Nazi-controlled government in Germany. The word *reich,* pronounced RIKE, means "empire" or "kingdom.") Frau Wilhelmine Haferkamp was 22 years old and pregnant with her fourth child in 1933 when her husband joined the Nazi party. (*Frau* is a term that refers to a German married woman. The title is equivalent to "Mrs.") Consistent with Nazi goals and ambitions, the Haferkamps had many more children during the 12 years of the Third Reich. Hitler's goal was to build a superrace of Aryans, or Germans. To achieve this goal, Hitler banned birth control and abortion among Germans and offered financial aid to worthy, racially pure Aryan families. Haferkamp received a bronze, silver, and gold Mother's Cross for her childbearing contributions. With each successive child, she received additional money, called *kindergeld,* from the government, which she saved in special bank accounts. By 1945, shortly after the end of World War II, she had given birth to her tenth child.

While Hitler was encouraging Aryan mothers to have as many children as possible, he was brutally suppressing and murdering those he perceived to be a threat to his beloved homeland. Shortly after becoming chancellor of Germany in 1933, Hitler instituted numerous legislative orders that silenced his political opponents. He also led an extensive anti-Jewish campaign that stripped German Jews of their rights and forced many to give up their jobs. Haferkamp put herself at risk by helping the non-Jewish prisoners of the Nazis (mainly people who disagreed with the Nazi political philosophy), but she implies in the following interview that the risks were too high to help those who were most persecuted—the Jews. While she and her husband received several stern warnings concerning her kindness toward prison laborers, it is unlikely that such leniency (or tolerance) would have been extended if she had aided Jews. Those caught violating Nazi law were subject to arrest, imprisonment without trial, internment (or confinement) at concentration camps, possible torture, and even death.

The story of Frau Wilhelmine is one that combines heroism with cowardice and happiness with pain and fear. She acknowledges the privileges she and her family enjoyed and relates her efforts to share her meager fortunes with those who were cast off as enemies by the Nazis. One of the most difficult questions still being explored today is the role ordinary people played in Nazi Germany. Like many first-hand accounts from this dark period of history, it is a story that is difficult to forget.

Things to Remember While Reading Haferkamp's Interview:

- This interview was conducted in German. The following selection is a literal (word-for-word) translation. It includes many German words such as *ja* ("yes") and the typical sentence ending of *nicht* ("no") to give readers the feeling that Haferkamp is actually speaking.

- The interviewer's questions appear in **bold**. Haferkamp's words appear within "quotation marks." Certain words have been underlined for emphasis.

- Notice the pressure placed on the Haferkamps to register their children in Nazi-sponsored youth programs. By connecting educational benefits with party registration, the Nazis gained control of Germany's young people. (See entry box titled "Hitler Youth.")

- The Nazis discriminated against people with mental and physical disabilities because they did not fit the Aryan ideal. Haferkamp refers to the horrendous treatment of individuals with chronic (always present) illnesses and hereditary diseases. Many children and adults deemed "unfit" were institutionalized or killed.

Frauen, Motherhood Times Ten, and Food to Spare

"**B**ut then all at once it happened. When one had ten children, well not ten, but a pile of them, one should join the [Nazi] party; '33 it was, **nicht**? I already had three children and the fourth on the way. When 'child rich' (**kinderreiche**) people were in the Party, the children had a great chance to advance. Stake claims and everything. **Ja**, what else could my husband do? They joined the Party, nicht? There was nothing else we could do. I got thirty **marks** per child from the Hitler government, came every month, and twenty marks' child aid from the city of Oberhausen. Was fifty marks per child. That was a lot of money. I sometimes got more 'child money' (Kindergeld) than my husband earned...."

What did she think when Hitler came to power?

"I didn't know him. I had a lot to do with the children. I always said, I had no time. To think about it, nicht? Ja, I often complained. There were meetings there and meetings there and there meetings.... Our 'Dicke,' one of the older children, when she was in school, had to be in the **BdM**. Otherwise she couldn't go to school... You <u>had</u> to be in the BdM. I still see ours running with the little shirts and the little blue skirts and the black scarves." Asked what she thought about the organization itself, she said she thought it was like the Girl Scouts, or a gymnastics or singing club. "They got their uniforms, nicht? And marched through the streets. They didn't learn anything harmful...."

Because Herr Haferkamp was a Party member, his children also got more schooling than they would have otherwise. "If you

Nicht: German for "no"; commonly used at the end of a sentence for extra emphasis.

Kinderreiche: German for "rich in children"; one who has many children.

Ja: German for "yes."

Marks: German unit of currency or money (comparable to the U.S. dollar).

BdM: Initials for Bund Deutscher Madel (League for German Girls), a girls' division of Hitler Youth.

went to high school, the parents had to pay. And if you were in the NSDAP [the Nazi Party], everything was paid."

Did she join the Party, too?

*"Never. My mother wasn't in it, either. To the **contrary**, a couple times I got a warning." With those words, Frau Haferkamp launched into stories that have become lore in her family.*

*Most of the stories involved slave laborers, prisoners of war or the human **booty** of Nazi **expansionism**, who did hard manual work in Germany, got meager rations, and lived an altogether miserable existence. To help insure their misery, the Nazi regime included them in the category of the "enemy" and forbade the German citizenry from having friendly relations with them. Some slave laborers worked on construction projects right outside the Haferkamp home, and especially caught the eye of Frau Haferkamp and her oldest boy. He had the chore of going to the baker's every morning for fresh breakfast rolls.*

*"I can still see him running with the net bag on his back, with rolls in it, and [past] the ditches in the streets where a new drainage system was being put in. And our boy always had pity. He always threw rolls [to the laborers] in the ditches." She said, laughing, "He just went by the row like a farmer sowing his crop." One of her sisters, at the house on a visit, was so distressed to see the freezing prisoners with "icicles in their beards" that she threw them the Christmas cookies she had brought. The gesture brought a **rebuke** from the Nazis—rather, another rebuke.*

By then, Frau Wilhelmine Haferkamp had also committed the crime of "füttern den Feind" [feeding the enemy].... "Now what really happened, [it] was <u>cold</u> outside. And every day I cooked a big pot of milk soup for the children, nicht? Nice and hot. Got a lot of milk on the children's ration cards. And then I put a whole cube of butter in it, the pot was full, and a lot of sugar, because sugar nourishes, nicht? And I lived upstairs. My mother-in-law lived down-

Contrary: Just the opposite.

Booty: Something taken by force.

Expansionism: Increasing the territory held by a nation.

Rebuke: An expression of strong disapproval.

Hitler Youth

The Nazis began sponsoring youth groups as early as 1922. Shortly after seizing power in 1933, they initiated a "coordinating" program that essentially disbanded most non-Nazi youth organizations. At first Catholic youth groups were allowed to exist, but they too were forbidden by 1937. The most significant Nazi youth organization, *Hitler Jugend,* or Hitler Youth, groomed boys to be soldiers and defenders of Nazism. Activities included camping, sporting competitions, evening social programs—all conducted with militarylike discipline, including the requirement that members wear uniforms.

The Nazis also created a group for girls called *Bund Deutscher Madel,* or League for German Girls. The League taught young girls the importance of being loyal Nazis and mothers of racially pure Germans. Much like the boys in Hitler Youth, girls wore standard uniforms and participated in parades, rallies, and other weekly group functions.

A law passed in 1936 made membership in the Hitler Youth compulsory (absolutely necessary), and over 7 million young boys were enrolled by 1939. German youth had to register with the Reich Youth Headquarters at the age of ten. This registration process included an extensive investigation of family background to assure racial purity. (Being "racially pure" meant not having Jewish ancestry.)

stairs.... *I looked out the window and pointed to 'the bandolios' [what she called the laborers] that I was putting something in the hallway. They were afraid to get out of the ditches and they wanted to eat it. Then I went to the watchman and I said, 'Listen, you too are married.' I said, 'I have many children.... And I cooked a big pot of milk soup.' I say, 'Can I not give it to the poor men? You wouldn't want me to throw it down the toilet....'*

"He looked at me, he said ... 'You are an **obstinate** *dame.... Go ahead and do what you have to, but I have seen* <u>nothing</u>.*' Then*

Obstinate: Stubborn.

antisemitism

(Continued from previous page)

Hitler Youth was organized into two age groups: one for ages ten to fourteen and one for ages fourteen to eighteen. At the age of eighteen, young men graduated from Hitler Youth to become members of the National Socialist German Workers' (Nazi) party. The next year, they enrolled in the State Labor Service (*Reichsarbeitsdienst*), which involved demanding physical labor and strict discipline. After completing the mandatory six-month term in the State Labor Service, the young Nazis then enrolled in the armed forces (*Wehrmacht*) to put in two years of military service.

Many who grew up as members of Hitler Youth went directly to the SS (*Schutzstaffel*), the police force of the Nazi party who operated the concentration camps. As the war progressed in Europe and German forces needed additional manpower to recover from losses, pressure grew to send members of Hitler Youth to work in military support functions at younger and younger ages. When the Allied armies captured areas of Germany in the spring of 1945, boys as young as eight were found in uniform, armed with weapons and fighting as adults.

For more information on Hitler Youth, see *Children of the Swastika* by Eileen Heyes, published by Millbrook Press (Brookfield, CT), 1993.

I made the soup so hot, put it down in the hallway and with a ladling spoon, not with individual bowls, and then I pointed to it. One by one, they jumped out of the ditches and took the big soup spoon ... until it was empty. One day, my husband got a card from the Party. They would like him to appear in the Party office.

*"And they said, 'Listen, your wife is sure doing fine things. How can she **fodder** our enemies?' 'Ja, well, I can't do anything about it, I'm not always home, I don't see it.' Then when my husband came home, he really yelled at me ..., he said, 'You will land*

Fodder: Feed.

me in the <u>devil's kitchen</u> if you keep doing that. And I am a Party member.... And what do you think will happen when they catch me? They will take me somewhere else....'"

Once, the enemy did something in return. Several of her children were playing near a construction site "canal" when a young daughter, trying to catch up with the older children, fell head-first into a deep hole. "The whole street cried, 'The best-looking Haferkamp child is dead.'" An "enemy" laborer whom Frau Haferkamp had been "foddering" jumped down after the girl and rescued her.

*No matter how **humanistic** and brave Frau Haferkamp was, the people she had spoken thus far of feeding were "Aryans," a "safer enemy" to help than Jews. But by then, were there any Jews in Oberhausen? For the first time since she began her story, her voice became soft. "Ja. There were Jews. There were even a lot of Jews. We even knew a Jew we did not know was a Jew. Eichherz was their name. Bought furniture [from their store] when we first married. And my husband went to the doctor. Dr. Floss was his name and [he] was also a Nazi.... And my husband laid his jacket over the chair. The [receipt] book fell out of his pocket, that you bought furniture you couldn't pay for all at once.... And the doctor saw that. Then he said ... ' <u>What?</u> You as a member of the Party, you buy from a Jew?' And he didn't know at all it was a Jew." She implied that her husband continued the payments.*

*She also implied that she had defied the **quasi-order** not to shop at Jewish stores. "You shopped where you liked something. They really made you crazy afterward. 'What? [they said.] You shopped at a Jew's store?' How did you know who was a Jew? Now, one knew what one was. What I always thought earlier, it's a difference like Catholic, Protestant. He's a Jew. Nicht?"*

[Frau Haferkamp went on:] "We had a ... Dr. Stein. We did not know that [he] was a Jew. [Stein is usually, but not always, a Jewish name.] My God, I was <u>furious,</u> was I ever furious, when I

Humanistic: Concerned with well-being of others.

Quasi-order: An order not strictly enforced.

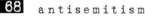

once went to Market Street and, because he was a Jew ... naked, and he had a sign hanging around his neck, 'I am the Jew Dr. Stein.'"

She began to shout. "Stark naked, down the middle of the street they chased him, and behind him with the whip. I <u>saw</u> it.... And that was our family doctor.... He had not done anything at all. They just found out who was a Jew.... That's what the Nazi **swine** did, really...."

When asked what happened to Dr. Stein, Frau Haferkamp looked distraught. "Ja, they took him away. They took him away. That was terrible." **Was it difficult not to be able to help him?** "They would have beat us dead.... You can believe it.... Do not get involved. Na, that's how we got through, as a little person...."

Frau Haferkamp knew of many more sad fates, including an example of the Nazis' early use of **euthanasia**.

"In the house where I lived, my brother-in-law's sister also lived and she had a sick child. Looked fifteen, but she was already nineteen. And she was in Essen, near Oberhausen. It was called the Franz Hals [?] House where children who are sort of.... She got her sickness through a **festering** in the middle ear. Anni von Thiel. And she came first to the Franz Hals House. And then in the Hitler time, if you inherited something or had something, nicht? I was standing below with my milk jug, the milkman came by at the door, and got milk with Frau von Thiel. And she got a letter from Essen. Anni has been ... transferred, let us say, to Krefeld, nicht? She had an inflammation of her lungs. And [Frau von Thiel] was **bawling**. She said, 'My God, look, she's been away a whole week. Couldn't they have told me earlier?...' I said, 'Wait, give me the letter and I'll show it to my husband....' [When shown the letter, he] said, 'What?' Looked at it again. 'She's not coming back. They're **gassing** them all....'

"That was that. When they said she was transferred, the child was already dead. And a couple days later she got another let-

Swine: Pigs; a derogatory term when applied to a person.

Euthanasia: The practice of killing or permitting death of sick or injured persons.

Festering: Contamination from an infected (pus-filled) sore.

Bawling: Crying.

Gassing: Killing in gas chambers.

Nonlethal inhumanities: Acts designed to torture—but not to kill—the intended victim.

Propagate: To multiply or continue a heritage.

Communist: An advocate of a political and economic theory that strives for the formation of a classless society through the communal, or group, ownership of all property.

ter. When the burial is going to be.... They gassed her.... Only because she had a disease."

[Frau Haferkamp] knew of **nonlethal inhumanities**, too. One classmate "also had a child every year" and "did not get a penny from Hitler, that is, from Hitler's side, because they all [all of the children] had inherited diseases. You had to be healthy, the children had to be healthy, so that you can **propagate** your heirs and no sick ones. I got all that child money and she got nothing at all."

What did such a nice family man, and Party member [Herr Haferkamp], think of Jews?

"I will honestly say, my husband actually had Jews as friends.... Well, we did not really think about what a Jew is. 'Zo vot [so what]?' we always said...."

Did she ever think she should have done something earlier against the Nazis?...

"You could not say a lot. Back then in the Nazi time, you were not even allowed to <u>have</u> your own opinion, nicht? If it already somehow was known that he or he complained about the Party, nicht? We knew one.... They always said to him, **Communist**, but he was not a Communist. The parents were <u>so</u> nice.... And one day the word was, they beat [him] up. Nobody knew where. Nobody knew how. He was in the hospital...." [He later died in the hospital.] (Owings, pp. 19-26)

What happened next....

When the bombing raids worsened across Germany, Frau Haferkamp and her children were evacuated to a farm in the rural area of southwestern Germany. Even on a remote farm, she continued to help prisoners in the area. Herr Haferkamp

Frau Wilhelmine Haferkamp (1911—)

Wilhelmine Haferkamp was born in Oberhausen, Germany. Her father and two brothers were train conductors. Hit hard financially in the aftermath of World War I, her family took drastic measures and sent her to live with relatives in Holland who owned a restaurant. The young girl returned to Germany a year later but always remembered the Dutch people fondly. As a teenager, she fell in love with Heinrich Haferkamp, a neighborhood boy who worked in the nearby stone mines. Wilhelmine's Catholic parents opposed their marriage because Heinrich was Protestant. Nevertheless, Wilhelmine converted to the Protestant faith, married Heinrich when she was 19, and together they had ten children. Herr Haferkamp died of lung disease shortly after World War II. Frau Haferkamp lives alone in a small town in Germany. As of the early 1990s, nine of her children were still alive, and five lived in the United States.

spent the war in the army, performing clerical services. When World War II ended in 1945, he rejoined his wife, arriving shortly after the birth of their last child. With the collapse of the German economy, bank accounts holding *kindergeld* were dissolved (meaning the money in the accounts no longer had value). Years later, during a trip to Stuttgart, Germany, Haferkamp encountered a man who seemed familiar to her. He turned out to be the prisoner who saved her daughter years ago. The man remembered Haferkamp as the only German woman who defied (went against) Nazi guards and helped feed starving prisoners.

Did you know...

- The Nazi party organized the *Lebensborn* ("Fountain of Life") program for the purpose of creating a German superrace through selective breeding. Unmarried "racially pure" women were encouraged to have children with certain elite Nazi men. Once pregnant, they were sent to one of twelve special state-sponsored maternity centers, where they received the best possible medical care.

- The *Lebensborn* program also engineered the kidnaping of hundreds of thousands of "racially acceptable" children with Aryan features from German-occupied countries to add to the breeding stock of the Third Reich.

- By 1936 more than 2 million German girls had enrolled in the Nazi-sponsored BdM program, or *Bund Deutscher Madel* ("League for German Girls"). In addition to party philosophy and service, young girls were schooled in physical fitness in preparation for motherhood.

- Girls ages 17 to 21 were enrolled in a special branch of the BdM called *Glaube and Schonheit* ("Faith and Beauty"), where they were educated in domestic arts and fashion design. This organization helped train women to conform to the Nazi version of ideal womanhood.

For Further Reading

Friedman, Ina R. *The Other Victims: First Person Stories of Non-Jews Persecuted by the Nazis.* Boston: Houghton Mifflin, 1990.

Gehrts, Barbara. *Don't Say a Word.* New York: M. K. McElderry Books, 1986.

Owings, Alison. *Frauen: German Women Recall the Third Reich.* New Brunswick, NJ: Rutgers University Press, 1993.

HOLOCAUST escalation

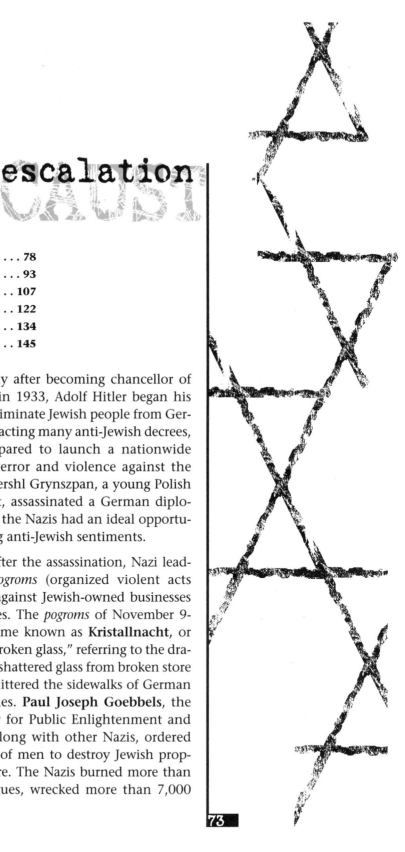

Immediately after becoming chancellor of Germany in 1933, Adolf Hitler began his campaign to eliminate Jewish people from Germany. After enacting many anti-Jewish decrees, the Nazis prepared to launch a nationwide campaign of terror and violence against the Jews. When Hershl Grynszpan, a young Polish Jewish student, assassinated a German diplomat in France, the Nazis had an ideal opportunity for stirring anti-Jewish sentiments.

Shortly after the assassination, Nazi leaders ordered *pogroms* (organized violent acts against Jews) against Jewish-owned businesses and synagogues. The *pogroms* of November 9-10, 1938, became known as **Kristallnacht**, or the "night of broken glass," referring to the dramatic scene of shattered glass from broken store windows that littered the sidewalks of German towns and cities. **Paul Joseph Goebbels**, the Reich Minister for Public Enlightenment and Propaganda, along with other Nazis, ordered roving groups of men to destroy Jewish property and culture. The Nazis burned more than 1,000 synagogues, wrecked more than 7,000

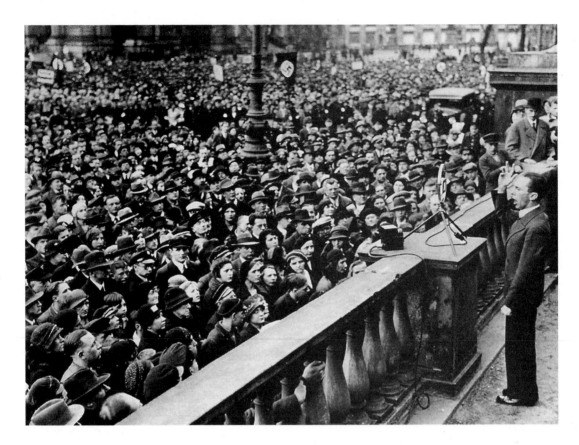

On April 1, 1933, Paul Joseph Goebbels delivered a speech to a crowd in the Berlin Lustgarte. Goebbels' speech supported a boycott of Jewish-owned businesses.

Jewish stores, and killed nearly 100 Jewish people. This reign of terror was witnessed firsthand by **Otto D. Tolischus**, a German-born reporter on the staff of the *New York Times*.

Jewish migration from Germany was very difficult once Hitler gained control of Germany. In order for Jewish people to leave Germany, other countries had to formally agree to accept these refugees. Some Jews who had the connections and financial resources for their travel expenses, passports, and visas could escape Germany and move to another country. Nearly 150,000 Jews managed to emigrate by the end of 1938, representing 30 percent of Germany's entire Jewish population. However, most countries maintained their existing quotas, which limited the number of persons allowed to enter those nations each year.

The ultimate goal of Hitler was to rule the world. The Nazis believed that a conspiracy of "worldwide Jewry" threatened to take over all countries, including Germany. Hitler

viewed Bolshevism, a form of communism that arose in Russia in the early 1900s, to be a Jewish-controlled political movement designed to obtain world power. Hitler's war plans served two goals: first to conduct a holy war against "Jewish Bolshevism," and second to create *Lebensraum,* or living space, for the German people.

Even as Germany prepared for war during the late 1930s, Hitler successfully expanded into Austria and Czechoslovakia without resorting to actual military conflict. A secret agreement with the Soviets set the stage for World War II when Germany invaded Poland in September 1939. To expand the German empire while cleansing the new territories of racial impurities, **Reinhard Heydrich**, chief of security police, issued orders titled the "Jewish Question in Occupied Territory." This directive reveals that the Nazis had a master plan for the annihilation, or utter destruction, of the Jews in Europe. Heydrich ordered the Nazis to concentrate Jews within cities that had railroad facilities "so that the later mea-

During Kristallnacht, the synagogue in Ober Ramstadt burned to the ground after the local fire department made no attempt to stop the blaze.

A Jewish policeman and a German soldier direct pedestrian traffic across the main street that divides the two sections of the Lodz (Poland) ghetto.

WOHNGEBIET DER
JUDEN
BETRETEN
VERBOTEN

sures will be easier." Throughout German-occupied Poland, the Nazis moved Jewish people to designated urban areas, which became known as *ghettos*.

Chaim Kaplan lived in Warsaw, Poland, and worked as a principal of a Hebrew school. Although he had started writing a diary as a way to record his private thoughts, he deliberately changed the style of his writing when war broke out, reporting on the mounting tragedy occurring around him. *The Warsaw Diary of Chaim Kaplan* contains a remarkable firsthand account of the lives of Jews within the Warsaw ghetto.

In her personal account, *A Square of Sky,* **Janina David** records the unforgettable horror and terror of living in the Nazi-controlled Jewish ghetto of Warsaw. David describes her experiences in the fall of 1940, when the Warsaw ghetto became "closed," or sealed off from surrounding neighborhoods. Her straightforward depiction conveys the harrowing and isolating experience of being surrounded by ghetto walls.

In occupied Poland, Hitler appointed his personal lawyer, Hans Frank, as governor-general of the "General Government" portion of Poland, where undesirable Poles and Jews were housed. Under his brutal command, Frank destroyed Poland as a national entity.

On June 24, 1941, the Nazis established two ghettos in Kovno (now Kaunas), Lithuania. About 30,000 Jews were imprisoned there when the ghetto was sealed off. One Lithuanian Jew, **Avraham Tory**, served as a member of the Nazi-sanctioned (or supported) Jewish Council. The Jewish Council, also called the *Judenrat,* played a critical role in managing the internal operations of the ghetto. Tory, a young American-educated lawyer, began writing a diary to document the events he witnessed.

To preserve political order and devotion to the German fatherland, the Nazis identified other so-called threats and targeted them for persecution. **Pastor Christian Reger**, a Christian minister, became disillusioned with Nazism and fought the repressive, violent government from his pulpit. In his story, he explains how he began to use his weekly sermons to preach the messages of his faith rather than the Nazi-directed ideas of hatred. After repeatedly harassing and arresting Reger, local party officials finally silenced him by condemning him to Dachau in 1940.

The Nazis also attempted to protect Aryan racial purity from the corrupting influences of "defective elements," namely people with hereditary disabilities. People with physical or mental disabilities were required by law to undergo sterilization. From 1934 to 1939, between 350,000 and 400,000 persons were forced to endure involuntary sterilization. At the age of 16, **Franziska Schwarz**, who was born deaf, also became caught in the tangle of Nazi racialism.

Otto D. Tolischus

Newspaper account of *Kristallnacht*

First published in the New York Times
November 11, 1938

A month after becoming German chancellor on January 30, 1933, Adolf Hitler began his campaign to eliminate Jewish people from Germany. Hitler, who was the leader of the Nazi (National Socialist German Workers') party, believed that Jews represented a distinct race from Germans. He viewed the German race, which he called "Aryan," as a superior race whose very survival was threatened by the corrupting influences of "inferior" peoples like the Jews. In fact, according to Hitler and other Nazi members, the Jews presented the most serious threat to the survival of the German people.

As the first of numerous nationwide anti-Jewish actions, the Nazi government ordered a boycott of all Jewish businesses for April 1, 1933. Shortly after the boycott, the Nazis passed laws forcing non-Aryans from civil service (government management) positions and certain professions such as law and medicine. The Nuremberg Laws, passed on September 15, 1935, deprived Jews of their rights as German citizens. Despite criticism from foreign countries, antisemitic (anti-Jewish) measures continued: random acts of violence against individuals, synagogues (Jewish houses of worship), and Jewish shops were common. The economic situation of the German Jews continued to deteriorate as tens of thousands of Jewish professionals lost their jobs.

While many large Jewish-owned businesses remained opened, countless other smaller firms were "voluntarily" transferred to Aryan owners at severely discounted prices. Throughout the first six months of 1938, the Nazis passed several decrees designed to aid the process of seizing ownership of Jewish business enterprises. As the Nazis escalated

The Hotel Royal in Evian-les Bains (France) was the site of the International Conference on Refugees. The conference was held July 6-13, 1938, with representatives from 32 nations in attendance.

their campaign against the Jews, they initiated several other important legislative (legal) measures that made it easier for authorities to identify Jews. A law passed July 23, 1938, required every Jew to obtain an identity card from the police. The Law Regarding Changes of Family Names and Given Names, passed the following month, stipulated all male Jews to take the name Israel and all female Jews to take the name Sarah. Later in the fall, all Jewish people with passports for foreign travel had to turn in their passports and have them marked with the letter "J" for Jew.

Jewish Migration from Germany

In order for Jewish people to emigrate from, or leave, Nazi-controlled Germany, other countries had to formally agree to accept them as refugees. (A refugee is a person who flees a country because of persecution.) Some Jews who had the financial resources for their travel expenses, passports, and visas were able to escape Germany and move to another country. Nearly 150,000 Jews managed to emigrate by the end of 1938. (That figure represented 30 percent of the entire Jewish population in Germany.)

Most countries, however, had quotas, which limited the number of immigrants allowed to enter each year. The 1938 annexation (incorporation within the territory of an existing state) of Austria by the German Reich (pronounced RIKE; the German term for "empire") overwhelmed the international immigration system. In 1938 American president Franklin D. Roosevelt organized an international conference to discuss how countries could best deal with the growing flood of refugees. From July 6-13, delegates from 32 nations met in Evian, France, to examine the situation. The conference was a dismal failure for Jews and their advocates, but it served as a persuasive tool for the Nazis, who could now boast that the rest of the world did little to support the Jews.

Following *Kristallnacht* (November 9, 1938; name means "night of broken

As part of their plans for the total exclusion of Jews from German society, the Nazis expelled about 17,000 Jews who had immigrated to Germany from Poland. On October 28, 1938, the party began rounding up Polish Jews by force, then transported them to the border of Poland. When the Polish government refused to readmit these Jews, the refugees were forced to live in appalling settlements.

A 17-year-old Polish Jewish student named Hershl Grynszpan had fled to Paris, France, before the expulsion. Once in France, Grynszpan received a letter from his father that described the freezing and destitute conditions of the

(Continued from previous page)

glass"), German Jews knew they could no longer remain safe in their native country. The German government took away their financial assets and prevented them from earning a living. Jews were also prohibited from leaving the country with more than ten marks (about four U.S. dollars), which closed many foreign doors since most countries would not accept destitute immigrants (those suffering from extreme poverty).

Cuba had a uniquely liberal (open) immigration policy and accepted German Jews who could afford the passage. In May of 1939, the steamship *St. Louis* left Hamburg, Germany, loaded with 936 passengers—930 of them Jewish—bound for Havana, Cuba. But although the passengers of the *St. Louis* had obtained their visas from a Cuban official in Germany, the Cuban government declared these visas to be invalid.

Cuba denied landing rights when the *St. Louis* arrived in Havana on May 27th. The government insisted the ship leave Cuba with its passengers still on board. After steaming along the coast of the United States for three days, the American government refused permission for the ship to dock. On June 6, 1939, the *St. Louis* set its course to return to Europe, reaching Antwerp, Belgium, 11 days later. The passengers then went ashore, only to fall victim to the Nazis in the coming years of the Holocaust.

no-man's-land where the refugees were being detained (held or restrained). Upset and overwhelmed by his family's ordeal at the hands of the Nazi government, Grynszpan went to the German embassy (the headquarters of diplomatic representatives) in Paris on November 7, 1938, to voice his outrage. When he was refused access to the ambassador, he took out a gun and shot another embassy official, Ernst vom Rath. Two days later, vom Rath died of his wounds. His death ignited a violent rampage against Jewish people, synagogues, and Jewish-owned businesses throughout Germany, Austria, and the Sudentenland (an area of German-speaking people adjoining, or lying next to, Germany).

*Paul Joseph Goebbels,
Reich Minister for Public
Enlightenment and
Propaganda (pictured here
with his daughter, Hedda),
used the murder of a
German diplomat by a Jew
to launch an all-out
attack on Jewish people.*

Paul Joseph Goebbels, Reich Minister for Public Enlightenment and Propaganda (pictured here with his daughter, Hedda), used the murder of a German diplomat by a Jew to launch an all-out attack on Jewish people.

The Nazis viewed the assassination of vom Rath as an ideal opportunity for stirring up anti-Jewish sentiments. The murder of a German diplomat by a Jew was exactly the type of incident Paul Joseph Goebbels, Reich Minister for Public Enlightenment and Propaganda, could turn into a sensational story to win public support for an all-out attack on Jewish people. Under the terms of a highly-organized secret plan, the Nazis vandalized and terrorized Jews over the course of two days. The party launched the first night of assaults on November 9, 1938, shortly after vom Rath died of his injuries.

*Jewish refugees aboard the **St. Louis** await their fate in the port of Havana (Cuba).*

   According to the strict orders of Nazi leaders, the attacks on stores and businesses were to appear spontaneous (unplanned). Over the course of two days, roving groups of organized and supervised men burned over 1,000 synagogues, wrecked over 7,000 Jewish stores, and killed nearly 100 Jewish people. The *pogroms* (organized violent attacks against Jews) of November 9-10 became known as *Kristallnacht,* or the "night of broken glass"—a name referring to the dramatic scene of shattered glass from broken store windows that littered the sidewalks of German towns and cities. The cost of the ruined plate glass windows alone was valued at 10 million marks (about 4 million U.S. dollars). The excerpt below contains firsthand observations of the tragedy by Otto D. Tolischus, a German-born reporter on the staff of the *New York Times*.

Things to Remember While Reading Tolischus's Account of *Kristallnacht*:

- While the Nazis tried to convince the news media and public that the attacks on Jewish buildings were spontaneous, notice Tolischus's firsthand observations of supervised gangs.

- According to Nazi instructions, local police did not try to stop the attackers and instead merely regulated traffic. The fire departments performed in a similar fashion. Rather than attempting to save burning Jewish buildings, firefighters worked only to prevent the spread of fire to Aryan buildings.

- Tolischus reports that there were two deaths associated with the wave of terror. Later reports put the death toll at 96 people.

The *New York Times* Account
of *Kristallnacht*

New York Times
November 11, 1938

NAZIS SMASH, LOOT AND BURN JEWISH SHOPS AND TEMPLES UNTIL GOEBBELS CALLS HALT

BANDS ROVE CITIES

**Thousands Arrested for "Protection"
as Gangs Avenge Paris Death**

EXPULSIONS ARE IN VIEW

Plunderers Trail Wreckers in Berlin—
Police Stand Idle—Two Deaths Reported

Reported by Otto D. Tolischus

Wireless to the New York Times

BERLIN, Nov. 10.—A wave of destruction, looting and **incendiarism unparalleled** in Germany since the **Thirty Years War** and in Europe generally since the **Bolshevist** revolution, swept over Great Germany today as **National Socialist cohorts** took vengeance on Jewish shops, offices and synagogues for the murder by a young Polish Jew of Ernst vom Rath, third secretary of the German Embassy in Paris.

Beginning systematically in the early morning hours in almost every town and city in the country, the wrecking, looting and burning continued all day. Huge but mostly silent crowds looked on and the police confined themselves to regulating traffic and making wholesale arrests of Jews "for their own protection."

All day the main shopping districts as well as the side streets of Berlin and innumerable other places resounded to the shattering of shop windows falling to the pavement; the dull thuds of furniture and fittings being pounded to pieces and the clamor of fire brigades rushing to burning shops and synagogues. Although shop fires were quickly extinguished, synagogue fires were merely kept from spreading to adjoining buildings.

Two Deaths Reported

As far as could be **ascertained** the violence was mainly confined to property. Although individuals were beaten, reports so far tell of the deaths of only two persons—a Jew in Polzin, Pomerania, and another in Bunzdorf.

In extent, intensity and total damage, however, the day's outbreaks exceeded even those of the **1918 revolution** and by nightfall there was scarcely a Jewish shop, cafe, office or synagogue in the country that was not either wrecked, burned severely or damaged.

Thereupon **Propaganda** Minister Joseph Goebbels issued the following proclamation:

The justified and understandable anger of the German people over the cowardly Jewish murder of a German diplomat in Paris found extensive expression during last night. In numerous cities and towns of the Reich **retaliatory** action has been undertaken against Jewish buildings and businesses.

Incendiarism: Setting fires.

Unparalleled: Unmatched.

Thirty Years War: 1618-1648; a power struggle between French and German ruling forces.

Bolshevist: Supporters of a form of communism— government characterized by "communal," or group, ownership of property— that originated in Russia; the Bolsheviks led the Russian Revolution of 1917, which resulted in the formation of the Soviet Union.

National Socialist: Nazi party.

Cohorts: A band or group of warriors.

Ascertained: Found out or learned with certainty; discovered.

1918 revolution: A period of profound disorder in Germany that occurred toward the end of World War I. It resulted in an end to the German monarchy.

Propaganda: Information intended to persuade.

Retaliatory: Designed to repay or to get revenge.

Legislation: Exercise of power; laws.

Ordinance: Order.

Brigades: Groups of people organized for a specific purpose.

Third Reich: The name given to the Nazi-controlled government in Germany, which lasted from 1933 to 1945.

Pharaohs: Kings of ancient Egypt.

Consulates: Offices of consuls, officials appointed by a government to represent that nation's interests in a foreign country.

Besieged: Surrounded by armed forces.

Pretense: A false show.

Communist: Political doctrine that originated in Russia and advocated a classless society.

German News Bureau: Newspaper controlled by Nazi party.

Now a strict request is issued to the entire population to cease immediately all further demonstrations and actions against Jewry, no matter what kind. A final answer to the Jewish assassination in Paris will be given to Jewry by way of **legislation** and **ordinance**.

What this legal action is going to be remains to be seen. It is known, however, that measures for the extensive expulsion of foreign Jews are already being prepared in the Interior Ministry, and some towns, like Munich, have ordered all Jews to leave within forty-eight hours. All Jewish organizational, cultural and publishing activity has been suspended. It is assumed that the Jews, who have now lost most of their possessions and livelihood, will either be thrown into the streets or put into ghettos and concentration camps, or impressed into labor **brigades** and put to work for the **Third Reich**, as the children of Israel were once before for the **Pharaohs**.

Thousands Are Arrested

In any case, all day in Berlin, as throughout the country, thousands of Jews, mostly men, were being taken from their homes and arrested—in particular prominent Jewish leaders, who in some cases, it is understood, were told they were being held as hostages for the good behavior of Jewry outside Germany.

In Breslau, they were hunted out even in the homes of non-Jews where they might have been hiding.

Foreign embassies in Berlin and **consulates** throughout the country were **besieged** by frantic telephone calls and by persons, particularly weeping women and children, begging help that could not be given them. Incidentally, in Breslau the United States Consulate had to shut down for some time during the day because of fumes coming from a burning synagogue near by.

All **pretense** ... to the effect that the day's deeds had been the work of irresponsible, even **Communist**, elements was dropped this time and the official **German News Bureau** ... said specifically:

Continued anti-Jewish demonstrations occurred in numerous places. In most cities the synagogue was fired by the population. The fire department in many cases was able merely to save adjoining buildings. In addition, in many cities the windows of Jewish shops were smashed.

Occasionally fires occurred and because of the population's extraordinary excitement the contents of shops were partly destroyed. Jewish shop owners were taken into custody by the police for their own protection.

Excesses in Many Cities

Berlin papers also mention many cities and towns in which anti-Jewish excesses occurred, including Potsdam, Stettin, Frank-

fort on the Main, Leipzig, Luebeck, Cologne, Nuremberg, Essen, Duesseldorf, Konstanz, Landsberg, Kottbus and Eberswalde. In most of them, it is reported, synagogues were raided and burned and shops were demolished. But in general the press follows a system of reporting only local excesses so as to disguise the national extent of the outbreak, the full spread of which probably never will be known.

On the other hand, the German press already warns the world that if the day's events lead to another **agitation** campaign against Germany "the **improvised** and **spontaneous** outbreaks of today will be replaced with even more drastic authoritative action." No doubt is left that the contemplated "authoritative action" would have a retaliatory character.

Says the Angriff, Dr. Goebbels's **organ**:

For every suffering, every crime and every injury that this criminal [the Jewish community] inflicts on a German anywhere, every individual Jew will be held responsible. All Judah wants is war with us and it can have this war according to its own moral law: an eye for an eye and a tooth for a tooth.

German pedestrians pass by the charred remains of a Jewish-owned business destroyed during Kristallnacht.

Agitation: The stirring up of public feeling.

Improvised: Arranged on the spot without preparation.

Spontaneous: Unplanned.

Possession of
Weapons Barred

One of the first legal measures issued was an order by Heinrich Himmler, commander of all German police, forbidding Jews to possess any weapons whatever and imposing a penalty of twenty years' confinement in a concentration camp upon every Jew found in possession of a weapon hereafter.

The dropping of all pretense in the outbreak is also illustrated by the fact that although shops and synagogues were wrecked or burned by so-called Rollkommandos, or wrecking crews, dressed in what the Nazis themselves call "Raeuberzivil," or "bandit **mufti**," consisting of leather coats or raincoats over uniform boots or trousers, these squads often performed their work in the presence and under the protection of uniformed Nazis or police.

The wrecking work was thoroughly organized, sometimes proceeding under the direct orders of a controlling person in the street at whose command the wreckers ceased, lined up and proceeded to another place.

In the fashionable Tauenzienstrasse the writer [Tolischus] saw a wrecking crew at work in one shop while the police stood outside telling a vast crowd watching the **proceeding** to keep moving.

"Move on," said the policemen, "there are young Volks-

genossen [racial comrades] inside who have some work to do."

At other shops during the wrecking process uniformed Storm Troopers and Elite Guards were seen entering and emerging while soldiers passed by outside.

Crowds Mostly Silent

Generally the crowds were silent and the majority seemed gravely disturbed by the proceedings. Only members of the wrecking squads shouted occasionally, "Perish Jewry!" and "Kill the Jews!" and in one case a person in the crowd shouted, "Why not hang the owner in the window?"

In one case on the Kurfuerstendamm actual violence was observed by an American girl who saw one Jew with his face bandaged dragged from a shop, beaten and chased by a crowd while a second Jew was dragged from the same shop by a single man who beat him as the crowd looked on.

One Jewish shopowner, arriving at this wrecked store, exclaimed, "Terrible," and was arrested on the spot.

In some cases on the other hand crowds were observed making passages for Jews to leave their stores **unmolested**.

Some persons in the crowds —peculiarly enough, mostly women—expressed the view that it was only right that the Jews should suffer what the Germans suffered

Organ: A periodical publication issued by a group or organization.

Mufti: Civilian clothes.

Proceeding: In this case, the term is used as a noun meaning events or happenings.

Unmolested: Without injury.

in 1918. But there were also men and women who expressed protests. Most of them said something about Bolshevism. One man—obviously a worker—watching the burning of a synagogue in Fasanenstrasse exclaimed, "Arson remains arson." The protesters, however, were quickly silenced by the wrecking crews with threats of violence.

Warned Against Looting

To some extent—at least during the day—efforts were made to prevent **looting**. Crowds were warned they might destroy but must not **plunder**, and in individual cases looters either were beaten up on the spot by uniformed Nazis or arrested. But for the most part, looting was general, particularly during the night and in the poorer quarters. And in at least one case the wreckers themselves tossed goods out to the crowd with the shout "Here are some cheap Christmas presents."

Children were observed with their mouths smeared with candy from wrecked candy shops or flaunting toys from wrecked toy shops until one elderly women watching the spectacle exclaimed,

"So that is how they teach our children to steal."

Foreign Jewish shops, it appears, were not at first marked for destruction and were passed over by the first wrecking crews. But in their destructive enthusiasm others took them on as well and even wrecked some "Aryan" shops by mistake....

No photographing of the wreckage was permitted and Anton Celler, American tourist, of Hamden, Conn., was arrested while trying to take such pictures, although he was soon released. Members of a South American diplomatic mission likewise got into trouble on that account.

Grave doubt prevails whether insurance companies will honor their policies. Some are reported to have flatly refused to reimburse for the damage because of its extent, and, considering the standing the Jew enjoys in German courts today, there is little likelihood of his collecting by suing. But there still remains to be settled the damage done to "Aryan" houses and other property. (Tolischus, pp. 1, 4)

Looting: Robbing, especially in the midst of a riot or similar disturbance.

Plunder: Taking goods by force.

What happened next...

As part of the reign of terror known as *Kristallnacht,* over 30,000 Jewish men were arrested and sent to the concentration camps at Dachau, Buchenwald, and Sachsenhausen. In

Paul Joseph Goebbels (1897-1945)

Paul Joseph Goebbels was one of Hitler's most intimate and influential advisors. Born into a strict Catholic working-class family from the Rhineland area of Germany, Goebbels was a brilliant intellectual. He attended Roman Catholic schools and earned a doctorate in literature and history at the University of Heidelberg. During World War I, he was rejected for army service due to physical disabilities—a crippled foot and a permanent limp. These physical deformities haunted Goebbels throughout his life.

Goebbels first attempted a career in literature and the arts before focusing exclusively on Nazi party activities. He helped spread Nazi ideology through an extensive propaganda campaign involving posters, pamphlets, parades, and organized street battles. From 1927 to 1935, he edited his own weekly newspaper, Der Angriff (The Assault) to promote Nazi beliefs.

When Hitler became German chancellor in 1933, he appointed Goebbels as Reich Minister for Public Enlightenment and Propaganda. In this powerful role, Goebbels controlled all aspects of German press and culture, including the newspapers, radio, films, theater, and sports. He was the chief architect of the May 10, 1933, book burning and the Kristallnacht incident that was staged five years later.

After Hitler committed suicide at the close of the war, Goebbels decided he too could not bear to live in a defeated Germany. He arranged to have members of the SS (the Elite Guard of the Nazi party) administer poisonous injections to his six children and then to shoot himself and his wife on May 1, 1945. Before his death, he is said to have commented: "We shall go down in history as the greatest statesmen of all time, or as the greatest criminals."

compliance with official instructions, the Nazis arrested able-bodied Jewish males, "especially rich ones," then referred to such arrests and imprisonments as a form of "protective custody." In reality the prisoners would only be released once they had arranged to leave Germany.

The leaders of the Nazi government who had planned *Kristallnacht* gathered on November 12, 1938, to discuss the future course of action regarding the "Jewish question." The group decided that the government would seize all insurance payments for damages to Jewish shops and businesses—valued at 25 million marks (about 10 million U.S. dollars). In addition, Jewish owners would be required to repair their stores themselves, and they would not be permitted to reopen their businesses unless they hired non-Jews as managers. Finally, a one billion mark fine (400 million U.S. dollars) was imposed upon the "Jews Who Are German Subjects" because the "hostile attitude of Jewry toward the German Volk and Reich, which does not shrink even from committing cowardly murder, necessitates determined resistance and harsh penalty." (The Nazis were saying that the Jewish people's ill will toward the German government—and the murder of Ernst vom Rath by a Jew—had to be dealt with severely.)

In addition to financial penalties, the Nazis also imposed many legislative measures that removed Jews from social life. Decrees were passed that barred Jewish children from public schools and prohibited all Jews from certain public places such as movie theaters, beaches, parks, general hospitals, resorts, and even sleeping-cars on trains. The Nazis also imposed curfew restrictions, thereby strictly controlling the movement of Jews. As a result of the worsening conditions for German Jews, many of them lost all hope and committed suicide.

Did you know...

- Although the Nazis officially prohibited people from photographing the wreckage associated with *Kristallnacht,* today many photographs survive, giving dramatic visual testimony to the violence and destruction of the "night of broken glass."

- At the time of *Kristallnacht,* most plate glass was imported from Belgium. One historian estimated that the amount of plate glass destroyed in the two nights of mayhem equaled half the annual production of the entire plate-glass industry of Belgium.

- In 1940 Otto Tolischus won the Pulitzer Prize for his articles in the *New York Times*—articles that traced the expansion of Nazi Germany into Europe.

- After covering Nazi Germany, Tolischus went to Tokyo to report on the rise of Japanese militarism (a policy of aggressive preparedness for war). On December 7, 1941, the day the Japanese attacked Pearl Harbor (marking American involvement in World War II), Tolischus was arrested by Japanese authorities and then tortured. He was released June 25, 1942, in an American-Japanese exchange of diplomats and nationals (citizens).

For Further Reading

Altshuler, David. *Hitler's War against the Jews: A Young Reader's Version of "The War against the Jews, 1933-1945" by Lucy S. Dawidowicz.* New York: Behrman House, 1978.

Tolischus, Otto D. "Nazis Smash, Loot, and Burn Jewish Shops and Temples until Goebbels Calls Halt," *New York Times,* November 11, 1938, pp. 1, 4.

Chaim Arron Kaplan

Excerpt from *The Warsaw Diary of Chaim A. Kaplan*, written September 1, 1939 to August 4, 1942

Translated and edited by Abraham I. Katsh
Published in 1965

German forces attacked Poland on September 1, 1939, starting World War II. While Britain and France declared war on Germany, they failed to provide Poland with the military support required to resist Nazi (National Socialist German Workers' party) forces. The Germans had several advantages on their side, including a bigger army and more modern equipment. By surrounding Poland on three sides, the Germans conquered the Polish troops within a month. Mobile killing units known as *Einsatzgruppen* accompanied the German army throughout Poland and targeted Jews, aristocrats (members of the upper class), intellectuals, and members of the clergy. These task forces murdered 16,000 Polish and Jewish civilians in more than 700 mass executions.

Germany annexed the western and northern parts of Poland and called this newly acquired Reich (pronounced RIKE; the German word for "empire") territory Warthegau. In the southeastern portion of Poland, the Germans formed a civil (or state) administration called Generalgouvernement, or General Government. More than 10 million Poles lived in Warthegau and 12 million lived in the Generalgouvernement. To eliminate the "harmful influence" of "alien" populations, Hitler ordered the expulsion of all non-Germans from Warthegau. He envisioned "the old and new Reich area" to be "cleansed of Jews, Polacks and company"; racially pure Germans could then establish colonies in land vacated by the Poles. The Nazis also instituted a racial "reclamation" project to screen Polish people and determine if they could undergo "re-Germanization." Certain Poles who resembled the German ideal—especially those who were blond and tall—were allowed to stay in segregated areas.

Germany Prepares for War

The Nazi party, or National Socialist German Workers' party, believed that a conspiracy of "worldwide Jewry" threatened to take over all countries, including Germany. Adolf Hitler viewed Bolshevism—a form of communism that arose in Russia in the early 1900s—as a Jewish-controlled political movement designed to win world power. Hitler's war plans served two goals: first, to conduct a holy war against "Jewish Bolshevism," and second, to create *Lebensraum,* or living space, for the German people.

Hitler ordered his top Nazi officials to orchestrate a massive propaganda campaign to convince the German people that "Jewish-Bolshevik world conspirators" were the primary evil threatening all of mankind. He then prepared German military forces for the conquest of neighboring countries. His first territorial expansions occurred without the onset of an actual war. He annexed (or added to Germany's territory) Austria in March of 1938 and acquired the Sudentenland, a German-speaking area in western Czechoslovakia, later that same year. Since the Germans viewed Austria as part of their rightful homeland, the invasion and annexation of Austria was called *anschluss,* or union.

Under the pressure of terror by the Gestapo, about 126,000 of the 185,000 Austrian Jews left Austria before the end of 1939. After further dismantling (destroying; stripping) Czechoslovakia by annexing western provinces and establishing a puppet government (a government in name only—one that is actually controlled by outside forces) in the east, Hitler began to make plans for the invasion of Poland. He even signed a secret agreement with Joseph Stalin, leader of the Soviet Union, specifying how the two countries would divide Poland after the invasion.

Of the 22 million people in German-occupied Poland, over 2 million were Jews. About 600,000 Jews lived in the Warthegau area and 1.5 million lived in the Generalgouvernement. While the September fighting was drawing to a close, Nazi leaders met in Germany to discuss the "Jewish

A Jewish businessman walks down a Berlin street wearing the Star of David.

problem" in Poland. A directive dated September 21, 1939, and issued by Reinhardt Heydrich, the chief of security police, contained instructions to the *Einsatzgruppen* chiefs regarding racial policy in Poland.

Heydrich's written orders—titled "The Jewish Question in Occupied Territory"—proved that the Nazis had already conceived of a master plan for the annihilation (complete destruction or extermination) of the Jews. In his memo, Heydrich ordered "as the first precondition for the end goal" that Jews from the countryside be concentrated at once into the larger cities. "So that the later measures will be easier," he noted that the resettlement efforts should only take place in those cities "which are either railroad junctions or at least along railroad lines." He also ordered the creation of Councils of Jewish Elders in each Jewish community, which would be "fully answerable for the exact and punctual performance of all orders already issued or to be issued."

Immediately after Poland surrendered, the German forces subjected Jewish people to violence and discrimination. Jews were driven away from food lines and randomly seized off the streets for forced labor. The Nazis also humiliated and assaulted Jews who were wearing traditional religious garb. Many Jews lost their jobs without receiving any compensation; they were left without any prospect of securing a new position. The Nazis issued numerous anti-Jewish decrees, including (1) the requirement that Jews wear white arm bands depicting a blue Star of David, (2) a ban on ownership of radios by Jews, and (3) a ban on travel by train for Jewish passengers. The most damaging of these orders restricted the economic rights and privileges of Jews and mandated (or ordered) the confiscation (seizure) of Jewish property. Throughout the Generalgouvernement in 1940 and 1941, local authorities began the process of confining Jewish people to ghettos, or designated areas within certain cities.

At this time, Chaim Arron Kaplan lived in Warsaw, Poland, and worked as a principal of a Hebrew school. He had started writing a diary in 1933 as a way to record his private thoughts. However, when World War II broke out, he deliberately changed the style of his writing to serve more as a chronicle or historical record. He no longer focused on his personal feelings and problems; instead, he devoted his efforts to reporting on the mounting tragedy occurring around him. Cautious and fearful of detection, Kaplan never mentioned his own name in the diary entries and kept them a secret from his family. *The Warsaw Diary of Chaim A. Kaplan* contains a remarkable firsthand account of Jewish life within the Warsaw ghetto.

Things to Remember While Reading Kaplan's Diary Entries:

- Notice the confusion concerning the decree on October 12, 1940, which ordered the formation of the ghetto in the heart of the Jewish section of Warsaw. While the Nazi government in Germany had issued a directive to concentrate Jews within Polish cities, it did not explicitly order the organization of ghettos. Local officials had to make that decision themselves.

- The Jews continued to practice their religion even amidst the oppressive conditions of occupied Warsaw. Although they were barred from using synagogues (Jewish houses of worship), they formed small groups within the Warsaw ghetto to pray out of the sight of guards and police.

- The Nazis created the *Judenrat* (Jewish Council), comprised of Jewish men, to help control the Jewish population in occupied territories. The *Judenrat* played a critical role in "closed" ghettos, where inhabitants became cut off from the rest of society.

- During 1940 and 1941, the ghettos functioned much like prisons or camps, where Jews were held under brutal conditions, including starvation and disease. Beginning in the spring of 1942, Germans began deporting Jews from ghettos to extermination (death) camps.

The Warsaw Diary of Chaim A. Kaplan

October 2, 1940
The Eve of the New Year, 5701

*We have no public worship, even on the high holy days. There is darkness in our synagogues, for there are no worshipers— silence and **desolation** within, and sorrow looking on from without. Even for the high holy days, there was no permission for **communal** worship. I don't know whether the **Judenrat** made any attempt to obtain it, but if it didn't try it was only because everyone knew in advance that the request would be turned down. Even in the darkest days of our exile we were not tested with this trial. Never before was there a government so evil that it would forbid an*

Desolation: Grief; sadness; devastation.

Communal: Group.

Judenrat: German for "Jewish Council."

*entire people to pray. But never before in our history, drenched in tears and blood, did we have so cruel and **barbaric** an enemy.*

*Everything is forbidden to us. The wonder is that we are still alive, and that we do everything. And this is true of public prayer, too. Secret **minyanim** by the hundreds throughout Warsaw organize services, and do not skip over even the most difficult hymns in the **liturgy**. There is not even a shortage of sermons. Everything is in accordance with the ancient customs of Israel. When there is no informer at work, the enemy doesn't know what is going on, and we can assume that no Jewish man, even if he is a Jew born in Poland, would inform on Jews standing before **their Maker** in prayer.*

*They pick some inside room whose windows look out onto the courtyard, and pour out their **supplications** before the God of Israel in whispers. This time there are no **cantors** and choirs, only whispered prayers. But the prayers are heartfelt; it is possible to weep in secret, too, and the gates of tears are not locked.*

*And so we give praise to the God of Israel "who kept us alive and supported us and brought us unto this season." During the year many individuals drank the cup of **hemlock**; many have gone to their graves. The community has been **debased** and impoverished. But it still exists.*

October 12, 1940
End of Yom Kippur, 5701

*...To our great sorrow, as the day drew to a close, at a time when the gates of tears were still open, we learned that a new **edict** had been issued for us, a barbaric edict which by its weight and results is greater than all the other edicts made against us up to now, to which we had become accustomed.*

At last the ghetto edict has gone into effect. For the time being it will be an open ghetto, but there is no doubt that in short order it will be closed. In Lodz the ghetto edict was not carried out all at

Barbaric: Uncivilized.

Minyanim: "Number"; refers to the number ten, which is the number of men required for congregational worship according to Judaism.

Liturgy: Religious service or ritual.

Their Maker: Their God.

Supplications: Humble requests; prayers.

Cantors: Soloists or official singers of Jewish religious services.

Hemlock: Poisonous herb.

Debased: Lowered in status or quality.

Edict: An order or command having the force of law.

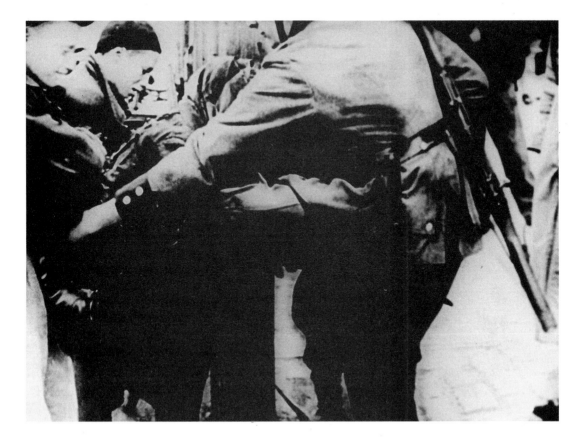

once, but rather step by step, and many signs indicate that it will be the same in Warsaw. After the ghetto plan was postponed two weeks ago, we were almost **tranquil**. But the enemy of Israel neither sleeps nor slumbers.

This new edict was issued in a somewhat humane form—perhaps for the sake of world opinion—but we know that in its new form it is still the last link of the chain of troubles and misfortunes.

Before the thirty-first of October the Jews who live in the streets outside the walls must move lock, stock, and barrel to the streets within the walls; and all the Aryans (read Poles) living in the streets within the walls must move to the Aryan quarter. To a certain extent the edict has hurt the Poles more than the Jews, for the Poles are ordered to move not only from the ghetto, but from the German quarter as well. Nazism wants to separate everyone—

German soldiers search Jewish boys at the entrance to the Warsaw ghetto.

Tranquil: Calm.

the lords by themselves, the underlings by themselves, the slaves by themselves. The blessed and the accursed must not mingle.

A hundred and twenty thousand people will be driven out of their homes and will have to find **sanctuary** *and shelter within the walls. Where will we put this great mass of people? Most of them are wealthy, accustomed to beautiful apartments and lives of comfort, and they will be totally impoverished from now on. Their businesses and livelihoods were directly connected with the areas where they lived. In leaving their homes they are also leaving their incomes.*

The **Gentiles** *too are in mourning. Not one tradesman or storekeeper wants to move to a strange section, even if it be to an Aryan section. It is hard for any man, whether Jewish or Aryan, to start making his life over. And so the panic in captured Warsaw, occupied by harsh masters, is great. As I have said, for the time being we are in an open ghetto; but we will end by being in a real ghetto, within closed walls.*

Hundreds of Germans are coming in, **refugees** *from the English bombs, half-mad women with their children. They complain angrily to their fat, comfortable relatives who are enjoying the spoils of a strange land out of all danger. An eyewitness reports that a German soldier dared to write these words on the wall of one of the trolley cars: 'We ride back and forth. We have no more homeland!'...*

October 24, 1940
The night of Simhat Torah, 5701

The Warsaw ghetto is making its full appearance. Everyone is vacating his forbidden apartment in advance of the deadline, and taking some new apartment in the Jewish area. So long as poverty can be locked in the innermost places, people forget it exists; but when it is brought outside it awakens disgust and **loathing.** *Now we see the used furniture and household utensils of the poor as they search through the streets for a new* **refuge.** *There is no sense to*

Sanctuary: A place of safety or protection.

Gentiles: Non-Jews.

Refugees: People who flee to a foreign country to escape danger and persecution.

Loathing: Hatred.

Refuge: Shelter.

this. For what reason are these miserable and oppressed creatures made to roam around like shadows, these who have nothing to keep themselves alive with even under their own roofs?

*The **naïve** among the Jews and Poles ask: Can the world sit silent? Will the evil and the corrupt always have the upper hand? Will the ax fall upon the entire world? O Leader of the city, where are you?*

But He Who sits in Heaven laughs.

*The torments of the creation of the ghetto are harder, perhaps, than the ghetto itself. At every hour new changes are made regarding one area or another. Thus Zelazna Street, a place of refuge for 60,000 Poles and 26,000 Jews, has been in limbo for several days, and no one knows what its fate will be. Is it ours, or our competitor's? There is a rumor that two **delegations**, one Jewish (Wielikowski and Sztolcman) and one Polish, went to Cracow, but neither managed to see the ruler, and both returned empty-handed. There are also various rumors about extension of the period of evacuation. Some say it was extended until November 15; others say the original date still stands. Yesterday the radio announced that the time stated before, October 31, remains in effect. Today people in Judenrat circles announce that on the twenty-eighth a notice will be published extending the time until November 15.*

And an additional doubt is gnawing at us:

*Will it be a closed ghetto? There are signs in both directions, and we hoped for a miracle—which doesn't always happen in time of need. A closed ghetto means gradual death. An open ghetto is only a halfway **catastrophe**.*

October 27, 1940

As long as the ghetto is open and there is still a gap, no larger than the eye of a needle, through which we may come in contact

Naïve: Simple and unsophisticated.

Delegations: Groups of persons chosen to represent others.

Catastrophe: A final, tragic event.

A Warsaw ghetto Judenrat official at work in his office.

Jurisdiction: Power

Nincompoops: Fools.

with the outside world, the Judenrat has **jurisdiction** only over internal affairs; from the time when the ghetto is closed, we will become a foreign national organism, separated from the civil life of the nation. We will stop paying taxes to the government, and be exempt from paying rent. "Sinners and criminals" are not obligated to bear the burden of debts and taxes, because they have been doomed to elimination, and all the arteries of life are stopped up before them. Thus it is that the Judenrat will be the representative of the Jewish people both within and without....

The Judenrat is not the same as our traditional Jewish Community Council, which wrote such brilliant chapters in our history. Strangers in our midst, foreign to our spirit, ... the president of the Judenrat and his advisors are musclemen who were put on our backs by strangers. Most of them are **nincompoops** whom no one *knew in normal times. They were never elected, and would not have dared dream of being elected, as Jewish representatives; had they dared, they would have been defeated. All their lives until now they were outside the Jewish fold; they did not rejoice in our happiness nor mourn our misfortunes....*

November 4, 1940

The face of Warsaw has changed so that no one who knows it would recognize it. People from the outside do not enter now, but if a miracle were to take place and one of its inhabitants who fled returned to the city, he would say, "Can this be Warsaw?"

Not even the Poles are in a hurry to rebuild their ruins. The holes and cracks in the burned and destroyed buildings have been patched up with bricks and lime; the rubble of destruction has been cleared; the broken sidewalks shine. The conquerors boast of the order they have instituted. Yes, the order of a graveyard....

Since the Jewish quarter was established, Jewish Warsaw has become a city unto itself, with characteristics quite different from those of Aryan Warsaw....

Jewish Warsaw has changed for the worse, in the direction of ugliness, tastelessness, and lack of beauty. Here too it is a graveyard, only here the skeletons of the dead walk about the streets. They have gathered from all parts of the country and come to Warsaw. They came empty-handed, broken and crushed, without a penny, without food for a single meal or clothes to cover their nakedness.

November 28, 1940

*The ghetto is empty of all Gentiles and has turned into a Jewish kingdom. The police are leaving and the Jewish police will inherit their place. The same applies to the post office; Jews working for the Judenrat will head it and all the jobs will be filled by Jews. An exceptional **concession** will apparently be made in the*

Concession: Acknowledgment; granting as a right or privilege.

Chaos: Utter confusion.

Privation: Being deprived; a lack of what is needed for existence.

Epidemics: Outbreaks of contagious disease affecting a large portion of a population.

Atrocities: Cruel and horrible acts or situations.

case of the tax bureau, and for the public utility departments—if the cruel conquerors do not forbid us to use gas and electricity. In short, [this is] a Jewish state complete in every detail, but a closed, cramped one, imprisoned, mummified within its narrow borders.

December 2, 1940

*Life in the ghetto is becoming "normal." The **chaos** lasted no more than a week. When half a million people are locked in a small cage, faced with hunger, **privation, epidemics, atrocities,** naturally it causes a stir. Even the conquerors were confused. This is a unique political experiment. The intention was to starve and impoverish us in body and in spirit, to segregate us from the outside world; to undermine our very existence. A great project of this sort demands extraordinary exertions and cannot be brought into effect by words alone. But to our sorrow, it must be admitted that the tyrants succeeded.... (Kaplan, pp. 202-29)*

What happened next...

Chaim Kaplan continued writing entries in his diary, faithfully reporting and reflecting on the events of ghetto existence. His last entry was dated August 4, 1942—one of the days the Nazis conducted a mass deportation from the Warsaw ghetto to extermination camps. The last sentence reads: "When my end comes—what will happen to the diary?" A day or two later, Kaplan and his wife were deported to the extermination camp Treblinka. Historians believe the Kaplans perished at Treblinka between December 1942 and January 1943.

After World War II ended in 1945, Kaplan's war diary was discovered inside a kerosene can on a farm outside Warsaw. Kaplan had managed to smuggle his diary out through a Jewish friend, who worked daily at forced labor outside the ghetto. Today this precious diary, which resembles the small notebooks similar to the ones used by grade-school children, is one of the rare original documents of its kind to have survived the Holocaust period.

Reinhardt Heydrich (1902-1942)

Reinhardt Heydrich was born in Halle, Saxony. His father was a renowned musician and founder of the Halle Conservatory of Music. Heydrich served as an officer in the German navy but was dismissed upon being found guilty of misconduct. After joining the Nazis in 1931, he befriended Heinrich Himmler, leader of the SS—the political police force of the Nazi party. Himmler placed Heydrich in charge of the SS branch responsible for espionage (spying) and intelligence.

Heydrich eventually rose to the inner circle of Nazi power, becoming the executive director of the Gestapo (the secret state police force of the Nazis). He played a key role in *Kristallnacht* activities, where Nazi soldiers used his prepared lists and the Gestapo placed thousands of Jews in "protective custody." In the following months, the Nazis established the Central Office for Jewish Emigration under Heydrich to coordinate and implement Jewish policy.

When Germany invaded Poland, Heydrich commanded the ghettoization of the Polish Jews. He was one of the main authors of a plan for the mass deportation of all European Jews to Madagascar (off the African coast). His ruthless proposal for the immediate extermination (rather than capture and imprisonment) of all Jews during the Russian invasion resulted in the deaths of millions of Russian Jews.

On January 20, 1942, Nazi leaders met in Wannsee, Germany, to coordinate the mass movement of all Jews under Nazi control to labor camps—and ultimately to death camps. Following this conference, Heydrich issued the protocol (decree) which ordered the "Final Solution" to the "Jewish Question."

Heydrich's enthusiasm and fanaticism resulted in his appointment as acting governor of Bohemia and Moravia, where he continued his policy of brutal repression and mass executions of the Jewish communities. On May 27, 1942, two Czech resistance fighters ignited a bomb under his car near Prague. He died of his wounds on June 4, 1942.

Did you know...

- Warsaw contained the largest Jewish community in Europe, numbering about 375,000 before the outbreak of World War II. The Nazi-instituted ghetto in Warsaw was the largest in German-occupied Europe, enclosing between 400,000 and 600,000 people. During the worst period, about 500 people starved to death each week.

- An 11-mile-long wall surrounded the Warsaw ghetto. It was 11.5 feet high and 10.6 inches thick and topped with barbed wire. Guards were posted at the gates and also patrolled the length of the wall around the clock.

- Approximately 30 percent of Warsaw's population was packed into 2.4 percent of the city's square area. No more than 73 of the 1,800 streets of Warsaw were made part of the ghetto.

- The Nazis did not always refer to Jewish living quarters as "ghettos." In Warsaw, Krakow, and other places, they referred to the ghettos as the *Judischer Wohnbezirk,* or Jewish residential quarter. The word "ghetto" originated in sixteenth-century Venice, Italy, where Jews were forced to live in a closed section of the city called *Geto Nuovo* ("New Foundry").

For Further Reading

Kaplan, Chaim A. *Scroll of Agony: The Warsaw Diary of Chaim A. Kaplan.* Translated and edited by Abraham I. Katsh. New York: Collier, 1973.

Treseder, Terry Walton. *Hear O Israel: A Story of the Warsaw Ghetto.* New York: Atheneum, 1990.

Zar, Rose. *In the Mouth of the Wolf.* Philadelphia: Jewish Publication Society of America, 1983.

Janina David

Excerpt from
A Square of Sky

Published in 1964

Janina David lived with her parents in western Poland near the German border. She grew up enjoying all the comforts and pleasures of a middle-class Jewish home. With the threat of a German invasion looming in 1939, nine-year-old Janina moved to Warsaw along with her parents and grandparents. The family survived the devastating German air raids only to find themselves in the grip of Nazi (National Socialist German Workers' party) enslavement. With the defeat of Poland, the David family—along with two million other Polish Jews—became subjects of Nazi rule.

Germany annexed the western and northern parts of Poland and called this territory Warthegau. In the southeastern portion of Poland, the Germans formed a civil administration called Generalgouvernement, or General Government. Under the supervision of Governor-General Hans Frank, this area became the designated repository (holding center) where the Nazis sent Jews and all others deemed unfit for Reich citizenship.

Unlike the Jewish people living in Germany, Polish Jews had little or no opportunity for escape before becoming entangled in the lethal antisemitic (anti-Jewish) measures imposed by the Nazi regime. Less than a year after the German invasion, the Nazis prohibited Jews from leaving Poland. A similar ban was introduced within Germany in 1941—a full eight years after the Nazis first seized power. Shortly after German occupation, Polish Jews were forced to give up their jobs. The German administration imposed numerous anti-Jewish decrees that robbed both Poles and Jews of their property and assets.

In addition to the Polish Jews, several million more Jews fell under Nazi rule when Germany invaded the Soviet Union in 1941. The Germans forced the Jews in occupied territories to move into certain sections of towns and cities, creating areas known as "ghettos" or "Jewish residential quarters." The powerful Nazi organization, determined to eliminate Jews from society, established more than 400 ghettos—most of them in Poland, but also several in the Baltic states (Lithuania, Latvia, and Estonia in northeastern Europe) and in the occupied parts of the Soviet Union.

The Nazis created most ghettos around existing Jewish neighborhoods. The Germans generally chose those areas containing the most run-down buildings and lacking basic facilities such as sewers and lighting. The Nazis often had to evict non-Jewish residents before forcing Jews to move in. They relied on the *Judenrat,* a Nazi-sanctioned Jewish Council, to organize the mass moves into the ghettos according to imposed deadlines. Streams of Jews were forced from their homes and trekked through Polish cities and towns, taking only those possessions they could carry with them. What awaited them is difficult to imagine: miserable, life-threatening conditions in densely crowded buildings and neighborhoods. In the Warsaw ghetto, the largest ghetto in occupied Poland, an average room had to accommodate eight to fourteen people.

Life in the ghettos meant a daily fight for survival—against hunger, contagious diseases, poor sanitation, and constant danger. The daily food rations allotted to Jews were hardly enough to keep a person alive; as a result, thousands died. The Generalgouvernement provided Jews with ration cards worth 7.5 percent the quota granted to Germans. These starvation-level rations forced Jews, including children, to find ways of smuggling food into the ghetto. In addition to hunger, prisoners sometimes froze to death due to the lack of heat in winter months. (Jews living in the Warsaw ghetto are said to have called coal "black pearls.")

In her personal account, *A Square of Sky,* Janina David speaks of the unforgettable horror and terror of living in the Nazi-controlled Jewish ghetto of Warsaw. In the excerpt below, David describes her experiences in the fall of 1940, when the Warsaw ghetto was "closed," or sealed off, from sur-

rounding neighborhoods. Her straightforward depiction conveys the harrowing and isolating experience of being surrounded by ghetto walls.

Things to Remember While Reading
A Square of Sky:

- Between 400,000 and 600,000 people lived in the Warsaw ghetto. Restrictions prevented Jews from traveling in and out of the ghetto freely. Only Jews who had work permits were allowed to leave and work at factories that supported the German war effort.

- Historians estimate that 100,000 children lived in the Warsaw ghetto. Many were orphaned and forced to beg on the streets.

- Unemployed teachers in the ghettos saved themselves from starving by secretly teaching small groups of children. Despite the ban against teaching Jewish children, numerous "illegal schools" existed in Warsaw and other ghettos.

- It is estimated that, at times, up to 500 persons per week starved to death in the Warsaw ghetto. Also, in 1941, 16,000 died of typhus (a serious disease marked by high fever and a rash). The Nazis rounded up infected persons and killed them or left them to die untreated.

A Square of Sky

Typhus: A serious disease (transmitted initially by body lice) marked by high fever, stupor, intense headache, and a dark red rash.

November [1940] came, and the gates of the ghetto closed. The trap was sprung. During the last weeks some 140,000 Jews moved into it and the crowding was indescribable. Refugee centres [centers] were set up. Despite the cold weather typhus was spreading, and we wondered what would happen in the spring. But the dominant feeling of those days was fear and depression. There was defeat on the faces of adults, and when I met my friends we avoided the subject. It was too painful and too frightening to admit that our parents and other all-powerful grown-ups were helpless

and afraid. It was inadmissable, and yet it was obvious. We did not know how to **reconcile** the two aspects of the situation.

Privately we assured each other that our parents were staying in the ghetto because at the moment it was the most convenient place for us to be. They could leave when they chose, of course, and no amount of German orders could stop them. And then the look on our parents' faces as they discussed the situation would raise doubts in our minds, doubts which we tried to suppress as soon as they arose, because they threatened our whole universe.

Late in November Father returned home one evening with an unmistakable 'surprise' look on his face. It was the look he had when he was planning a special treat or brought an unexpected present. Standing in the centre [center] of the room, he slowly drew out of his pocket three small packages and dropped them in our laps. We unwrapped the tissue paper. Inside were two cakes of Yardley lavender soap and a bottle of Lavender Water.

We threw ourselves on Father, begging for explanations. We had not seen such luxuries since the war started, and they brought a flood of memories. Scented bathrooms and warm nursery evenings swam in my mind as I pressed my nose to the little cake of soap and sniffed **rapturously**. Father, enjoying his success, would not at first answer any questions. We had to let him undress and eat his dinner. Then, stretching his legs and lighting a cigarette, he finally **condescended** to let us into the secret.

'Do you remember Lydia?' he asked, turning to Mother.

She looked puzzled: 'Lydia? No, I don't think so....'

'Oh surely,' Father insisted, 'the wife of your hairdresser, a very tall blonde....'

A little light shone in Mother's eyes, and suddenly her face was tense. Lydia did not **evoke** pleasant memories.

Reconcile: Resolve.

Rapturously: With great joy.

Condescended: Lowered oneself.

Evoke: To call forth or bring to mind.

Jewish youths look over the wall that divides the Warsaw ghetto into large and small areas.

'I met her today,' continued Father, 'here, in the ghetto. You can imagine my surprise. She saw me first, screamed, and threw herself into my arms. Created quite a stir, too. Everybody was staring at us. Me, in my shabby coat and that beautiful woman in her sables, diamonds flashing all over, weeping on my shoulder.'

Father obviously enjoyed the memory and the impression it was having on us.

'What was she doing here?' Mother wanted to know. Her voice was hard. There was no doubt she remembered Lydia well and did not like her at all.

'Oh, visiting someone, I suppose. Anyway, she was very surprised to hear we were here. She said she was sure we were abroad. And she wants to come and see us.'

'What—here?' Mother looked with dismay around her. 'I could never receive her here.'

Father leaned forward, suddenly grave:

'I know how you feel, Celia, but this is important. Lydia's husband is very prosperous. They have one of the biggest hairdressing salons in Warsaw and a Beauty Institute—whatever that may be. Lydia certainly looks like a successful film star. She told me she may be able to help us if we ever wanted to get out of here, and she was certain we shall have to leave quite soon. I have a feeling she knows quite a lot of things which may be useful. It may be a very important contact.'

'Isn't her husband a German? I seem to remember—'

'He was naturalized years ago, and refused to take German nationality when the war started, which speaks for itself.'

'But what will she think of us when she sees this room?'

'She will think that the rich Davids have come down in life, which is precisely what has happened. And she may feel quite at home here. She started life in just such a room, only it was in the basement. Her mother ran an agency **procuring domestics** and such like.... She gave me the soap and lavender water for you and asked to see me tomorrow. Shall I tell her to come here on Sunday?'

Mother sighed, nodding.

On Sunday afternoon Father brought Lydia home, and at first sight of her I ran and buried my face in her coat.

'Love at first sight,' they all laughed as Mother, embarrassed, apologized for my behaviour [behavior] and assured Lydia that I was always very shy with visitors and she didn't know what had got into me.

Procuring: Obtaining.

Domestics: Housekeepers.

Lydia was as tall as Father. She stood in the centre [center] of the room smiling slowly at him as he took her coat. She had a radiant smile, large blue eyes and hair of a most extraordinary honey shade. It was very long and she wore it pinned in intricate coils on the top of her head, like a shining crown. In our dark cavern of a room she glowed like a being from a different world.

'Is this what they all look like, those from the "Outside"?' I wondered, forgetting that only two years ago we too had lived outside and that whatever differences existed between us they were of the spiritual order rather than of the physical.

*Waves of scent spread through the room. There were different ones flowing from her hair, her dress and her coat with its silver fox trimming. I buried my nose **furtively** in the long hair of the animal and remembered immediately when I did just that the last time. There was my parents' bedroom back home, and a black coat trimmed with a silver fox lay in readiness on a chair. Mother was dressing before the long mirror. I was sitting on the floor, stroking the fox and playing with his paws. It gave off a sharp, unfamiliar smell and I couldn't decide whether I liked it or not. The room was filled with Mother's favourite [favorite] scent; it was French and was called 'Mitsouko.' I was given the empty box, brown and gold, to play with and I sat flushed with happiness and admiration as Mother finished her dressing, smoothed the new black dress over her hips and began putting on her jewellrey [jewelry]. One of the rings, a sapphire set in a circle of diamonds, was for me. Mother promised to give it to me when I **matriculated**. In the meantime she wore it herself, while I contented myself with a tiny sapphire in a gold flower. Originally I had asked for a tin ring with the picture of [popular American child actress] Shirley Temple which all my friends wore. Father would not hear of it, and Mother bought me a gold one instead. I still wanted a ring with Shirley but realized that ... it was not for me.*

Furtively: Secretly.

Matriculated: Enrolled at college.

Lydia opened a large box she had brought with her, and waves of **Guerlain** retreated before the scent of poppy-seed cake. I came back to reality and approached the table.

Mother served 'tea.' I watched our guest politely sipping the hot water coloured [colored] with a few drops of caramelized sugar. This, together with **ersatz** coffee, was all we could offer.

Conversation was difficult. Lydia could not avoid looking around her and Mother watched her, tight-lipped, resenting every glance.

Father struggled manfully—asking questions, trying to remember old times, but the memories seemed embarrassing to them all. Lydia began talking of recent events, and the tension gradually vanished. She left our town, with her husband and two sons, two years before the war. They established themselves in Warsaw and, from modest beginnings, reached their present success. They lived in a fashionable part of town. Business was expanding. The hairdressing shop now included a beauty salon and a cosmetic store where all foreign makes were still obtainable.

'How?' Mother asked.

'Oh, a trade secret,' laughed Lydia. 'I can't tell you, but if you need anything I can get it for you—French perfume, make-up, soap, everything.'

Mother smiled and shook her head. At the moment she had everything she needed. I thought of the gritty, greyish-green soap and felt disappointed. So we were going to be 'poor but proud.' Good. I buried my face in Lydia's lap and she patted my hair.

'Would you like to come home with me and meet my boys?'

I nodded, speechless.

Guerlain: A type of perfume.

Ersatz: Substitute; artificial.

'Can I have her for Christmas?' Asked Lydia. Mother looked uneasy, thanked her and promised to think it over. It could be dangerous. She wouldn't wish to cause trouble.

'No trouble at all. She will be quite safe with me.'

Curfew approached, but Lydia appeared unconcerned. She began to talk in earnest now. Why did we stay in the ghetto? Why did we allow ourselves to be trapped? How could we live in these conditions?

*'I don't mean this room,' she added quickly, seeing Mother blush. 'I mean the whole thing—the overcrowding, the **epidemics**, the walls. And the danger. Don't you know that you are here like rats in a trap? The Germans have a definite plan. They won't let you stay here to die peacefully of typhus. They will put an end to the whole thing, and pretty soon too. You must get out!'*

Father shook his head:

*'Dear Lydia, you are quite right and we agree. But we can't get out. To do this we would need a fortune. False papers cost a lot. And then one must live. And if we were caught or recognized we should need another fortune to pay off blackmailers. You don't seem to understand that we have no money at all. If we had a little more we wouldn't be living in this **hovel**!'*

*Lydia looked **incredulous**. 'But you—why, Mark, you were millionaires, you couldn't have lost it all?'*

*Father shrugged his shoulders. 'We weren't as rich as you think, and anyway most of our wealth was in real estate. All that is German now. Other things were lost in bombing here in Warsaw, and in **requisitions** back home. Lots of smaller things, jewellery [jewelry] and such, Sophie lost at the frontier when she tried to smuggle it through. And we are living on the remainder. I am not earning enough to keep us, even here.'*

Epidemics: Outbreaks of contagious disease affecting a large portion of a population.

Hovel: A small, inferior quality, often dirty house.

Incredulous: Unwilling to accept what is offered as true.

Requisitions: Requirements. The Nazi government imposed various financial fees on Jews.

Hans Frank (1900-1945)

Hans Frank was born in Karlsruhe, a city in southwestern Germany. He served briefly in the German army during World War I and joined the Nazi storm troopers in 1923. When Frank began practicing law in Munich in 1926, he quickly earned the reputation as the top defense counsel of the Nazi party. He successfully defended Hitler in several hundred legal actions and became Hitler's personal lawyer. After the Nazis seized control of the German government in 1933, Hitler rewarded Frank with several prestigious and powerful positions.

Following the invasion of Poland in 1939, Hitler appointed Frank as governor-general of those parts of Poland not incorporated into Germany. In this position, Frank destroyed Poland and exploited (or used) its people and resources for the German war effort. He confiscated Polish properties and businesses and demolished Polish cultural and scientific institutions. And in the midst of severe food shortages, he hosted lavish feasts in the governor's palace in Cracow.

He also took over valuable art pieces and added them to his personal collection, including works by Italian master Leonardo da Vinci and Dutch painter Rembrandt.

Frank ruthlessly terrorized the Poles, whom he regarded as slaves for Germany. He once boasted to a Nazi journalist, "If I put up a poster for every seven Poles shot, the forests of Poland would not be sufficient to manufacture the paper for such posters." Frank especially despised Jews, whom he wished to destroy "wherever we meet them and whenever opportunity offers." By December 1942, more than 85 percent of the Jews in Poland had been sent to death camps.

Following the fall of the Third Reich (as the Nazi-controlled government in Germany was called), Frank was arrested and charged with war crimes. He confessed his guilt but also announced his conversion to Catholicism and begged for forgiveness. Frank was found guilty of war crimes and crimes against humanity and hanged at Nuremberg, Germany, on October 16, 1946.

Gendarme: Border guard.

Lydia shook her head, her eyes wide with disbelief.

'We shall have to do something about you,' she decided, putting her coat on. It was long past curfew and Father expressed his concern.

She smiled and patted his shoulder. 'Don't you worry. I have a pass. I shall be quite safe.'

She allowed him to take her to the gate, where she waved something at the **gendarme** *and crossed to the 'other side.'*

We were too excited to sleep much that night. The room was full of wonderful, expensive scents, the poppy-seed cake was still on the table and I thought, as my eyes slowly closed, that fairy god-mothers really existed and the world was not so hopelessly bad after all. (David, pp. 121-25)

What happened next...

Mass deportations (forced exits) of Jews from the ghettos to extermination camps began in the spring of 1942. This process came to be known as "liquidation." By 1944, few ghettos remained in Eastern Europe. The liquidation of the ghettos represented the beginning of the "Final Solution," the Nazi code-word for the organized effort to murder all European Jews.

The Nazis transported Jews by freight trains and trucks to six main extermination camps in Poland: Chelmno, Treblinka, Sobibor, Belzec, Auschwitz-Birkenau, and Majdanek-Lublin. Once the deportees arrived at the camp, most were killed on the spot by poisonous gas. This murderous campaign began first in the ghettos but then spread to other Nazi-occupied countries such as the Netherlands, Greece, Czechoslovakia, Romania, and Hungary. Most of the Jewish people living in Denmark and Bulgaria, however, managed to survive since the local population offered them protection.

As rumors and reports of deportations from other ghettos reached Warsaw, tension and fear grew among the hopelessly entrapped Jews. In the months immediately preceding (coming before) the deportations, the German police conducted murderous night raids. In the Warsaw ghetto, the first and worst such raid occurred on April 18, 1942. The police broke into apartments, hauled off their victims according to a prepared list, and shot them at a nearby location. Fifty-two people were killed that night, which came to be known as "bloody night." According to underground Jewish leaders, the purpose of these raids was to instill terror among the ghetto population and eliminate the people most likely to lead attempts at organized resistance.

From July to September 1942, during the first wave of deportations at the Warsaw ghetto, over 300,000 Jews were sent to the extermination camp known as Treblinka. But when the second wave began on January 18, 1943, the Germans met resistance. Refusing to assemble, some Jewish people went into hiding while others engaged in hand-to-hand fighting with the German escorts. On April 19, on the eve of Passover (a Jewish holiday commemorating the liberation of the Hebrews from slavery in Egypt), German military forces assembled to attempt the final liquidation of the ghetto.

The remaining Jews organized an extensive hiding operation involving a network of bunkers (fortified chambers) beneath the buildings. Members of underground (illegal) organizations had also managed to obtain limited weapons and were prepared to fight to their death. The Jews of the Warsaw ghetto held out for an entire month of fighting but finally yielded to the raging fires set by Nazi forces. By mid-May of 1943, the Warsaw ghetto was liquidated.

Janina David's parents managed to smuggle her out of the ghetto on January 18, 1943—the day the second wave of deportations began. In the pitch-black darkness of predawn, thirteen-year-old David tearfully said goodbye to her mother and gave her a gold medallion engraved with the word "Shadai," the name of the Lord in Hebrew. Then she rode with her father and other men in a truck transporting laborers outside the camp to work. When the truck arrived in a residential section of Warsaw outside the ghetto, David's father carefully lifted her over the side rail and placed her on the sidewalk. Paralyzed with sorrow and shock, young Janina watched as the truck pulled away. A family friend appeared out of the shadows of early dawn and led her to the home of Lydia, the "fairy godmother" she had met a few years earlier. While Lydia's children delighted in their new guest and prepared for a celebratory breakfast, "Janie" struggled to speak and act as if all were normal.

Janina David's parents did not survive the Holocaust. David left Poland in 1946 and spent two years in Paris at an international orphanage. After immigrating to Australia, she obtained citizenship just before her eighteenth birthday. First working in factories to support herself, David eventually won a state scholarship and graduated from Melbourne University. In 1958, she settled in England and began working as a social worker in a large hospital in London.

Did you know...

- Some 20,000 Jews escaped the Warsaw ghetto during the last few months of its existence. About 4,000 found refuge through Zegota, a relief organization created by underground political parties. Jews also took an active part in the Warsaw Polish uprising a year later in August 1944.

- It was more difficult to help Jews in Poland than in other occupied countries because of its Nazi-imposed laws—sheltering a Jew was punishable by death.

- The Warsaw ghetto revolt became a legend throughout Poland and Europe, inspiring Jews and non-Jews alike. The work of the resistors helped save lives even after the failed uprising. Some Jews were able to survive by hiding and living in the abandoned bunkers.

- Since children were forced to leave their cherished toys behind at home, they created toys in the ghetto. Some used the tops of cigarette boxes as playing cards. Others invented a "clacking" toy comprised of two pieces of wood, which were held between the fingers of the same hand and clapped together—a feat that required some effort to master.

For Further Reading

David, Janina. *A Square of Sky*. New York: Norton, 1964.

Eisner, Jack. *The Survivor*. New York: William Morrow, 1980.

Orlev, Uri. *The Island on Bird Street*. Translated from Hebrew by Hillel Halkin. Boston: Houghton Mifflin, 1984.

Avraham Tory

Excerpt from *Surviving the Holocaust: The Kovno Ghetto Diary*

Published in 1990

When Adolf Hitler, leader of Nazi Germany (1933-1945) prepared to invade Poland in 1939, he first made an agreement with Premier Joseph Stalin of the Soviet Union. The Hitler-Stalin Pact provided both leaders with assurances that the two countries were essentially allies (supporters of a common cause). A secret protocol, or treaty, also specified how the two superpowers would divide Eastern Europe into German and Soviet spheres. Even before German troops reached Polish soil, the fate of Poland was sealed. In addition to sharing a portion of Poland with Stalin, Hitler gave Stalin control over Lithuania—a small country located on the southeastern shore of the Baltic Sea, bordering both Poland and what is today known as Belarus.

The German-Soviet invasion of Poland in September of 1939 officially started World War II. Shortly thereafter, the Soviets established military bases throughout Lithuania. By the summer of 1940, Lithuania was officially annexed to (or added to the territory of) the Soviet Union as the Lithuanian SSR (Soviet Socialist Republic).

Under Soviet rule, the situation for Lithuanian Jews changed dramatically. The Soviets abolished the esteemed Hebrew educational system, closed down cultural organizations, and eliminated most Yiddish (Jewish-language) daily newspapers. During a massive deportation (forced exit) of "enemies of the people," some 7,000 Jews were exiled to Siberia and other areas of Soviet Asia; among those sent away were business leaders, Zionist activists, merchants, and public figures. (Zionists were members of an international movement for the establishment of a Jewish national community in Palestine; they later supported efforts to form modern Israel.) A week later Germany invaded Lithuania, spreading antisemitic (anti-Jewish) destruction and terror in the process.

Antisemitic sentiment raged in Lithuania after the Nazis took over in 1941. In fact, many anti-Jewish nationals (or citizens of Lithuania) considered the Germans heros for rescuing the country from the Soviets. Shortly after the German invasion, many Jews made a desperate attempt to flee Lithuania. While 15,000 Jews managed to escape to the Soviet Union, some 220,000 more remained within Lithuanian borders.

Within the first two months of German occupation, an estimated 10,000 Jews were murdered by rioting Lithuanian anti-Semites and Nazis. Much of the violence took place in the city of Kovno at the Seventh Fort (one of the forts circling the city that dated back to czarist, or royal, rule, which ended with the formation of the Soviet Union in 1917). The Nazis quickly implemented an organized program for the complete elimination of all Jews from Lithuania.

On June 24, 1941, the Nazis established two ghettos (sections of a city in which Jews were forced to live) in Kovno (now Kaunas). The "large ghetto" and "small ghetto" were located in the district of Slobodka, just outside the city. When the ghetto was sealed, about 30,000 Jews were imprisoned there. One Lithuanian Jew, Avraham Tory, was a member of the Nazi-sanctioned Jewish Council. The Jewish Council, or *Judenrat*—a group of high-ranking Jews (also referred to as "representatives" or "elders")—was chosen to oversee the actions of the Jewish people. The *Judenrat* played a critical role in the implementation of Nazi policy, managing the internal operations of the ghetto. Tory, a young American-educated lawyer, began writing a diary to accurately and objectively document the events he witnessed.

Things to Remember While Reading *Surviving the Holocaust: The Kovno Ghetto Diary*:

- The governing Jewish Council had the difficult assignment of managing the internal affairs of the ghetto. Council members relied on keen negotiation skills to deal with Nazi captors and to manage the needs of their fellow Jews.

- The "action" witnessed by Tory on October 28, 1941, reduced the size of the ghetto to include only those who could work and contribute to its operation. The nearly 10,000 people removed from the ghetto—about half of whom were children— died in mass executions.

- Notice that council members focused their efforts on keeping as many people alive as possible. However, their "privileged" role served to protect them from the greater part of Nazi terror. For example, in the lineup of prisoners—where one row of people would end up dead and the other row of people would be spared—council members and their families were automatically granted life.

Surviving the Holocaust: The Kovno Ghetto Diary

October 28, 1941
MEMOIR

*On Friday afternoon, October 24, 1941, a **Gestapo** car entered the Ghetto. It carried the Gestapo chief, Captain Schmitz, and Master Sergeant Rauca. Their appearance filled all onlookers with fear. The **Council** was worried and ordered the **Jewish Ghetto police** to follow all their movements. Those movements were rather unusual. The two Ghetto rulers turned neither to the Council offices nor to the Jewish police, nor to the German labor office, nor even to the German commandant, as they used to in their visits to the ghetto. Instead, they toured various places as if looking for something, **tarried** awhile in Demokratu Square, looked it over, and left through the gate, leaving in their wake an **ominously** large question mark: what were they **scheming** to do?*

The next day, Saturday afternoon, an urgent message was relayed from the Ghetto gate to the Council: Rauca, accompanied by a high-ranking Gestapo officer, was coming....

Gestapo: Secret police of the Nazis.

Council: The Nazi-sanctioned Jewish Council (Judenrat), which managed Jewish affairs and carried out Nazi orders.

Jewish Ghetto police: Internal Jewish security force authorized to maintain order within the ghetto.

Tarried: Delayed; lingered; waited.

Ominously: Threateningly; predicting evil.

Scheming: Plotting or planning.

*The two Germans entered the offices of the Council. Rauca did not waste time. He opened with a major **pronouncement**: it is **imperative** to increase the size of the Jewish labor force in view of its importance for the German war effort—an allusion to the indispensability of Jewish labor to the Germans. Furthermore, he continued, the Gestapo is aware that food rations allotted to the ghetto inmates do not provide proper nourishment to heavy-labor workers and, therefore, he intends to increase rations for both the workers and their families so that they will be able to achieve greater output for the Reich. The remaining ghetto inmates, those not included in the Jewish labor force, would have to make do with the existing rations. To **forestall** competition and envy between them and the Jewish labor force, they would be separated from them and transferred to the small Ghetto [a smaller, separate, and secure section of the Kovno Ghetto]. In this fashion, those contributing to the war effort would obtain more spacious and comfortable living quarters. To carry out this operation a roll call would take place. The Council was to issue an order in which all the Ghetto inmates, without exception, and irrespective of sex and age, were called to report to Demokratu Square on October 28, at 6 A.M. on the dot. In the square they should line up by families and by the workplace of the family head. When leaving for the roll call they were to leave their apartments, closets, and drawers open. Anybody found after 6 A.M. in his home would be shot on the spot.*

*The members of the Council were shaken and overcome by fear. This order **boded very ill** for the future of the Ghetto. But what did it mean? Dr. Elkes attempted to get Rauca to divulge some information about the intention behind this roll call, but his efforts bore no fruit. Rauca refused to add another word to his communication and, accompanied by his associate, left the Council office and the Ghetto.*

The members of the Council remained in a state of shock. What lay in wait for the Ghetto? What was the true purpose of the roll call? Why did Rauca order the Council to publish the

Pronouncement: Formal declaration; authoritative announcement.

Imperative: Necessary.

Forestall: Obstruct; prevent.

Boded very ill: Predicted bad luck; indicated trouble was coming.

order, rather than publish it himself? Was he planning to abuse the trust the Ghetto population had in the Jewish leadership? And if so, had the Council the right to **comply** *with Rauca's order and publish it, thereby becoming an* **accomplice** *in an act which might spell disaster?*

Some Council members proposed to disobey the Gestapo and not publish the order, even if this would mean putting the lives of the Council members at risk. Others feared that in the case of disobedience the arch-henchmen would not be contented with punishing the Council alone, but would vent their **wrath** *also on the Ghetto inmates, and that thousands of Jews were liable to pay with their lives for the* **impudence** *of their leaders. After all, no one could fathom the intentions of Rauca and his men; why, then, stir the beasts of prey into anger? Was the Council entitled to take responsibility for the outcome of not publishing the order? On the other hand, was the Council entitled to take upon itself the heavy burden of moral responsibility and go ahead with publishing the order?...*

Immediately after their visit to the chief **rabbi***, members of the Council convened for a special meeting and decided to publish the decree. So it was that on October 27, 1941, announcements in Yiddish and German were posted by the Council throughout the Ghetto. Their text was as follows:*

> *The Council has been ordered by the authorities to publish the following official decree to the Ghetto inmates:*
>
> *All inmates of the Ghetto, without exception, including children and the sick, are to leave their homes on Tuesday, October 28, 1941, at 6 A.M. and to assemble in the square between the big blocks and the Demokratu Street, and to line up in accordance with police instructions.*
>
> *The Ghetto inmates are required to report by families, each family being headed by the worker who is the head of the family.*

Comply: Conform to or go along with.

Accomplice: One person closely associated with another, especially in wrongdoing.

Wrath: Anger.

Impudence: Boldness or pride.

Rabbi: A Jewish religious leader.

It is forbidden to lock apartments, wardrobes, cupboards, desks, etc....

After 6 A.M. nobody may remain in his apartment.

Anyone found in the apartments after 6 A.M. will be shot on sight.

The wording was chosen by the Council so that everyone would understand that it concerned a Gestapo order; that the Council had no part in it.

*The Ghetto was **agog**. Until the publication of this order everyone had carried his fears in his own heart. Now those fears and **forebodings** broke out.... The Ghetto remembered well the way the previous "actions" had been prepared, in which some 2,800 people had met their deaths. An additional sign of the impending disaster was that on that very same day workers in various places were furnished with special papers issued by their German employers—military and **paramilitary**—certifying that their holders were employed on a permanent basis at such-and-such a German factory or workplace....*

*Tuesday morning, October 28, was rainy. A heavy mist covered the sky and the whole Ghetto was shrouded in darkness. A fine sleet filled the air and covered the ground in a thin layer. From all directions, dragging themselves heavily and falteringly, groups of men, women, and children, elderly and sick who leaned on the arms of their relatives or neighbors, babies carried in their mothers' arms, **proceeded** in long lines. They were all wrapped in winter coats, shawls, or blankets, so as to protect themselves from the cold and the damp. Many carried in their hands lanterns or candles, which cast a faint light, illuminating their way in the darkness.*

Many families stepped along slowly, holding hands. They all made their way in the same direction—to Demokratu Square. It was a procession of mourners grieving over themselves. Some thirty

Agog: Highly excited.

Forebodings: Sense of impending evil; feeling that something evil is about to occur.

Paramilitary: A militarylike force used for backup.

Proceeded: Went on in an orderly, regulated way.

thousand people proceeded that morning into the unknown, toward a fate that could already have been sealed for them by the bloodthirsty rulers.

*A deathlike silence pervaded this procession tens of thousands strong. Every person dragged himself along, absorbed in his own thoughts, pondering his own fate and the fate of his family whose lives hung by a thread. Thirty thousand lonely people, forgotten by God and by man, delivered to the **whim of tyrants** whose hands had already spilled the blood of many Jews....*

*The Ghetto inmates were lined up in columns according to the workplace of the family heads. The first column consisted of the Council members, followed by the column of the Jewish policemen and their families. On both sides and behind stood the workers in the Ghetto institutions, and many columns of the various Jewish labor **brigades** together with their families, since on that day the Ghetto was sealed off. No one was allowed to go out to work....*

Whim of tyrants: Sudden and unreasonable ideas of unjust rulers.

Brigades: A group of people organized for a specific purpose.

Entourage: A group of attendants.

Partisans: Fighters who attack the enemy within occupied territory.

Emplacements: A prepared position for weapons.

Three hours went by. The cold and the damp penetrated their bones. The endless waiting for the sentence had driven many people out of their minds. Religious Jews mumbled prayers and Psalms. The old and the sick whimpered. Babies cried aloud. In every eye the same horrible question stood out: "When will it begin?! When will it begin?!"

*At 9 A.M. a Gestapo **entourage** appeared at the square: the deputy Gestapo-chief, Captain Schmitz, Master Sergeant Rauca, Captain Jordan, and Captain Tornbaum, accompanied by a squad of the German policemen and Lithuanian **partisans**.*

*The square was surrounded by machine-gun **emplacements**. Rauca positioned himself on top of a little mound from which he could watch the great crowd that waited in the square in tense and anxious anticipation. His glance ranged briefly over the*

column of the Council members and the Jewish Ghetto police, and by a movement of his hand he motioned them to the left, which, as it became clear later, was the "good" side. Then he signaled with the baton he held in his hand and ordered the remaining columns: "Forward!" The selection had begun.

The columns of employees of the Ghetto institutions and their families passed before Rauca, followed by other columns, one after another. The Gestapo man fixed his gaze on each pair of eyes and with a flick of the finger of his right hand passed sentence on individuals, families, or even whole groups. Elderly and sick persons, families with children, single women, and persons whose physique did not impress him in terms of labor power, were directed to the right. There, they immediately fell into the hands of the German policemen and the Lithuanian partisans, who showered them with shouts and blows and pushed them toward an opening especially made in the fence, where two Germans counted them and then reassembled them in a different place.

At first, nobody knew which was the "good" side. Many therefore rejoiced at finding themselves on the right. They began thanking Rauca, saying "Thank you kindly," or even "Thank you for your mercy." There were many men and women who, having been directed to the left, asked permission to move over to the right and join their relatives from whom they had been separated. Smiling sarcastically, Rauca gave his consent....

The selection process was completed only after nightfall, but not before Rauca made sure that the quota had been fulfilled and that some 10,000 people had been transferred to the small Ghetto. Only then were those who had passed through the selection, and had remained standing in the square, allowed to return to their homes.

About 17,000 out of some 27,000 people slowly left the vast square where they had been standing for more than twelve hours. Hungry, thirsty, crushed, and dejected, they returned home, most of

Avraham Tory (1909—)

Avraham Tory was born Avraham Golub in Lazdijai, Lithuania. He attended religious schools, graduating in 1927, then studied law in Kovno and in the United States at the University of Pittsburgh. Tory completed his law studies in 1933. He was active in promoting sports activities and the local Zionist (pro-Israel) movements. His activities led him to travel throughout Europe representing Lithuanian Jews.

Tory was attending a Zionist conference in Geneva when the German army invaded Poland in September of 1939. Delegates from Eastern European countries debated about whether to return home or stay in neutral Switzerland. Tory decided to return to Kovno. Lithuania soon fell to the Soviets, who set up military bases and installed communist rule. (Communism is a political and economic theory that strives for the formation of a classless society through the communal, or group, ownership of all property.)

With the German invasion of Lithuania in June of 1941, Nazi repression (the act of subduing or putting down by force) replaced Soviet repression. The Nazis immediately moved all Jews into ghettos in segments of major cities. Tory became a member of the Jewish Council of the Kovno ghetto. It was in this capacity that he wrote his diary and collected whatever photographs, paintings, and sketches he could. Tory escaped the ghetto on March 23, 1944. Unfortunately, most of his collection of evidence, aside from his diary, was lost in the "liquidation" of the ghetto.

Following the war he immigrated to Israel, where he abandoned his Russian name (Golub, Russian for "dove") and adopted the Hebrew translation, Tory. He continued to practice law in Tel Aviv, Israel, at the time his diary was published in 1990.

them bereaved or orphaned, having been separated from a father, a mother, children, a brother or a sister, a grandfather or grandmother, an uncle or an aunt. A deep mourning descended on the Ghetto. In every house there were now empty rooms, unoccupied

beds, and the belongings of those who had not returned from the selection. One-third of the Ghetto population had been cut down....

*[The next morning, there] was an autumnal, foggy, and gloomy dawn.... German policemen and drunken Lithuanian partisans broke into the small Ghetto, like so many ferocious beasts, and began driving the Jews out of their homes. The assault was so unexpected and brutal that the wretched inmates did not have a single moment to grasp what was going on. The partisans barked out their orders to leave the houses and to line up in rows and columns. Each column was immediately surrounded by partisans, shouting "Forward march, you scum, forward march," and driving the people by rifle butts out of the small Ghetto toward the road leading to the Ninth Fort. It was in the same direction that the Jews had been led away in the "action" ... on September 26, 1941, and in the "action" of the **liquidation** of the small Ghetto on October 4, 1941. The same uphill road led Jews in one direction alone—to a place from which no one returned.*

It was a death procession. The cries of despair issuing from thousands of mouths were hovering above them. Bitter weeping could be heard from far off. Column after column, family after family, those sentenced to death passed by the fence of the large Ghetto. Some men, even a number of women, tried to break through the chain of guards and flee to the large Ghetto, but were shot dead on the spot. One woman threw her child over the fence, but missed her aim and the child remained hanging on the barbed wire. Its screams were quickly silenced by bullets....

In the fort, the wretched people were immediately set upon by the Lithuanian killers, who stripped them of every valuable article—gold rings, earrings, bracelets. They forced them to strip naked, pushed them into pits which had been prepared in advance, and fired into each pit with machine guns which had been positioned there in advance. The murderers did not have time to shoot everybody in one batch before the next batch of Jews arrived. They

Liquidation: In this case, the destruction of the ghetto by first sending prisoners to death camps and then burning the buildings.

were accorded the same treatment as those who had preceded them. They were pushed into the pit on top of the dead, the dying, and those still alive from the previous group. So it continued, batch after batch, until the 10,000 men, women, and children had been butchered. (Tory, pp. 43-58)

What happened next...

Following the "action" taken on October 28, 1941, the Kovno ghetto inmates enjoyed a period of relative calm, with fewer murders, beatings, and indignities suffered at the hands of their Nazi captors. The ghetto itself was "liquidated" in July of 1944, just before the Soviet army recaptured the city. Those prisoners still able to work were sent to German concentration camps. The ghetto buildings were burned, and many inmates were killed. When the German concentration camps were finally liberated, only about 2,000 Kovno Jews had survived. The Soviets, who recaptured Lithuania in the summer of 1944, estimated that 22,000 out of an original 220,000—or only 10 percent—of Lithuanian Jews survived the war.

Tory chronicled the life in the Kovno ghetto with almost daily entries to his diary from July 1941 until his escape on March 23, 1944. Because of his access to the Jewish Council, his obsession with maintaining accuracy and objectivity, and his law background, his diary is considered among the most authentic and complete documentaries of ghetto life. In fact, Tory's diary has been used as a reference in several war-crime trials.

Did you know...

- In the Kovno ghetto in February 1942, Nazi leaders banned all reading material. Jews were forced to turn over their books, manuscripts, and all other printed material. Later that year the party closed the synagogues and outlawed public prayer.

- Kovno, as well as Riga (the capital of Latvia), became the destination for many German Jews who were deported from Germany during late 1941.

- The German military objected to the use of ammunition for mass executions; they argued that bullets, grenades, and the like were needed for the war effort and should not be wasted on Jews. The mass extermination of Jewish populations was later conducted using the more "efficient" method of gassing.

For Further Reading

Suhl, Yuri. *On the Other Side of the Gate: A Novel.* New York: Franklin Watts, 1975.

Tory, Avraham. *Surviving the Holocaust: The Kovno Ghetto Diary.* Translated by Jerzy Michalowicz. Cambridge, MA: Harvard University Press, 1990.

Pastor Christian Reger

Barracks 26

From The Other Victims
Compiled by Ina R. Freidman
Published in 1990

Shortly after becoming chancellor of Germany in 1933, Adolf Hitler launched an intensive campaign to control all of the nation's political, social, and cultural activities. This massive effort, called *Gleichschaltung,* or Coordination, attempted to infuse every aspect of German life with Nazi (National Socialist German Workers' party) philosophy. Only by creating a blindly devoted populace could Hitler ensure his ultimate goal of achieving world domination for Germany.

Within months of taking power, the Nazis seized control of the media (newspapers and radio broadcasts) and banned all other political parties. They also regulated cultural activities, the arts, and education. After determining what news Germans would receive, what books they would read, and what movies and plays they would see, the Nazis planned to take eventual control of the citizens' religious beliefs. Hitler strove to create a single Reich (pronounced RIKE; means "empire" in German) church that reflected and supported his ideas about race and German nationalism. (Nationalism is a sense of loyalty or devotion to a nation—in this case, it represents glorification of German pride, culture, and interests above all others.)

At first, most German clergy eagerly embraced Nazism; the nationalistic fervor gave hope and jobs to downtrodden and impoverished Germans. To some extent Christian clergymen were also antisemitic (opposed to Jewish people) because they viewed everyone who did not convert to Christianity as unworthy of salvation.

Newly-arrived prisoners—including a clergyman (second from left)—stand during roll call at Buchenwald.

Early in his rise to power, Hitler outwardly promised to protect Christian religions. In 1933, he formally agreed to provide German Catholics with the freedom and right to practice their religion. In fact, he signed an accord, or *Concordat,* with the Vatican (the headquarters of the Roman Catholic church, located in Rome, Italy) in 1933. However, days after the treaty was signed, the Nazis banned the Catholic Youth League. Hitler ordered church schools to remove all crucifixes in 1936, but this decree was rescinded (appealed or canceled) due to public protest. The Nazis did succeed in eliminating all Catholic newspapers in 1938, and the following year they prohibited all religious processions (marches, parades, or other public ceremonies honoring figures important in the Catholic faith).

In an attempt to seize control of Protestant churches, the Nazis created the German Faith Movement (*Deutsche Glaubensbewegung*). The movement denounced the teachings of the Old Testament and advocated rewriting the New Testament according to Nazi ideology. Proponents planned to replace references to Jesus with mentions of Hitler and the German Fatherland. Nazi leaders banned nativity plays and carols (celebrating the birth of Jesus) from schools and attempted to convert Christmas into a pagan solstice festival (a Godless festival marking annual solar patterns). Civil servants and teachers, those people most dependent on the Nazi government for employment, were expected to join the German Faith Movement.

While some 3,000 Protestant ministers joined the German Faith Movement, an equal number joined an opposing group, called the Confessional church (*Bekenntniskirche*). In a bold move, the Confessional church leaders declared Christianity to be incompatible with Nazi principles. The Nazis quickly persecuted those belonging to this countermovement, sending many clergy members to Dachau, a concentration camp where the majority perished.

Christian Reger was one pastor who fought the Nazi regime from his pulpit. When the Nazis came to power, Reger had a small congregation in the eastern German town of Stegelitz. In his story, which is excerpted below, he explains how he first embraced the hope offered by Nazism but soon rejected its ideals. He began to use his weekly public sermons to preach the messages of his faith—not the Nazi-directed ideas of hatred. After the local officials repeatedly harassed and arrested Reger, they finally silenced him by condemning him to Dachau in 1940.

Things to Remember While Reading *Barracks 26*:

- As Germany invaded and conquered other countries, foreign religious leaders who opposed Nazism were also sent to concentration camps. The Nazis sent over 2,250 priests and pastors from 19 different occupied countries to Dachau.

- The concentration camp Dachau, located outside of Munich, had a special barrack (temporary housing) set up for clergymen—Barracks 26, where Reger resided.

- Inmates in camps were identified by the colored triangles they were forced to wear on their camp uniforms. Reger was required to wear a red triangle, the color assigned to political prisoners.

Pastor Christian Reger: Barracks 26

*For my first sermon in Stegelitz, I wore my **Brown Shirt** uniform.... The congregation burst into applause. Mina, my wife beamed. Only a few years before, as a young **seminary** student, I had heard Adolf Hitler speak. Although I did not like his ranting and raving, I saw how much hope he gave the hungry, threadbare men and women in the audience. The huge **swastika** flags flying from the rafters, the splendidly uniformed soldiers, and the brass band, inspired everyone to stand up and cheer, "Germany, awake!"*

*I was proud to be a part of this new **nationalistic** spirit. In 1932, I wore my uniform to show I was one with the people. Hitler had not yet been elected chancellor, but he promised Germany prosperity and power. A few months after his election in 1933, however, Mina and I were walking in the woods. As we strolled toward our favorite glade, we heard voices. We stopped. A young father, in a Brown Shirt uniform, placed a flag with a swastika across a tree stump. Then, holding up his newborn son, he proclaimed, "I baptize thee, Wilhelm Smit, in the name of the Fatherland and to the glory of Germany."*

*I was shocked. **Baptism** was the rite of the church. Christians could only be **consecrated** to Jesus Christ. There were tears in Mina's blue eyes as we turned back. When we came home, she packed away my uniform. The next Sunday, I preached about the*

Brown Shirt: Uniform associated with the army of the Nazi party, the storm troopers.

Seminary: A training institute for priests, ministers, or rabbis.

Swastika: An ancient Christian symbol of a cross with bent arms. It was later adopted by the Nazis and took on a negative meaning.

Nationalistic: Characterized by an intense feeling of loyalty and devotion to a nation.

Baptism: Religious ceremony to initiate a newborn to Christianity.

Consecrated: Initiated or dedicated to service.

sacredness of baptism. That night, a terrible banging awakened us. Lights flooded the bedroom window. "Traitors of Germany, traitors of Germany!" voices shouted in the darkness. "We'll smash you."

Petrified, Mina huddled beneath the covers. I crept over to the window and cautiously peeped outside. Young storm troopers, their faces filled with hate, beat their clubs and sticks against the metal truck over and over, rousing the sleeping village. Then it stopped. "This is a warning, Pastor Reger," shouted a voice that had a familiar sound. I heard the motor start and drive off.

"What should we do, Mina?" I asked. "Leave? Stop protesting the teachings of Hitler?"

"What do you want to do, Christian Reger? Keep quiet?"

"Mina, I have to speak up. I can't be silent in the face of evil."

"Then we stay and fight."

It was not easy. There was constant pressure by the Nazis to join the German Christian Faith Movement. The movement had been established by the Nazis to wipe out Christian beliefs. The Old Testament was to be abolished, the New Testament was to be rewritten to praise Hitler instead of Christ. **Blasphemy**!

Pastor Martin Niemueller, who had been a submarine captain in World War I, organized the Confessional Church. Three thousand Protestant clergy joined the Confessional Church and three thousand joined the German Christian Faith Movement. Eleven thousand Protestant clergymen remained silent.

The years 1933, 1934, 1935 passed. I continued to preach against the Nazis. As the people became more and more enthusiastic about the jobs the Nazis brought them, the membership in my church grew smaller. Marching bands and huge rallies made the people ignore the persecution of the Jews. After the disgrace of

Blasphemy: Showing a lack of respect or reverence for God.

losing World War I, everyone wanted to believe that Germans were superior to other people. One Sunday morning, I stood in the pulpit and pleaded for sanity. "Christianity teaches, 'Thou shalt not kill, thou shalt not steal.' The Nazis preach otherwise. What is the Lord's should remain the Lord's."

*With seven hundred other clergymen, I was imprisoned. Suddenly, from all over Germany, people protested our arrests. In a rare instance of responding to public **indignation**, the Nazis released most of the pastors, including me, but twenty-seven were sent to Dachau.*

I could not keep quiet. Every Sunday there was a new outrage. After Crystal Night, the night when synagogues were burned and twenty thousand Jewish men sent to concentration camps, I again protested. "All men are equal in the sight of the Lord." For a second time, I was arrested. After a brief imprisonment, I was released....

Sometimes I wondered how I, a small-town pastor, a man who had never been a leader, could stand up against Hitler. The only thing I excelled in, in all my life, was gymnastics. Was I being foolish to go against the tide? But how could I be a soldier of Christ and not fight against the Nazis? Mina agreed.

*In 1940, the **Gestapo** arrested me for a third time. For weeks, I paced up and down the narrow prison cell wondering if I would ever see Mina again. I wasn't allowed to receive any mail. The isolation was frightening and I worried about Mina. Was she all right, or had the Nazis imprisoned her? I grew more and more depressed. One morning, a letter fluttered through the prison peephole. I opened the envelope. Mina had copied, in tiny letters, Acts 4:26-30, " ... grant unto Thy servants to speak Thy Word with all boldness...." The passage renewed my courage. I would have need of courage, for a few days later, I was sentenced to Dachau....*

Indignation: Anger aroused by injustice.

Gestapo: The Nazi secret police force.

A view of the Dachau concentration camp.

How does one describe Dachau? The barking dogs and striking guards, being forced to run through the gates? The photographing, the turning of a man into a number? No longer Pastor Christian Reger, I became 26 661. Even a dog has a name. The shaving of the hair, the beating, standing there naked while a prisoner in charge of clothing threw out a pair of pants, a shirt, and a hat.

"Number 26 661, what is your crime?"...

"Crime? I'm a clergyman. I am Pastor Christian Reger."

"Political prisoner!" the guard shouted, handing me a red triangle. "Answer only to your number."...

It was 1940, in the year of our Lord. I walked down the main road toward the Pastors' Barracks, Barracks 26. A moat, filled with water, surrounded the camp. Electrified barbed wire encircled the area *around the moat. Guard towers, with armed **sentries**, overlooked each corner of the camp. A terrible stench, as though someone were burning **putrid** meat, assaulted my nose. I started to choke....*

"Welcome to the Pastors' Barracks. I'm Werner Sylten." A small slim man offered me his hand.

"I'm Christian Reger from Stegelitz." As I stood in the "living" area, I saw another room filled with tiers of wooden boards.

The prisoners crowded around me asking for news. They knew that Germany had invaded Poland because there were Polish priests in the barracks.

"Is Germany losing the war?" they asked.

I shook my head, "No, we've taken Norway, Holland, France, Belgium, and Denmark."

Their faces fell. How thin and emaciated they all looked. I turned to Werner. "Why are you here?"

"I had a Jewish grandmother."

*Another man came over. "I am Father Fritz Seitz. I was arrested for hearing the confession of a Pole. Hitler declared Poles **subhuman**. We're not allowed to give them any rites of the church."...*

"There are Catholics in the Pastors' Barracks?"

"Yes, and Greek Orthodox. Hatred knows no discrimination. We come from many countries," Fritz Seitz said.

Everyone went out of their way to warn me: "In the Pastors' Barracks, you can trust your fellow man. Outside, trust no one...."

That night, I lay on the top tier of the wooden boards, unable to turn over because so many were crowded together. I thought of Mina....

Sentries: Guards.

Putrid: Rotten or foul.

Subhuman: Less than human; failing to attain the level of normal humans, especially in civility and intelligence.

Vatican Issues Holocaust Declaration

On March 16, 1998, the Vatican issued a document titled "We Remember: A Reflection on the Shoah." The result of more than a decade of work by the Commission for Religious Relations With the Jews, the text was described as an "act of repentance" (or remorse) for the failure of Roman Catholics—including Pope Pius XII—to prevent the mass killing of European Jews during World War II. Edward Idris Cardinal Cassidy, head of the commission, told a news conference that "as members of the Church, we are linked to the sins as well as the merits of all her children."

Not everyone was pleased with the document. Some critics, including Chief Rabbi Meir Lau of Israel, felt that "We Remember" was too general in addressing the Church's attitude toward Jewish persecution during the Holocaust. Rabbi Lau was also disappointed that there was no "explicit apology for the shameful attitude of the Pope at that time." The last Vatican document relating to Jews, called "In Our Times," was released in 1965 under the auspices of the Second Vatican Council and Pope Paul VI.

The next morning, the guards marched the German priests out of the camp.... The wind blew dust into my face, intensifying the terrible smell still hanging over the camp. "What is that awful odor? Is there a chemical plant nearby?" I asked Werner Sylten. "It chokes my lungs."

"Humanity," he said, looking straight ahead.

"I'm sorry, I didn't understand you." I walked slowly, my hoe over my shoulder. I was starving. I had had only a piece of bread since I arrived.

"Faster, faster," the guards called, lifting their clubs. "You think this is a resort. On the double."

"Those who die of disease or malnutrition or hangings or beatings or from experiments, the Nazis have a long list ... those who die are burned in crematoriums."

"People are dying?" I was careful not to stop. "But it's uncivilized to kill prisoners. This is a civilized country."...

*"This is the Third Reich. The Germany that we knew, or thought we knew, is dead. The **barbarians** are in command."...*

On Christmas Eve, 1942, we knelt, Catholic and Protestant, on the wooden floor and prayed for our families and our parishes. I thought of Mina, I tried to radiate a special message of love to her. It was the only Christmas present I could send. The loneliness of the years overwhelmed me. I began to cry. I prayed, how I prayed that evil would be no more. I even prayed for our Lord to forgive our oppressors. As I stood up, I felt a great peace. I was a man of God. I would not let my oppressors make me hate. (Reger in Friedman, pp. 34-46)

Barbarians: A primitive and uncivilized people; in this case, a reference to the Nazis.

What happened next...

During the course of World War II, the barracks at Dachau became even more crowded. As the Third Reich suffered defeats on the battlefields, their vast empire shrank. Prisoners from the Russian front as well as from Italy and France were shipped to Dachau rather than released to advancing Allied forces (the forces that fought against Germany in World War II). Christian Reger survived Dachau for five years—far longer than most inmates. He was freed on April 2, 1945, shortly before the Reich collapsed. Following his release, he was reunited with his wife Mina in their hometown of Stegelitz.

After the war, the city of Stegelitz became part of East Germany, which was under communist control. (Communism is a political and economic theory advocating the formation of a classless society through the communal, or group, ownership of all property.) Because of his concentration camp experience, communist officials felt Reger could be trusted. He served a congregation in East Berlin until 1985, dying at the age of 80. His wife, Mina, died in 1970.

Did you know...

- The majority of Protestant pastors in Germany remained neutral by joining neither the Nazi-inspired German Faith Movement or the anti-Nazi Confessional church. Their silence probably helped save their lives.

- The Vatican issued only one public objection against Nazi racial policies. While papal officials did condemn the Nazis for not honoring the *Concordat,* the Pope (the leader of the Roman Catholic church) never spoke out against Nazi persecution of the Jews.

- The Nazis singled out Jehovah's Witnesses for especially severe treatment. Despite their long Germanic ancestry, Hitler labeled them "a degenerate race." Members of this Christian pacifist (antiwar) faith do not salute any political authority or bear weapons. By refusing to salute Hitler or join the Nazi forces, many Jehovah's Witnesses were persecuted and sent to concentration camps.

For Further Reading

Friedman, Ina R. *The Other Victims.* Boston: Houghton Mifflin, 1990.

Rossel, Seymour. *The Holocaust.* New York: Franklin Watts, 1981.

Franziska Schwarz

"A Silent Protest against
Sterilization"

From *The Other Victims*

Compiled by Ina R. Friedman
Published in 1990

Adolf Hitler, leader of Nazi Germany from 1933 to 1945, believed devoutly in the idea of a superior race. According to Nazi ideology, German people were descendants of a master race called the "Aryan" race. Nazi racialists felt that the Aryans had grown weak over the centuries from mixing their blood with that of inferior races. Fiercely intent on preserving the purity of the Aryan race, the Nazis began to eliminate the "corrupting influences" of "foreign elements" in Germany. According to Hitler, the Jews represented the most sinister threat to the purity and strength of the Aryan race. Nazi racial doctrine advocated anti-Jewish measures, as well as the rejection of "defective elements" in German society (that is, childbearing by "less-than-perfect" people—people they believed weakened Germany's reproductive gene pool).

The Nazi government enlisted scientists and medical professionals to identify inferior non-Germans. Elimination of these inferior elements was thought necessary in order to assure that the German master race would maintain its purity in future generations.

Nazi leaders and race specialists decided that it was imperative (absolutely necessary) to forbid certain non-German groups—including the Jews, the Slavs, and the Gypsies—from interbreeding with the German race. Proponents of racial doctrine established "scientific" criteria to identify members of the true Aryan race. In classrooms, teachers were actually required to measure and record physical attributes of their students (skull size, hair, and eye color, among them) to determine inferiority. The Nuremberg Laws, passed in 1935, prohibited marriages and sexual relationships between Jews

The facial features of a German youth are measured during a racial examination.

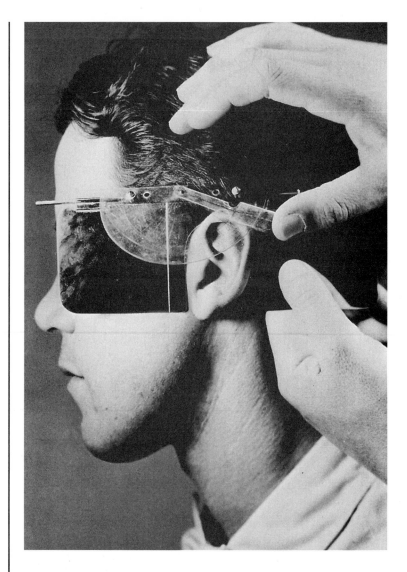

and non-Jews in attempt to prevent "race defilement" (dirtying or contamination).

In July 1933 the Nazis enacted the Law for the Prevention of Offspring with Hereditary Defects. This decree required sterilization for people who had inherited blindness, deafness, physical or mental disabilities, or alcoholism. Government officials and medical specialists reviewed individual cases to determine how to best treat each patient while preserving the racial purity of Germany. Nazi authorities required teachers in schools for the deaf to turn over rosters of their deaf pupils. Reports of a physical disability required the students, and often their parents as well, to undergo sterilization. From 1934 to 1939, between 350,000 to 400,000 persons underwent involuntary sterilization.

Franziska Schwarz was 14 years old when Hitler came to power in 1933. Born deaf, she grew up in a loving family and went to a school for the hearing impaired. In her account below, Schwarz tells how she and her mother received a summons in 1935 to appear at a health center and arrange for their own sterilizations. With her entire life ahead of her at the age of 16, Schwarz tried desperately to oppose Nazi policy and protect her reproductive rights.

Things to Remember While Reading *Franziska: A Silent Protest against Sterilization*:

- Some doctors in Nazi Germany were reportedly sympathetic to the plight of disabled people. Schwarz's first surgeon may have been such a person. Although he allegedly performed a sterilization procedure, she became pregnant a few years later.

- When Schwarz became pregnant after the failed sterilization, her second gynecologist reported her to the authorities. Responding to a request that she undergo a medical examination, Schwarz was forcibly locked inside a dressing room and held against her will.

- Most victims did not have lawyers present to defend their cases at the hearings before a health tribunal (court of justice). Schwarz brought along her uncle who could hear as well as sign.

Franziska: A Silent Protest against Sterilization

I never saw anything wrong with being deaf. My younger sister, Theresa, and most of my friends were deaf. Though my parents were hard of hearing, my younger brother, Theo, had normal hearing. My father was one of six brothers. Four of them were hearing.

*When they came to visit, every hand was busy sharing news of the deaf community or giving advice. Our eyes were glued to the hands and faces of the **signers**. Everyone had so much to say.*

In deaf school, the teachers got mad if I signed. They wanted me to read lips and to use my voice. I got so tired of watching the teacher's lips. I couldn't look away for a minute. It was even harder when she tried to teach me to say the letters correctly. The teacher put a strip of paper in front of my lips. "To make the 'B' sound, purse your lips and blow just enough to make the paper quiver. To make a 'P,' blow a little harder and make the paper shake." Day after day, the teacher drilled me.

*I felt like a **bellows**. I liked it better after school when the teachers weren't around. My friends and I would make signs and chat with our fingers.*

*When I was fourteen, Hitler took over Germany. Theo, my eleven-year-old hearing brother, liked to go to the Munich Stadium to the **rallies**. Once Theo came home all excited because he had shaken Hitler's hand. My favorite uncle, Karl, who could hear, got mad.*

He shouted at my brother and signed at the same time. "Hitler is a disgrace to Germany. Don't waste your time and hearing listening to him."

My father put his fingers on my brother's lips. "Don't ever repeat what you have just heard. Swear by the Holy Father!"

Theo looked scared. "But in school, they tell us to report anything bad [that] people say about Hitler."

"If you don't repeat it, no one will know your uncle said it."...

*For me, the trouble started in 1935. I came home from the **convent** and found Mother crying. "What's the matter?" I signed.*

She handed me the letter that read, "Frau Schwarz and her daughter Franziska are to come to the health office to arrange for

Signers: People who use hand motions as a language to communicate.

Bellows: A device for producing a strong current of air.

Rallies: The joining together of people for a common cause; such meetings are intended to increase enthusiasm among the members of a group.

Convent: Religious school or community.

*their sterilization. **Heil** Hitler." I couldn't make out the signature at the bottom....*

*The day of the hearing, my mother, my father, and all my uncles accompanied me to court. "She's only sixteen years." Uncle Karl talked and signed at the same time so I could understand. "Deafness is not always inherited. I'm her uncle, and I can hear perfectly well. As for her mother, she is going through the **menopause**. Though she is a good Catholic, she promises not to have any more children."*

The two men on the judges' bench whispered to each other. They frowned and shook their heads. After a few minutes, the one with the big nose and bald head stood up. "Petition denied for the minor, Franziska Schwarz. Since the mother promises not to have any more children, she will not have to be sterilized."

I started to cry. The previous year, I had met a boy I liked, Christian Mikus. As a child, he had scarlet fever and lost his hearing in one ear. Christian and I liked to walk in the park. We'd sign for hours. Whenever he saw children playing, he'd smile and sign, "One day, we will have children, too." Of course we couldn't get married then. He didn't make much money working in a clothing factory.... If I were sterilized, I didn't think Christian would want to go with me anymore....

A letter came from the department of health. "Franziska Schwarz is to report to the Women's Hospital in Munich for the sterilization."

"I won't go," I cried. "I want to be able to have babies."

Father looked sad. "If you don't go, the police will drag you to the hospital."

I screamed all the way to the hospital. The nurse locked me in a room with two other deaf teenagers. The three of us cried all

Heil: The German word for "hail," used in the phrase "Heil Hitler," which took the place of other common greetings and ceremonial expressions during the Nazi regime.

Menopause: The point in a woman's life when her period stops and she can no longer have children.

night. When the nurse came to give us tranquilizers, I tried to fight her off. She held me down and gave me the injection. In the morning, I woke up in a room full of beds. My stomach hurt. I touched the bandages and started to cry. The nurse who brought me water was crying, too. "I'm sorry, there's nothing I could do to help you. With Hitler, you have to be quiet." Her finger pointed to the portrait of Hitler hanging over the bed. She tapped her temple with her finger, to indicate, "He's crazy."

I had so much pain, I couldn't go to the convent. I asked the public health insurance office for the standard sick pay.

"Why should you get sick pay?" The social worker sneered. "You can have all the fun you want. You don't have to worry about getting pregnant."

When Christian came to the house, I started to cry. "The doctors sterilized me. I guess you won't want to be my boyfriend anymore."

Christian made the sign for love. "Whatever happens, we'll be together. As soon as you're twenty-one, we'll get married."

In 1938, in spite of being sterilized, I missed my period. Christian became excited. "Now we can get married." He began to look for an apartment.

My mother was out of town helping a sick relative. When she returned, a few months later, she saw my swollen stomach. "How could you do this?"

I blushed. "Please, please, don't be angry. We want a baby so much. I was afraid I'd never have one. Now Christian and I can get married."

"All right, but I want to be sure you have proper care. I want you to go to a gynecologist."

The gynecologist who examined me was very jolly. "Congratulations. The Fuehrer wants every young girl to have a baby."

Then I saw my mother say, "I'm surprised Franziska got pregnant. She's been sterilized."

"Sterilized!" The doctor jumped up and opened the door. "You'll have to leave at once."

Within a few days, I had a letter from the health office. "Fraulein Schwarz is to come to the Women's Hospital for an examination."

I took off my clothes and went into the examining room. The doctor felt my stomach. "Yes, you're pregnant. The pregnancy appears normal. Go into the other room."

In the dressing room, I couldn't find my clothes. I looked in all the drawers and under the seats. They were gone.

I banged on the doctor's door. "Clothes, clothes."

The doctor shook his head. He wrote on a pad. "You stay here. We have to check your urine for three days."

I wrote back. "I don't believe you. I want to go home. I can have my urine checked at home."

The doctor pushed me inside the changing room and locked the door. I looked out the window. I was on the fifth floor, too far to jump. I hid behind the door. When the nurse brought lunch, I escaped and ran toward the stairs. All the nurses ran after me. They caught me and locked me in the room.

For three days, I lay there, biting my nails and screaming. No one came to check my urine or examine me. Then the doctor came in. He pointed to my stomach. His lips moved, saying, "Out."

"What do you mean?"

Uterus: In humans and other mammals, the organ in which the fetus develops prior to birth.

"Out." He left.

I ran to the window. Even though it was on the fifth floor, I was going to jump. The nurse caught me. She dragged me by the hair into the hall and put me in a room with barred windows. I saw a piece of paper and a pencil on the desk. I wrote a note and then tried the door. It was unlocked. I ran into the hallway. A friend was coming up the steps to see me. I handed her the note. "Please, take it to my mother."

A nurse snatched the note. "You'd better leave," she told my friend. "She's acting a little crazy." I had no time to sign and tell my friend that the doctor was going to take my baby.

All night long I banged on the wall so they would let me out. The nurse shoved me into bed and gave me an injection. I woke up just as the stretcher was being wheeled into the operating room. There was a big tray next to the operating table. My baby is going to be on that tray, I thought, instead of inside me. "No, no," I tried to shout. "Christian, stop them."

*When I woke up, I had terrible pains. "Christian, Christian," I moaned. "My **uterus** feels as though it's burning...."*

When I woke up from a nap, I saw Christian standing next to the bed. My face was so white he dropped the flowers he had brought me. "Franziska, I'm sorry they took the baby. But we'll still get married. We can't stop Hitler, but he can't stop us from loving each other."

The nurse handed me a notice when I left the hospital. "You are to return to this hospital within 10 weeks to be sterilized." I crumpled the paper and threw it in the trash can. (Schwarz in Friedman, pp. 67-74)

What happened next...

Following her forced abortion, Franziska Schwarz was ordered to undergo sterilization a second time. Ignoring the order, she and her boyfriend, Christian Mikus, decided to get married. They were unable to obtain a marriage license, however, because of her existing "file" with the Nazi authorities. Schwarz's uncle obtained yet another hearing regarding her sterilization, but again her appeal was denied. When the judges pronounced the sterilization order to be final, Schwarz's uncle became enraged and shouted, "God damn Hitler! How can he do this to a young girl?" The judges immediately ordered his arrest because he had slandered (spoken publicly against) Hitler. After he was beheaded, the family was actually billed for the execution.

Schwarz underwent sterilization again on March 21, 1941. Shortly after the surgery, Franziska Schwarz and Christian Mikus were married. Franziska Schwarz Mikus and her husband survived the war, which ended in 1945. She devoted herself to the education of the deaf, serving as secretary to three different organizations promoting causes for the hearing-impaired community. Christian became a well-known soccer coach for the deaf, and his teams competed in international competitions. His death in the late 1980s was mourned by deaf people throughout Germany and all of Europe.

Did you know...

- At the outbreak of war in 1939, the Nazis escalated (raised or intensified) their efforts at eliminating the mentally disabled. They organized a program of "mercy killing," or euthanasia, to get rid of people they considered "useless eaters."

- The Nazis' targets for elimination included those people who were mentally retarded, mentally ill, or physically disabled. While the term "euthanasia" means the practice of killing those who are hopelessly sick as an act of mercy, the Nazis used this word to conceal the fact that they were murdering thousands of "less-than-perfect" citizens.

- The National Coordinating Agency for Therapeutic and Medical Establishments organized the Nazi euthanasia program. The code name "T-4" refers to its Berlin address—Tiergartenstrasse 4.

- The T-4, or euthanasia, program murdered more than 200,000 disabled people between 1940 and 1945 because they did conform to the ideal of a "master race." Certain T-4 techniques, including death in the gas chamber, served as models for use at extermination camps, where Jews, Gypsies, and other so-called undesirables were gathered for mass murders.

For Further Reading

Friedman, Ina R. *The Other Victims*. Boston: Houghton Mifflin, 1990.

Bachrach, Susan D. *Tell Them We Remember: The Story of the Holocaust*. Boston: Little, Brown, and Company, 1994.

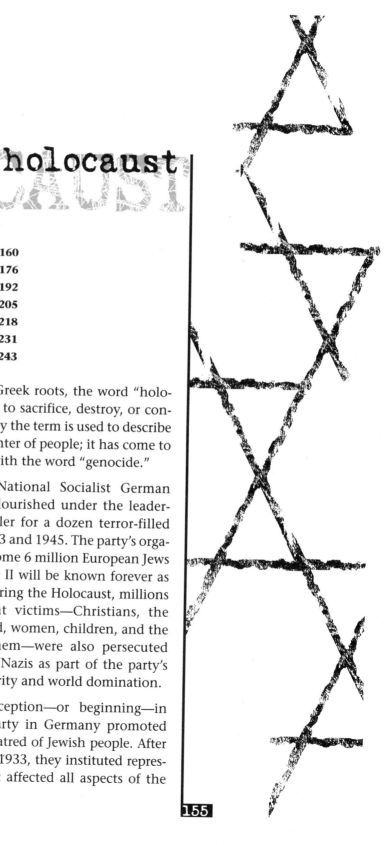

holocaust

Derived from Greek roots, the word "holocaust" means to sacrifice, destroy, or consume by fire. Today the term is used to describe the massive slaughter of people; it has come to be synonymous with the word "genocide."

The Nazi (National Socialist German Workers') party flourished under the leadership of Adolf Hitler for a dozen terror-filled years between 1933 and 1945. The party's organized murder of some 6 million European Jews during World War II will be known forever as the Holocaust. During the Holocaust, millions of other innocent victims—Christians, the physically disabled, women, children, and the elderly among them—were also persecuted and killed by the Nazis as part of the party's quest for racial purity and world domination.

From its inception—or beginning—in 1920, the Nazi party in Germany promoted antisemitism, or hatred of Jewish people. After rising to power in 1933, they instituted repressive measures that affected all aspects of the

Gypsy prisoners sit in an open area at the Belzec concentration camp.

social, political, and economic life of German Jews. When Germany invaded Poland in 1939, tactics to quash the dreams and goals of the Jewish people became more and more drastic. Jews and other victims such as Gypsies and Poles were forced into designated ghettos or camps. By 1940, Germany had conquered France, Belgium, Luxembourg, the Netherlands, Denmark, and Norway. With each military success, the Germans increased the number of Jews who fell under their rule.

At the height of its power, Nazi Germany invaded the Soviet Union in 1941. No longer content with forced emigration and imprisonment of Jews, the Nazis turned to mass murder. The launch of mobile killing squads, known as the *Einsatzgruppen,* represented the start of the Nazi plan to systematically murder all European Jews. However, bloody killings by gunfire placed a psychological burden on the executioners. As a result, the Nazis began experimenting with poisonous gas in their effort to find a more efficient and less taxing method for murdering their victims.

In his role as commandant of the Auschwitz concentration camp, **Rudolph Höss** oversaw early experiments involving a poisonous gas called Zyklon-B. He helped construct and then operate special airtight gas chambers at the Birkenau death camp, which was built as an addition to the Auschwitz complex. In *Death Dealer: The Memoirs of the SS Kommandant at Auschwitz*, Höss describes his experiences as overseer of what became the largest killing center during the Holocaust.

In 1941, Hitler and his top-level Nazi leaders approved a secret plan for the "final solution" to the "Jewish question."

An aerial photograph of the Auschwitz area taken by Allied reconnaissance units sometime between April 4, 1944, and January 14, 1945.

Polish children in Auschwitz. By July 1944, approximately 40,000 children had been imprisoned in the camp.

The Final Solution served as a code name for their scheme to annihilate—or totally wipe out—all European Jews. On January 20, 1942, a small group of Nazi party and government officials met at a villa on the Wannsee Lake near Berlin. At this meeting, which came to be known as the Wannsee Conference, the leaders discussed their plans for transporting 11 million Jews from all over German-occupied Europe to "extermination" camps. Once all the camps became fully operational by mid-1942, the Nazis began massive roundups and deportations (forced exits) of Jews from territories under German control.

To escape deportation, many Jews went into hiding. One such family was that of Otto and Edith Frank, who escaped Germany in 1933 and sought refuge in the Netherlands. Shortly before the family went into hiding in 1942, **Anne Frank** began keeping a diary. Millions of people around the world have come to know Frank by reading her *Diary of a Young Girl*.

To disguise their murderous intentions, the Nazis funneled Jews through a series of ghettos and transit camps that channeled victims into the various death camps. **Etty Hillesum**, a young Jewish women living in Amsterdam, worked at the transit camp Westerbork. She witnessed the arrival of thousands of Jews and their departures on trains headed to extermination camps located in Poland. Her observations were finally published 40 years after the war in *Etty Hillesum: An Interrupted Life—The Diaries, 1941-1943 and Letters from Westerbork*.

In November 1941, the city of Theresienstadt in Czechoslovakia became a ghetto, or restricted area for Jews. The Nazis originally planned to present Theresienstadt as a "model Jewish settlement." **Gonda Redlich**, a highly-esteemed educator, arrived in the ghetto in December. *The Terezin Diary of Gonda Redlich* contains the poignant diary Redlich wrote to his son, who was born in the ghetto in March 1944.

Very few of the people who were sent to the extermination camps in Poland survived. **Primo Levi** was one of the fortunate few who lived to tell of his experiences at Auschwitz. As he notes in the book *Survival in Auschwitz*, prisoners who were spared from death in the gas chambers (most were given labor assignments) still fought daily to survive starvation, disease, exposure, and the violence of guards.

Although Nazi racialists considered Jews to be the primary and most dangerous enemy of the Aryan (German) race, they targeted other groups for abuse as well. **Elisabeth Kusserow** and her family suffered persecution as members of a Christian denomination known as Jehovah's Witnesses. In accordance with their religious beliefs, Jehovah's Witnesses refrained from joining political parties and refused to partake in military service. The Nazis therefore considered the Witnesses to be traitors, an offense punishable by execution.

Many people throughout Europe put their lives at risk to help protect Jews from their persecutors. Such acts of courage and kindness saved a Jewish teenager named **Hirsch Grunstein**, who fled with his family from Poland to Belgium in the early 1930s. After the Nazi invasion of Belgium in the spring of 1940, Grunstein's parents placed him in the care of generous strangers who promised to keep him safe.

Rudolph Höss

*Death Dealer: The Memoirs of
the SS Kommandant at
Auschwitz*

Edited by Steven Paskuly
Translated by Andrew Pollinger

Nazi Germany was at the height of its power in 1941. The German army invaded the Soviet Union on June 22 and with lightning speed advanced closer and closer toward the capital city of Moscow. With the Soviet invasion, the Nazis succeeded in occupying or dominating almost the entire European continent from the west to the east. In preparing for the Soviet invasion, German leader Adolf Hitler ordered his forces to perform "special tasks" in the "final struggle that will have to be carried out between two opposing political systems." He reorganized the mobile killing units known as the *Einsatzgruppen,* or Special Action Squads, to perform these "special tasks," which consisted of killing Jews found in the conquered territory. No longer content with forced emigration and imprisonment of Jews, the Nazis turned to mass murder. Weeks before the invasion, the men of the *Einsatzgruppen* received a directive demanding "ruthless and energetic measures against Bolshevik agitators, guerrillas, saboteurs, Jews, and the complete elimination of every active or passive resistance." The launch of the *Einsatzgruppen* forces in 1941 represented the start of the Nazi plan to systematically murder every European Jew—a lethal plan for mass murder often referred to by Nazis as the "final solution" to the "Jewish question."

Four separate Special Action Squads, ranging in size from 800 to 1,200 men apiece, accompanied the German army into Soviet territory and easily carried out their brutal tasks. The roving squads of killers acted swiftly as they raided towns and cities throughout the Nazi-occupied Soviet Union. They ordered Jews to assemble in a central area for the purpose of "resettlement." Once gathered, the Jews were forced to sur-

The Final Solution

On January 20, 1942, a small group of high-ranking Nazi party and government officials met to discuss the "final solution" to the European "Jewish question." The officials gathered at a villa in a wealthy section of Berlin near Wannsee Lake. The purpose of this top-secret gathering, which became known as the Wannsee Conference, was to inform key German government leaders of Adolf Hitler's plan for the elimination of all European Jews.

Rather than use explicit (clear and to the point) language, Nazi leaders used the code name "Final Solution" in their official reports. The Nazis proposed to transport 11 million Jews from all over German-occupied Europe to "extermination" camps. The enormity and scope of the "overall plan" required the cooperation of all attendees—not one of the fifteen participants objected.

Official preparations for a "final solution" had actually begun the year before. Soon after invading the Soviet Union in the spring of 1941, the Nazis employed mobile killing squads known as the *Einsatzgruppen.* These special task forces used firing squads to systematically murder Soviet Jews. The Nazis next experimented with various poisonous gas techniques, including mobile gas vans and stationary gas chambers. In December of 1941, in Chelmno, Poland, the Nazi party opened the first camp designed specifically for killing large numbers of Jews.

In the coming months, the Nazis built five additional "extermination" camps, all located in Poland: Treblinka, Sobibor, Belzec, Auschwitz-Birkenau, and Majdanek-Lubin. Many of the first victims came from the ghettos located throughout Poland. (Ghettos were sections of cities in which Jews were required to live.) Once all six camps became fully operational by mid-1942, the party began massive deportations from territories under German control—France, Belgium, Holland, Norway, Hungary, Romania, Italy, North Africa, and Greece.

render their valuables and remove their outer clothing, which would be sent for use in Germany. The killing squad members would then march the men, women, and children to a remote

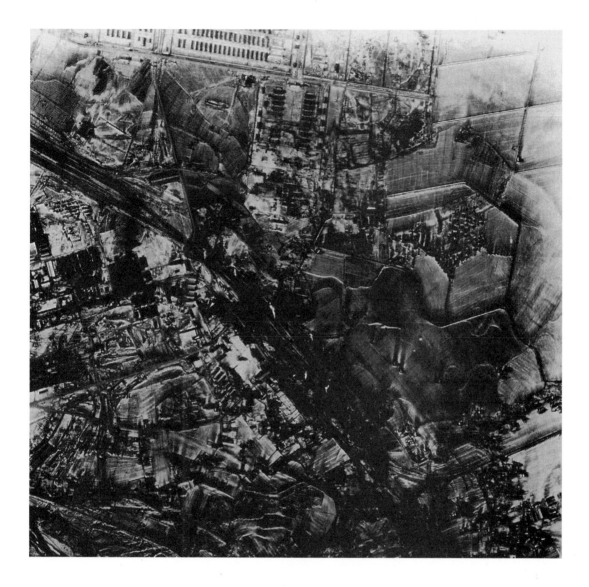

An aerial view of Auschwitz II—Birkenau.

location for execution. Nazis lined their victims up in front of antitank ditches, ravines, or newly dug mass graves and shot them to death one by one. In the small town of Ejszyski, in what is now Lithuania, the *Einsatzgruppen* killed nearly 4,000 Jews over two days. At Babi Yar, near the city of Kiev, 34,000 Jews were killed in only two days of shooting. By the time the Germans began their retreat from Soviet territory in 1943, the Special Action Squads had killed more than one million Jews and hundreds of thousands of other Soviet nationals (citizens), including Communist party leaders and Gypsies. (Communism is a political and economic theory that strives for the formation of a classless society through the communal, or group, ownership of all property.)

Killing by gunfire placed an enormous psychological burden on the members of the *Einsatzgruppen*. The men of these task forces complained of the "mental anguish" caused by having to shoot and kill women, children, and ill people. In August 1941, Nazi leaders ordered the development of alternative methods for mass execution. By the fall of that year, they began to use gas vans as a means for mass murder. These specially-equipped trucks piped poisonous exhaust fumes into airtight sections of the truck where the victims were being held. All four killing squads involved in the Soviet initiative employed these mobile killing vans.

Heinrich Himmler, head of the SS (*Schutzstaffel*, or protection squad) and overseer of the Nazi concentration camp system, visited the notorious camp at Auschwitz in 1941. He ordered the camp commandant, Rudolph Höss, to add a much larger section to the existing concentration camp. The new section, known as Auschwitz II or Birkenau, was to be set up for the extermination of large masses of human beings. The first gassing experiment using the poison known as Zyklon-B took place in Auschwitz on September 3, 1941. The initial victims of this experiment were 600 Soviet prisoners of war and 250 hospital patients. While awaiting trial and then execution after the war, Höss wrote a detailed account of all aspects of death camp operations, including the gas chambers. The following excerpt is from *Death Dealer: The Memoirs of the SS Kommandant at Auschwitz*, a complete edition of his memoirs and other Nazi documents.

Things to Remember While Reading
Höss's Memoirs:

- To conduct their "final solution" against the Jews, the Nazis needed a killing method that would spare them the psychological strain of shooting large numbers of civilians. Höss describes the first experiments using the poisonous gas Zyklon-B, which involved Russian political prisoners of war. He also reports on the routine gassings held at Auschwitz, which became the largest death camp where Jews were exterminated.

- The success of the experiments pleased Höss, who was relieved not to have to endure the annihilation (total destruction) of European Jews through the use of firing squads. By his own admission, execution by shooting made him squeamish. He preferred the relative efficiencies of gas chambers and the use of nearby crematoriums to burn the bodies.

- Keep in mind that Höss's manuscript reflects his views after the war, when the executions had stopped. His personal reflections should be read with the understanding that he did not know if expressions of compassion would reduce his sentence.

- Höss considered Soviets to be *untermenschen,* or subhuman, and Jews to be less than human. Notice how he refers to Jews as "leeches" and to his horses as "darlings." In contrast to his description of the mass murders he organized, Höss seems most passionate—and almost unfathomably selfish—when describing the suffering he and other Nazi officers experienced.

Politruks: Members of the Communist party.

Commissars: Officials of the Communist party.

Einsatzgruppen: Special Action Squads; special mobile killing squads of the Nazi SS.

POW: Prisoner of war; person taken by enemy forces during wartime.

Liquidation: To put an end to by death; killing.

Death Dealer: The Memoirs of the SS Kommandant at Auschwitz

*B*efore the mass destruction of the Jews began, all the Russian *politruks* and political **commissars** were killed in almost every camp during 1941 and 1942. According to the secret order given by Hitler, the **Einsatzgruppe** searched for and picked up the Russian politruks and commissars from all the **POW** camps. They transferred all they found to the nearest concentration camp for **liquidation**. The reason for this action was given as follows: the Russians were murdering any German soldier who was a member of the Nazi Party, especially **SS** members. Also, the political section of the **Red Army** had a standing order to cause unrest in every way in any POW camp or places where the POWs worked. If they were caught or imprisoned, they were instructed to perform acts of **sabotage**. This is why these political officials of the Red Army were sent to Auschwitz for liquidation. The first small transports were shot by firing squads of SS soldiers.

While I was on an official trip, my second in command, Camp Commander Fritzsch, experimented with gas for these killings. He used a gas called **Cyclon B**, **prussic acid**, which was often used as an insecticide in the camp to exterminate lice and **vermin**. There was always a supply on hand. When I returned Fritzsch reported to me about how he had used the gas. We used it again to kill the next **transport**.

The gassing was carried out in the basement of Block 11. I viewed the killings wearing a gas mask for protection. Death occurred in the crammed-full cells immediately after the gas was thrown in. Only a brief choking outcry and it was all over. This first gassing of people did not really sink into my mind. Perhaps I was much too impressed by the whole procedure.

I remember well and was much more impressed by the gassing of nine hundred Russians which occurred soon afterwards in the old **crematory** because the use of Block 11 caused too many problems. While the unloading took place, several holes were simply punched from above through the earth and concrete ceiling of the **mortuary**. The Russians had to undress in the **antechamber**, then everyone calmly walked into the mortuary because they were told they were to be **deloused** in there. The entire transport fit exactly in the room. The doors were closed and the gas poured in through the openings in the roof. How long the process lasted, I don't know, but for quite some time sounds could be heard. As the gas was thrown in some of them yelled "Gas!" and a tremendous screaming and shoving started toward both doors, but the doors were able to withstand all the force. It was not until several hours later that the doors were opened and the room aired out. There for the first time I saw gassed bodies in mass. Even though I imagined death by gas to be much worse, I still was overcome by a sick feeling, a horror. I always imagined death by gas a terrible choking

SS: Nazi political police who also ran the concentration camps.

Red Army: Military forces of Communist Russia.

Sabotage: Actions taken to defeat or hinder enemy forces.

Cyclon B: Or Zyklon B. Brand name of a crystal pellet form of prussic acid, a poison.

Prussic acid: Hydrocyanic acid (HCN), a highly volatile, poisonous liquid.

Vermin: Various small animals or insects such as rats and cockroaches that are annoying or dangerous to health.

Transport: In this use, a train full of people, usually Jews.

Crematory: A furnace for the cremation, or burning, of corpses.

Mortuary: A place where dead bodies are kept prior to cremation or burial.

Antechamber: A smaller room that serves as an entryway into a larger room.

Deloused: Underwent removal of lice.

The Birkenau arrival ramp.

Convulsions: Abnormal and uncontrollable contraction of muscles.

Eichmann, Adolf: SS officer responsible for organizing deportation of Jews to death camps.

suffocation, but the bodies showed no signs of **convulsions***. The doctors explained to me that prussic acid paralyzes the lungs. The effect is so sudden and so powerful that symptoms of suffocation never appear as in cases of death by coal gas or by lack of oxygen.*

At the time I really didn't waste any thoughts about the killing of the Russian POWs. It was ordered; I had to carry it out. But I must admit openly that the gassings had a calming effect on me, since in the near future the mass annihilation of the Jews was to begin. Up to this point it was not clear to me, nor to **Eichmann***, how the killing of the expected masses was to be done. Perhaps by gas? But how, and what kind of gas? Now we had discovered the gas and the procedure. I was always horrified of death by firing squads, especially when I thought of the huge numbers of women and children who would have to be killed. I had enough of hostage*

executions, and the mass killings by firing squad ordered by **Himmler** *and* **Heydrich**.

Now I was at ease. We were all saved from these bloodbaths, and the victims would be spared until the last moment. That is what I worried about the most when I thought of Eichmann's accounts of the mowing down of the Jews with machine guns and pistols by the Einsatzgruppe. Horrible scenes were supposed to have occurred: people running away even after being shot, the killing of those who were only wounded, especially the women and children. Another thing on my mind was the many suicides among the ranks of the SS Special Action Squads who could no longer mentally endure wading in the bloodbath. Some of them went mad. Most ... members ... drank a great deal to help get through this horrible work....

In the spring of 1942 [January] the first transports of Jews arrived from **Upper Silesia**. *All of them were to be exterminated. They were led from the ramp across the meadow, later named section B-II of Birkenau, to the farmhouse called Bunker I. [Camp Commander] Aumeier, Palitzsch, and a few other block leaders led them and spoke to them as one would in casual conversation, asking them about their occupations and their schooling in order to fool them. After arriving at the farmhouse they were told to undress. At first they went very quietly into the rooms where they were supposed to be disinfected. At that point some of them became suspicious and started talking about suffocation and extermination. Immediately a panic started. Those still standing outside were quickly driven into the chambers, and the doors were bolted shut. In the next transport those who were nervous or upset were identified and watched closely at all times. As soon as unrest was noticed these troublemakers were* **inconspicuously** *led behind the farmhouse and killed with a small-caliber pistol, which could not be heard by the others. The presence of the* **Sonderkommando** *and their soothing behavior also helped calm the restless*

Himmler, Heinrich: The senior leader of the SS responsible for the annihilation of the Jews.

Heydrich, Reinhard: Deputy head of the SS; directed the Einsatzgruppen.

Upper Silesia: Section of southwestern Poland bordering Germany.

Inconspicuously: Without being readily noticeable; without calling attention to.

Sonderkommando: German for "special squad." Groups of prisoners, usually Jewish, assigned to assist in the loading and unloading of the gas chambers, crematoriums, and burial pits.

and suspicious. Some of the Sonderkommando even went with them into the rooms and stayed until the last moment to keep them calm while an SS soldier stood in the doorway. The most important thing, of course, was to maintain as much peace and quiet as possible during the process of arriving and undressing. If some did not want to undress, some of those already undressed as well as the Sonderkommando had to help undress them.

With quiet talk and persuasion even those who resisted were soothed and undressed. The Sonderkommando, which was composed of prisoners, took great pains that the process of undressing took place very quickly so that the victims had no time to think about what was happening. Actually the eager assistance of the Sonderkommando during the undressing and the procession into the gas chambers was very peculiar. Never did I see or ever hear even a syllable breathed to those who were going to be gassed as to what their fate was. On the contrary, they tried everything to fool them. Most of all, they tried to calm those who seemed to guess what was ahead. Even though they might not believe the SS soldiers, they would have complete trust in those of their own race. For this reason the Sonderkommando was always composed of Jews from the same country as those who were being sent to the gas chamber.

The new arrivals asked about life in the camp and most of them asked about their relatives and friends from earlier transports. It was interesting to see how the Sonderkommando lied to them and how they emphasized these lies with convincing words and gestures. Many women hid their babies under piles of clothing. Some of the Sonderkommando watched carefully for this and would talk and talk to the woman until they persuaded her to take her baby along. The women tried to hide the babies because they thought the disinfection process would harm their infants. The little children cried mostly because of the unusual setting in which they were being undressed. But after their mothers or the Sonderkommando encouraged them, they calmed down and continued playing, teasing each other, clutching a toy as they went into the gas chamber.

I also watched how some women who suspected or knew what was happening, even with the fear of death all over their faces, still managed enough strength to play with their children and to talk to them lovingly. Once a woman with four children, all holding each other by the hand to help the smallest ones over the rough ground, passed by me very slowly. She stepped very close to me and whispered, pointing to her four children, "How can you murder these beautiful, darling children? Don't you have any heart?"...

Occasionally some women would suddenly start screaming in a terrible way while undressing. They pulled out their hair and acted as if they had gone crazy. Quickly they were led behind the farmhouse and killed by a bullet in the back of the neck from a small-caliber pistol. Sometimes, as the Sonderkommando were leaving the room, the women realized their fate and began hurling all kinds of curses at us. As the doors were being shut, I saw a woman trying to shove her children out of the chamber, crying out, "Why don't you at least let my precious children live?" There were many heartbreaking scenes like this....

In the spring of 1942 hundreds of people in the full bloom of life walked beneath the budding fruit trees of the farm into the gas chamber to their death, most of them without a hint of what was going to happen to them. To this day, I can still see these pictures of the arrivals, the selections, and the procession to their death.

As the selection process continued at the unloading ramps, there were an increasing number of incidences. Tearing apart families, separating the men from the women and children, caused great unrest.... Separating those who were able to work only increased the seriousness of the situation. No matter what, the families wanted to stay together. So it happened that even those

Rudolph Höss (sometimes spelled in English as "Hoess") 1900-1947

Rudolph Höss was born in Baden-Baden, a city located in the Black Forest of southwestern Germany. His father, a devout Catholic and strict disciplinarian, hoped that his son would become a priest. The elder Höss frequently took his son on religious pilgrimages throughout Europe. During World War I, fifteen-year-old Höss managed to join the army, even though he was underage. He was wounded several times and received the Iron Cross, a military honor, for his bravery. After the defeat of Germany, Höss joined a paramilitary nationalist organization called the "Freikorps" (Free Corps).

In 1923 he and other members of the Freikorps brutally murdered a German teacher who was accused of collaborating with the French during war. Höss was found guilty and served several years in prison before being pardoned in 1928.

Höss and his wife, Hedwig, joined a nationalist group that was committed to agricultural work and settlement in the East on Polish territory. (Nationalism is an extreme—in this case, fanatical—loyalty to one's country.) After spending six years as a farm worker and political activist, he formally joined the SS (Schutzstaffel, or protection squad, of the Nazi party) in June 1934. For the next four years, he held various administrative positions at the Dachau concentration camp. During his post as SS commandant at Auschwitz from 1940 to 1943, Höss methodically organized all camp operations concerning mass executions.

When he was executed in 1947, Höss died still committed to the principles of National Socialism (Nazism). The loyal Nazi SS officer was also an enthusiastic animal lover and devoted family man. He left behind his wife and five children.

selected to work ran back to the other members of their family, or the mothers with their children tried to get back to their husbands, or to the older children. Often there was such chaos and confusion that the selection process had to be started all over again. The limited amount of standing room did not permit better ways to separate them. There was no way to calm down these overly excited masses. Oftentimes order was restored by sheer force.

As I have said repeatedly, the Jews have a very strong sense of family. They cling to each other like leeches, but from what I observed, they lack a feeling of **solidarity***. In their situation you would assume that they would protect each other. But no, it was just the opposite. I heard about, and also experienced, Jews who gave the addresses of fellow Jews who were in hiding....*

This incident I witnessed myself: As the bodies were being pulled out of one of the gas chambers, one member of the Sonderkommando suddenly stopped and stood for a moment as if thunderstruck. He then pulled the body along, helping his comrades. I asked the **Kapo** *what was wrong with him. He found out that the startled Jew had discovered his wife among the bodies. I watched him for a while after this without noticing anything different about him. He just kept dragging his share of bodies. After a while I again happened on this work party. He was sitting with the others and eating as if nothing had happened. Was he really able to hide his feelings so completely, or had he become so hardened that something like this really didn't bother him?*

Where did the Jews of the Sonderkommando get the strength to perform this horrible job day and night? Did they hope for some special luck that would save them from the jaws of death? Or had they become too hardened by all the horror, or too weak to commit suicide to escape their existence? I really have watched this closely, but could never get to the bottom of their behavior. The ways the Jews lived and died was a puzzle I could never solve.

I could relate countless more of these experiences and occurrences.... These are only excerpts from the total process of the annihilation. They are only glimpses.

The mass annihilation with all the accompanying circumstances did not fail to affect those who had to carry it out. They just did not watch what was happening. With very few exceptions all who performed this monstrous "work" had been ordered to this

Solidarity: Unity as a people or community.

Kapo: Prisoners selected by the Nazis to oversee other prisoners in work groups.

detail. All of us, including myself, were given enough to think about which left a deep impression. Many of the men often approached me during my inspection trips through the killing areas and poured out their depression and anxieties to me, hoping that I could give them some reassurance. During these conversations the question arose again and again, "Is what we have to do here necessary? Is it necessary that hundreds of thousands of women and children have to be annihilated?" And I, who countless times deep inside myself had asked the same question, had to put them off by reminding them that it was Hitler's order. I had to tell them that it was necessary to destroy all the Jews in order to forever free Germany and the future generations from our toughest enemy.

It goes without saying that the Hitler order was a firm fact for all of us, and also that it was the duty of the SS to carry it out. However, secret doubts tormented all of us. Under no circumstances could I reveal my secret doubts to anyone. I had to convince myself to be a rock when faced with the necessity of carrying out this horribly severe order, and I had to show this in every way, in order to force all those under me to hang on mentally and emotionally.

Everyone watched me. They all wanted to see what kind of impression this made on me, and how I reacted.... Everything I said was thoroughly discussed. I had to make a tremendous effort to pull myself together in order not to show, not even once, in all the excitement after an incident, or to allow my inner doubts and depressions to come out in the open. I had to appear cold and heartless during these events which tear the heart apart in anyone who had any kind of human feelings.... Coldly, I had to stand and watch as the mothers went into the gas chambers with their laughing or crying children.

On one occasion two little children were involved in a game they were playing and their mother just couldn't tear them away

from it. Even the Jews of the Sonderkommando didn't want to pick up the children. I will never forget the pleading look on the face of the mother, who certainly knew what was happening. The people in the gas chamber were becoming restless. Everyone was looking at me. I had to act. I gave the sergeant in charge a wave, and he picked up the screaming, kicking children in his arms and brought them into the gas chamber along with the mother, who was weeping in the most heart-breaking fashion. Believe me, I felt like shrinking into the ground out of pity, but I was not allowed to show the slightest emotion.

Hour upon hour I had to witness all that happened. I had to watch day and night, whether it was the dragging and burning of the bodies, the teeth being ripped out, the cutting of the hair; I had to watch all this horror. For hours I had to stand in the horrible, haunting stench while the mass graves were dug open, and the bodies dragged out and burned. I also had to watch the process of death itself through the peephole of the gas chamber because the doctors called my attention to it. I had to do all of this because I was the one to whom everyone looked, and because I had to show everybody that I was not only the one who gave the orders and issued the directives, but that I was also willing to be present at whatever task I ordered my men to perform....

I had to watch it all with cold indifference. Even minor incidents, which others probably would not have noticed or been affected by, stayed on my mind for a long time.

And yet, I really had no reason to complain about being bored at Auschwitz.

When something upset me very much and it was impossible for me to go home to my family, I would climb onto my horse and ride until I chased the horrible pictures away. I often went into the horse stables during the night, and there found peace among my darlings.

Often at home my mind would suddenly recall some incident at the killing sites. That's when I had to get out because I couldn't stand being in the loving surroundings of my family.... (Höss, 155-63)

What happened next...

Rudolph Höss served as commandant of Auschwitz from 1940 to 1943. In November of 1943, he was appointed chief of the SS Economic and Administrative Main Office. He was sent back to Auschwitz in June of 1944 on a temporary assignment to manage the extermination of the Jews of Hungary. Senior SS leadership relied on Höss, a perfectionist and loyal bureaucrat, to accomplish the difficult task of murdering 430,000 Hungarian Jews brought to Auschwitz over the course of 56 days. The operation was named in his honor—Aktion (Operation) Höss. During his tenure at Auschwitz, Höss was responsible for liquidating some 2 million people, most of them Jews. Thousands of non-Jews were also victims of Auschwitz, including 20,000 Gypsies from Germany and Austria and 16,000 Soviet prisoners of war.

For his "outstanding service" in carrying out his "duties" at Auschwitz, Höss received praise from his superiors. An SS report in 1944 commended Höss for his accomplishments as "a true pioneer in this area because of his new ideas and educational methods."

When Germany fell in 1945, Höss took an assumed name, Franz Lang. (His father's first name was Franz.) After being released from a prisoner-of-war collection point, Höss managed to find work in agriculture. He was recognized and arrested in March 1946 near Flensburg in what was then called West Germany. Two months later he was extradited (delivered for trial) to Poland. While awaiting this trial, and then his execution, Höss wrote his autobiography and a series of profiles of SS commanders. In March of 1947, the supreme court in Warsaw, Poland, sentenced Höss to death. He felt hanging was somehow shameful and requested to be executed by firing squad. The Polish tribunal declined his request. On

April 16, 1947, Höss was brought to Auschwitz and hanged on gallows placed within yards of the first gas chamber.

Did you know...

- The Nazis first used poisonous gas in the "euthanasia" (mercy-killing) program aimed at eliminating people with physical and mental disabilities. The first recorded mass murder by gas took place in December 1939, when prison laborers used carbon monoxide to kill Polish mental patients. The gassings took place in facilities disguised as shower rooms.

- Before deciding on the use of Zyklon-B for mass killings, the Nazis experimented with several other methods, including firing squads, forced inhalation of pure carbon monoxide or exhaust fumes, and electrocution. In 1941 they began using specially equipped mobile vans that circulated exhaust gas into the sealed rear portion of the vehicle. A total of 20 gas vans were used to kill some 700,000 people, mainly in the Soviet Union and the Chelmno extermination camp.

- The profits of the firm that manufactured Zyklon-B increased significantly as the Nazis began to use the lethal gas in their mass executions of European Jews. Management was probably aware of the use of their product because the SS ordered the gas to be made without the standard warning odor, or "indicator." By removing the warning odor, the Nazis helped prevent victims from being alerted to their fate in the camp gas chambers.

For Further Reading

Höss, Rudolph. *Death Dealer: The Memoirs of the SS Kommandant at Auschwitz*. Edited by Steven Paskuly. Translated by Andrew Pollinger. New York: Da Capo Press, 1996.

Korschunow, Irina. *Night in Distant Motion: A Novel*. Translated by Leigh Hafrey. Boston: David R. Godine, 1983.

Sender, Ruth Minsky. *The Cage*. New York: Macmillan, 1986. Reprinted, Bantam Books, 1988.

Anne Frank

Excerpt from *The Diary of a Young Girl*, written between 1942-1944

Edited by Otto H. Frank and Mirjam Pressler
This version published in 1997

The Nazi (National Socialist) government of Germany (1933-1945) nearly achieved its goal of attaining world domination. Beginning with the Austrian annexation (adding onto existing territory) in 1938 and the Polish invasion in 1939, Nazi Germany set out to seize control of Europe and beyond. By 1940, Germany had conquered France, Belgium, Luxembourg, the Netherlands, Denmark, and Norway. With each military success, the Germans increased the number of Jews who fell under their rule. Many Jews who had fled Nazi Germany in the 1930s to settle in neighboring countries found themselves again under the brutal repression of antisemitic, or anti-Jewish, policies. One such family was that of Otto and Edith Frank, who escaped Germany and sought refuge in the Netherlands (also known as Holland). Millions of people have come to know this family by reading the diary their daughter, Anne Frank.

Otto and Edith Frank, along with their young daughters, Margot and Anne, left Germany in 1933 soon after Adolf Hitler came to power. The Frank family settled in Amsterdam, where Otto started two small food-production businesses. The Frank sisters attended local schools, learned the Dutch language, and made many friends in their new home. Seven years of stable family life ended abruptly when the Nazis invaded Holland in May 1940.

As in other conquered nations, the Nazis quickly abolished (put an end to) the rights of Jews. They passed a law ordering Jews to surrender their businesses to non-Jews, a process known as "Aryanization." With the help of friends, Otto Frank completed the paperwork required by the decree

yet retained control of his businesses. Another law mandated (ordered) that Jewish children could attend only Jewish schools, thus forcing Anne and Margot to switch schools.

By the middle of 1942, the Nazis had opened several camps throughout Poland that were specially designed for mass murder. The Nazis planned to use these "extermination camps" for the deliberate destruction of all European Jews. To conceal their intentions, they used the code name the "Final Solution" to refer to this horrendous, lethal plan. With the cooperation of numerous local and national bureaucracies (administrations or governments), they undertook the enormously complex task of transporting Jews from occupied countries to various death camps.

The Nazis created transit camps as a way to control and organize the flow of victims to the awaiting gas chambers and crematorium. Often, Jews boarded trains supposedly bound for "resettlement in the East" or relocation to forced labor assignments. Some Jews managed to escape after witnessing death camp operations and returned to inform others of the fate awaiting those ordered to relocate. The first massive deportation to death camps targeted the Jews imprisoned in the ghettos (certain restricted sections of cities where Jews were housed) of Poland. The Nazis began the mass deportation of Jews living in France, Belgium, and Holland in July 1942.

On July 5, 1942, Margot Frank received orders from a Nazi bureau to register for "labor expansion measures." This ominous letter prompted the Franks to go into hiding immediately.

For over a year, the Franks had planned for such an event. Piece by piece, Otto Frank had moved his family's belongings into a shelter he constructed in the unused upper floors of his office building. At the top of a staircase, he built a bookcase that, when slid aside, revealed a secret entrance to the annex. For two terrifying years, the Franks and four other friends lived as *onderduikers*, meaning "ones who dive under."

Shortly before going into hiding, Anne Frank received a diary from her father for her thirteenth birthday. Over the next two years she poured her heart into this red and orange checkered book, describing her darkest moments and brightest hopes for the future. *The Diary of a Young Girl* is one of the best-known personal accounts of the Nazi era. With remarkable insight and clarity, Frank wrote about the troubles of adolescence and the horrendous circumstances caused by Nazi terror. Her refreshing honesty and passion for life continue to touch readers around the world.

Things to Remember While Reading Frank's Diary:

- Frank addresses her diary entries to "Kitty"—an imaginary friend in whom she confides and who she hopes "will be a great support and comfort."

- Frank's diary reveals that her relationships with other family members are typical of any teenager, despite the very unusual circumstances under which they live. She competes relentlessly with her sister, adores her father, and feels that nobody—especially her mother—understands her.

- Another family joined the Frank family in hiding—Mr. and Mrs. van Daan and their teenage son, Peter. Albert Dussel, an elderly dentist, completed the group of eight.

- Otto Frank confided in four employees who helped the hideaways by bringing them food, clothing, and other items during their two years of seclusion. The four helpers—Victor Kugler, Johannes Kleiman, Elli Voskuijl, and Miep Gies—risked their own lives to try to save their Jewish friends.

- Perhaps the most remarkable aspect of Frank's life was her ability to hold onto her ideals. Amidst the destruction and killing inflicted by the Nazis, she remained hopeful that one day peace and freedom would return.

The Diary of a Young Girl

SATURDAY, NOVEMBER 7, 1942

Dearest Kitty,

*Mother's nerves are very much on edge, and that doesn't **bode well** for me. Is it just a coincidence that Father and Mother never scold Margot and always blame me for everything? Last night, for example, Margot was reading a book with beautiful illustrations; she got up and put the book aside for later. I wasn't doing anything, so I picked it up and began looking at the pictures. Margot came back, saw "her" book in my hands, **knitted her brow** and angrily demanded the book back. I wanted to look through it some more. Margot got madder by the minute, and Mother butted in: "Margot was reading that book; give it back to her."*

Bode well: Indicate that things would go smoothly.

Knitted her brow: Drew her eyebrows together, making wrinkles.

Father came in, and without even knowing what was going on, saw Margot was being wronged and lashed out at me: "I'd like to see what you'd do if Margot was looking at one of your books!"

I promptly gave in, put the book down and, according to them, left the room "in a huff." I was neither huffy nor cross, but merely sad.

It wasn't right of Father to pass judgment without knowing what the issue was. I would have given the book to Margot myself, and a lot sooner, if Father and Mother hadn't intervened and rushed to take Margot's part, as if she were suffering some great injustice.

*Of course, Mother took Margot's side; they always take each other's sides. I'm so used to it that I've become completely indifferent to Mother's **rebukes** and Margot's moodiness. I love them, but only because they're Mother and Margot. I don't give a darn about them as people. As far as I'm concerned, they can go jump in a lake. It's different with Father. When I see him **being partial to** Margot, approving Margot's every action, praising her, hugging her, I feel a gnawing ache inside, because I'm crazy about him. I model myself after Father, and there's no one in the world I love more. He doesn't realize that he treats Margot differently than he does me: Margot just happens to be the smartest, the kindest, the prettiest and the best. But I have a right to be taken seriously too. I've always been the clown and mischief maker of the family; I've always had to pay double for my sins: once with scoldings and then again with my own sense of **despair**. I'm no longer satisfied with the meaningless affection or the supposedly serious talks. I long for something from Father that he's incapable of giving. I'm not jealous of Margot; I never have been. I'm not envious of her brains or her beauty. It's just that I'd like to feel that Father really loves me, not because I'm his child, but because I'm me, Anne.*

I cling to Father because my contempt of Mother is growing daily and it's only through him that I'm able to retain the last ounce

Rebukes: Sharp criticisms; reprimands.

Being partial to: Favoring.

Despair: Hopelessness.

holocaust

of family feeling I have left. He doesn't understand that I sometimes need to vent my feelings for Mother. He doesn't want to talk about it, and he avoids any discussion involving Mother's failings.

And yet Mother, with all her shortcomings, is tougher for me to deal with. I don't know how I should act. I can't very well confront her with her carelessness, her sarcasm and her hard-heartedness, yet I can't continue to take the blame for everything.

I'm the opposite of Mother, so of course we clash. I don't mean to judge her; I don't have that right. I'm simply looking at her as a mother. She's not a mother to me—I have to mother myself. I've cut myself adrift from them. I'm charting my own course, and we'll see where it leads me. I have no choice, because I can picture what a mother and a wife should be and can't seem to find anything of the sort in the woman I'm supposed to call "Mother."

*I tell myself time and again to overlook Mother's bad example. I only want to see her good points, and to look inside myself for what's lacking in her. But it doesn't work, and the worst part is that Father and Mother don't realize their own **inadequacies** and how much I blame them for letting me down. Are there any parents who can make their children completely happy?*

Sometimes I think God is trying to test me, both now and in the future. I'll have to become a good person on my own, without anyone to serve as a model or advise me, but it'll make me stronger in the end.

*Who else but me is ever going to read these letters? Who else but me can I turn to for comfort? I'm frequently in need of **consolation**, I often feel weak, and more often than not, I fail to meet expectations. I know this, and every day I **resolve** to do better.*

They [Frank's parents] aren't consistent in their treatment of me. One day they say that Anne's a sensible girl and entitled to

Inadequacies: Shortcomings; faults; deficiencies.

Consolation: To be consoled; to be comforted.

Resolve: Determine; pledge; promise.

know everything, and the next that Anne's a silly goose who doesn't know a thing and yet imagines she's learned all she needs to know from books! I'm no longer the baby and spoiled little darling whose every deed can be laughed at. I have my own ideas, plans and ideals, but am unable to **articulate** them yet.

Oh well. So much comes into my head at night when I'm alone, or during the day when I'm obliged put up with people I can't **abide** or who **invariably** misinterpret my intentions. That's why I always wind up coming back to my diary—I start there and end there because Kitty's always patient. I promise her that, despite everything, I'll keep going, that I'll find my own way and choke back my tears. I only wish I could see some results or, just once, receive encouragement from someone who loves me.

Don't condemn me, but think of me as a person who sometimes reaches the bursting point!

Yours, Anne

SATURDAY, JANUARY 30, 1943

Dearest Kitty,

I'm **seething** with rage, yet I can't show it. I'd like to scream, stamp my foot, give Mother a good shaking, cry and I don't know what else because of the nasty words, mocking looks and accusations that she hurls at me day after day, piercing me like arrows from a tightly strung bow, which are nearly impossible to pull from my body. I'd like to scream at Mother, Margot, the van Daans, Dussel and Father too: "Leave me alone, let me have at least one night when I don't cry myself to sleep with my eyes burning and my head pounding. Let me get away, away from everything, away from this world!" But I can't do that. I can't let them see my doubts, or the wounds they've inflicted on me. I couldn't bear their sympathy or their good-humored **derision**. It would only make me want to scream even more.

Articulate: To express clearly.

Abide: Tolerate; bear with patience.

Invariably: Always.

Seething: Intensely hot; boiling; agitated.

Derision: Ridicule.

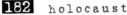

*Everyone thinks I'm showing off when I talk, ridiculous when I'm silent, **insolent** when I answer, **cunning** when I have a good idea, lazy when I'm tired, selfish when I eat one bite more than I should, stupid, cowardly, calculating, etc., etc. All day long I hear nothing but what an **exasperating** child I am, and although I laugh it off and pretend not to mind, I do mind. I wish I could ask God to give me another personality, one that doesn't **antagonize** everyone.*

Insolent: Arrogant, bold, or proud; lacking proper respect.

Cunning: Shrewd; skilled at deception.

Exasperating: Irritating.

Antagonize: To bring on dislike or hostility.

But that's impossible. I'm stuck with the character I was born with, yet I'm sure I'm not a bad person. I do my best to please everyone, more than they'd ever suspect in a million years. When I'm upstairs, I try to laugh it off because I don't want them to see my troubles.

*More than once, after a series of absurd **reproaches**, I've snapped at Mother: "I don't care what you say. Why don't you just wash your hands of me—I'm a hopeless case." Of course, she'd tell me not to talk back and virtually ignore me for two days. Then suddenly all would be forgotten and she'd treat me like everyone else.*

*It's impossible for me to be all smiles one day and **venomous** the next. I'd rather choose the **golden mean**, which isn't so golden, and keep my thoughts to myself. Perhaps sometime I'll treat the others with the same contempt as they treat me. Oh, if only I could.*

Yours, Anne

MONDAY, JULY 26, 1943

Dear Kitty,

*Yesterday was a very **tumultuous** day, and we're still all wound up. Actually, you may wonder if there's ever a day that passes without some kind of excitement.*

The first warning siren went off in the morning while we were at breakfast, but we paid no attention, because it only meant that the planes were crossing the coast. I had a terrible headache, so I lay down for an hour after breakfast and then went to the office at around two. At two-thirty Margot had finished her office work and was just gathering her things together when the sirens began wailing again. So she and I trooped back upstairs. None too soon, it seems, for less than five minutes later the guns were boom-

Reproaches: In this case, a noun meaning an expression of disapproval.

Venomous: Spiteful.

Golden mean: The course between extremes.

Tumultuous: Full of confusion, commotion, or turbulence.

*ing so loudly that we went and stood in the hall. The house shook and the bombs kept falling. I was clutching my "escape bag," more because I wanted to have something to hold on to than because I wanted to run away. I know we can't leave here, but if we had to, being seen on the streets would be just as dangerous as getting caught in an air raid. After half an hour the **drone** of engines faded and the house began to hum with activity again. Peter emerged from his lookout post in the front attic, Dussel remained in the front office, Mrs. van D. felt safest in the private office, Mr. van Daan had been watching from the loft, and those of us on the landing spread out to watch the columns of smoke rising from the harbor. Before long the smell of fire was everywhere, and outside it looked as if the city were enveloped in a thick fog.*

A big fire like that is not a pleasant sight, but fortunately for us it was all over, and we went back to our various chores. Just as we were starting dinner: another air-raid alarm. The food was good, but I lost my appetite the moment I heard the siren. Nothing happened, however, and forty-five minutes later the all clear was sounded. After the dishes had been washed: another air-raid warning, gunfire and swarms of planes. "Oh, gosh, twice in one day," we thought, "that's twice too many." Little good that did us, because once again the bombs rained down, this time on the other side of the city. According to British reports, Schiphol Airport was bombed. The planes dived and climbed, the air was abuzz with the drone of engines. It was very scary, and the whole time I kept thinking, "Here it comes, this is it."

I can assure you that when I went to bed at nine, my legs were still shaking. At the stroke of midnight I woke up again: more planes! Dussel was undressing, but I took no notice and leapt up, wide awake, at the sound of the first shot. I stayed in Father's bed until one, in my own bed until one-thirty, and was back in Father's bed at two. But the planes kept on coming. At last they stopped firing and I was able to go back "home" again. I finally fell asleep at half past two.

Drone: Continued humming or buzzing sound.

*Seven o'clock. I awoke with a start and sat up in bed. Mr. van Daan was with Father. My first thought was: burglars. "Everything," I heard Mr. van Daan say, and I thought everything had been stolen. But no, this time it was wonderful news, the best we've had in months, maybe even since the war began. **Mussolini** has resigned and the King of Italy has taken over the government [of Italy].*

We jumped for joy. After the awful events of yesterday, finally something good happens and brings us ... hope! Hope for an end to the war, hope for peace.

Mr. Kugler dropped by and told us that the Fokker aircraft factory had been hit hard. Meanwhile, there was another air-raid alarm this morning, with planes flying over, and another warning siren. I've had it up to here with alarms. I've hardly slept, and the last thing I want to do is work. But now the suspense about Italy and the hope that the war will be over by the end of the year are keeping us awake...

Yours, Anne

MONDAY EVENING, NOVEMBER 8, 1943

Dearest Kitty,

Miep often says she envies us because we have such peace and quiet here. That may be true, but she's obviously not thinking about our fear.

I simply can't imagine the world will ever be normal again for us. I do talk about "after the war," but it's as if I were talking about a castle in the air, something that can never come true.

I see the eight of us in the Annex as if we were a patch of blue sky surrounded by menacing black clouds. The perfectly round spot

Mussolini, Benito: (1883-1945) Fascist dictator of Italy from 1922 to 1943. (Fascism is a political philosophy that places nation and race above the individual. Fascist governments are run by a single, dictatorial leader and are characterized by extreme social and economic restrictions.)

*on which we're standing is still safe, but the clouds are moving in on us, and the ring between us and the approaching danger is being pulled tighter and tighter. We're surrounded by darkness and danger, and in our desperate search for a way out we keep bumping into each other. We look at the fighting down below and the peace and beauty up above. In the meantime, we've been cut off by the dark mass of clouds, so that we can go neither up nor down. It looms before us like an **impenetrable** wall, trying to crush us, but not yet able to. I can only cry out and **implore**, "Oh, ring, ring, open wide and let us out!"*

Yours, Anne

SATURDAY, JULY 15, 1944

Dearest Kitty,

"Deep down, the young are lonelier than the old." I read this in a book somewhere and it's stuck in my mind. As far as I can tell, it's true.

*So if you're wondering whether it's harder for the adults here than for the children, the answer is no, it's certainly not. Older people have an opinion about everything and are sure of themselves and their actions. It's twice as hard for us young people to hold on to our opinions at a time when ideals are being shattered and destroyed, when the worst side of human nature **predominates**, when everyone has come to doubt truth, justice and God.*

Anyone who claims that the older folks have a more difficult time in the Annex doesn't realize that the problems have a far greater impact on us. We're much too young to deal with these problems, but they keep thrusting themselves on us until, finally, we're forced to think up a solution, though most of the time our solutions crumble when faced with the facts. It's difficult in times like these: ideals, dreams, and cherished hopes rise within us, only

Impenetrable: Not capable of being penetrated or entered.

Implore: To plead or beg for urgently.

Predominates: Shows itself; wins out.

Frank

Anne Frank (1929-1945)

Annelies Marie Frank was born to Otto and Edith Frank in Frankfurt, Germany. Along with Anne's older sister, Margot, the family fled Germany in 1933, shortly after the Nazis took control of the government. They moved to Amsterdam, where Mr. Frank opened a small food-production company, specializing in materials for jams and jellies. He later opened another business, specializing in spices. Anne attended local schools in Amsterdam and was reported to be an average student with a strong interest in reading and writing.

The Nazis invaded the Netherlands on May 10, 1940. The Franks chose to remain in Amsterdam, but their children had to attend a Jewish Lyceum (or school) established by the Nazis. Anne's first diary entry was written on June 12, 1942, her thirteenth birthday. The family decided to hide in July 1942, when the then-sixteen-year-old Margot received a summons to report for work "in the East." With the help of friends, the Franks and four others spent two years secluded in the attic of an office which adjoined (was connected to) Otto Frank's business.

The Nazis discovered the hideaways and arrested them on August 4, 1944. The Frank family was sent first to the Westerbork transit camp and then to the Auschwitz-Birkenau death camp. Anne Frank died of typhus (a serious illness characterized by extremely high fever and a red rash) in early March 1945 at the Bergen-Belsen work camp.

to be crushed by grim reality. It's a wonder I haven't abandoned all my ideals, they seem so absurd and impractical. Yet I cling to them because I still believe, in spite of everything, that people are truly good at heart.

It's utterly impossible for me to build my life on a foundation of chaos, suffering and death. I see the world being slowly transformed into wilderness, I hear the approaching thunder that, one day, will destroy us too, I feel the suffering of millions. And yet, when I look up at the sky, I somehow feel that everything will

change for the better, that this cruelty too shall end, that peace and **tranquility** *will return once more. In the meantime, I must hold on to my ideals. Perhaps the day will come when I'll be able to realize them!*

Yours, Anne M. Frank

> *(Frank, pp. 60-327)*

Tranquility: Calmness.

What happened next...

Anne wrote her last diary entry on Tuesday, August 1, 1944. A few days later, the Gestapo (secret police force of the Nazi party) in Amsterdam received an anonymous tip about the hideaway Jews in the annex and immediately raided the building. The Frank family was transported to the Westerbork transit camp on August 8, 1944. They were detained in Westerbork for a month before being transported to the Auschwitz-Birkenau extermination camp. Records indicate they were among the last trainload of prisoners to be transported from Westerbork to Auschwitz-Birkenau.

Faced with the prospect of losing the war in the fall of 1944, the Nazis rushed to finish their murderous goal of racial cleansing and destroy the evidence of mass murder at the death camps. They stopped deportations from transit camps, accelerated exterminations, and forced remaining able-bodied prisoners to relocate away from advancing Allied forces. As part of the effort to close the death camps, Anne and Margot Frank were sent to the Bergen-Belsen labor camp in October 1944. Their mother died at Auschwitz-Birkenau in January 1945, and Margot died of typhus at Bergen-Belsen in early March. Believing she was the only remaining family member alive, Anne died a few days later. Witnesses report she was buried in one of the mass graves at Bergen-Belsen. Anne's father, Otto Frank, remained in Auschwitz until liberation by the Soviet Army on January 27, 1945. He was the only one of the eight hideaways to survive the Holocaust.

Miep Gies, one of the people who helped conceal the Franks, managed to save Anne's diary and other writings. After liberation, Otto Frank returned to Amsterdam knowing he was a widower but still hopeful that his daughters were alive. The same day that the deaths of Anne and Margot were confirmed, Gies returned Anne's diary to Otto. In keeping with Anne's wishes to be a writer, he published several portions of the diary in 1947 as *The Annex*. By 1952, a more complete version, *The Diary of a Young Girl*, received worldwide critical acclaim. A stage version of Anne's diary won the 1955 Pulitzer Prize for best play of the year, and a film version followed in 1959.

In 1986, the Netherlands State Institute for War Documentation, which retained the original diary following the death of Otto Frank, released a complete unedited version. Proceeds of the publication of *The Diary of a Young Girl* help fund the Anne Frank Foundation, dedicated to fighting anti-semitism and racism throughout the world. The foundation maintains the original Annex building in Amsterdam and operates offices in Basel, Switzerland, and New York City.

Did you know...

- Anne heard a radio report in 1944 urging people to collect diaries and letters about their war experiences for possible future publication. Encouraged by her family and friends, she began to edit the earlier diary entries. On May 11, 1944, she wrote, "My greatest wish is to become a journalist some day and later a famous writer." Today some 20 million copies of her diary are in circulation in more than 50 editions.

- In preparation for possible publication, Anne used pseudonyms (false names) for most of the persons in the diary. The present edition retains the pseudonyms Anne assigned to the people in hiding, while using the real names of the four helpers.

- The diary itself is on display in Amsterdam, at the location of the office annex.

- Miep Gies, who held onto Anne's original diary, also saved some of her other writings: *Stories and Adventures from the Annex* and *Book of Beautiful Phrases*. Gies wrote about her experiences in *Anne Frank Remembered*, which became the basis of an Academy Award-winning documentary film.

For Further Reading

Frank, Anne. *The Diary of a Young Girl.* Edited by Otto H. Frank and Mirjam Pressler. Translated by Susan Massotty. New York: Bantam, 1997.

Gies, Miep, with Alison Gold. *Anne Frank Remembered.* New York: Simon & Schuster, 1987.

Lindwer, Willy. *The Last Seven Months of Anne Frank.* Translated by Alison Meersschaert. New York: Random House, 1991.

Etty Hillesum

Excerpt from *An Interrupted Life--The Diaries, 1941-1943 and Letters from Westerbork*

This version published in 1996

From its inception—or beginning—in 1920, the Nazi (National Socialist) party in Germany promoted anti-semitism, or hatred of Jewish people. After rising to power in 1933, they instituted repressive measures that affected all aspects of the social, political, and economic life of German Jews. When Germany invaded Poland in 1939, tactics to suppress Jews became more and more drastic. With each country they conquered, the Nazis brought additional Jews under their domination. While Nazi leader Adolf Hitler made repeated threats against the Jews, as early as 1939 he began to imply that he intended the "annihilation [complete destruction] of the Jews in Europe." In 1941, Hitler and other Nazi leaders approved a secret plan for the mass murder of all European Jews, a plan code-named the "Final Solution."

To accomplish their goals, the Nazi government coordinated the resources of a far-reaching bureaucracy (administrative body or government). Millions of Jews were removed from German-occupied countries and transported by train to a network of specially-built camps. The Nazis created several different types of camps, including "extermination" camps, which were specifically designed for mass murder. Immediately after their arrest, Jews in Western Europe were first retained in "transit" camps. Situated near populated areas and adjacent to (lying next to) major train lines, transit camps served as waiting stations; the Jews were then sent on trains to labor camps or directly to death camps in Poland. Jews and other Nazi victims in Eastern Europe stayed first in ghettos (special sections of a city) before deportation to death camps or labor camps. In Nazi-occupied areas of the Soviet

Union, however, most Jews faced immediate execution by mobile killing squads.

The transit camps gave Jews a taste of life under Nazi control—a life that included constant hunger, systemized humiliation, disease, and death. To keep order within the camps, the Nazis carefully hid their intentions by referring to the inevitable deportation as "resettlement" to the East. Prisoners were allowed to keep whatever possessions they brought with them—although most assets had been confiscated before their arrests. The camp administrators also opened schools for Jewish children and allowed inmates to wear civilian clothes.

The Nazis invaded and conquered the Netherlands in May 1940. After moving quickly to suspend the Dutch parliament, the Germans set up their own government and appointed Dutch Nazis to key positions. A series of anti-Jewish decrees stripped Dutch Jews of their political and economic rights. Amidst a series of violent struggles with the Jews, the Nazis formed a *Joodsche Raad,* or Jewish Council. Composed of Dutch-Jewish leaders, the Council was held responsible for executing Nazi orders.

In February 1941, a strike broke out in reaction to Nazi organized anti-Jewish violence in Amsterdam, the official capital of the Netherlands. The Nazis intensified their pressure against Jews and resistors, launching their first major roundup of Jews in April 1942. Jews were required to wear a yellow star and relocate to Amsterdam, thereby making the provinces (or outlying areas) *judenrein,* or "free of Jews."

In July 1942 the Nazis began sequestering Jews in Westerbork, a camp originally set up a decade earlier by the Dutch government to house Jewish refugees from Germany. Also in July, a young Jewish woman, Etty Hillesum, secured a job as a typist for the Jewish Council. Hillesum was 28 years old, well educated, and active in the cultural life of Amsterdam. As part of the Jewish Council, she assisted new arrivals to Westerbork and tended to the prisoners during their brief stay. Perhaps most difficult of all, she comforted fellow Jews and other victims as they boarded trains that would likely take them to their deaths. While her association with the influential Jewish Council spared her life for a period of time, she knew her survival depended on the deaths of others—a situation that she found increasingly difficult to accept.

Things to Remember While Reading Hillesum's Diaries and Letters:

- Train arrivals and departures became the central focus of life in transit camps such as Westerbork. The Nazis used Jewish workers to assure stability in the transit camp environment. Knowing that chaos and disorder would jeopardize the orderly progression of inmates to the death camps, the Nazis attempted to trick victims into believing that they were simply being relocated to Eastern Europe for forced labor.

- Hillesum's brother Mischa was a famous and gifted pianist known throughout Europe. Since the Nazis considered him to be a "cultural Jew," they offered to allow him to stay with other Jewish artists and intellectuals in a castle in the small town of Barneveld. He pleaded for his parents to be given the same protection, but the Nazis refused his request.

- Hillesum wrote her final postcard from inside a transport headed to the Auschwitz-Birkenau death camp. She threw the card, addressed to her friend, out of the train car. Farmers found the card and posted it, enabling Hillesum's last thoughts to be heard.

Etty Hillesum: An Interrupted Life--The Diaries, 1941-1943 and Letters from Westerbork

[18] December, 1942

*One summer evening I sat eating red cabbage at the edge of the yellow **lupin** field that stretched from our dining hut to the **delousing** station, and with sudden inspiration I said, "One ought to write a chronicle of Westerbork." An older man to my left—also eating red cabbage—answered, "Yes, but to do that you'd have to be a great poet."*

*He is right, it would take a great poet. Little journalistic pieces won't do. The whole of Europe is gradually being turned into one great prison camp. The whole of Europe will undergo this same bitter experience. To simply record the bare facts of families torn apart, of possessions **plundered** and liberties **forfeited**, would soon become **monotonous**. Nor is it possible to pen **picturesque** accounts of barbed wire and vegetable **swill** to show outsiders*

Lupin: A type of flowering plant.

Delousing: To rid of lice, a type of parasite.

Plundered: Taken by force.

Forfeited: Lost; given up.

Monotonous: Tiresome or tedious because they all sound the same.

Picturesque: Resembling a picture; suggesting a painted scene.

Swill: A semiliquid food for animals.

what it's like. Besides, I wonder how many outsiders will be left if history continues along the paths it has taken....

*Finding something to say about Westerbork is also difficult because of its **ambiguous** character. On the one hand it is a stable community in the making, a forced one to be sure, yet with all the characteristics of a human society. And on the other hand, it is a camp for a people in transit, great waves of human beings constantly washed in from the cities and **provinces**, from rest homes, prisons, and other prison camps, from all the nooks and crannies of the Netherlands—only to be deported a few days later to meet their unknown destiny.*

*You can imagine how dreadfully crowded it is in half a square kilometer. Naturally, few follow the example of the man who packed his **rucksack** and went on transport of his own **accord**. When asked why, he said that he wanted the freedom to decide to go when <u>he</u> wanted to go. It reminds me of the Roman judge who said to a **martyr**, "Do you know that I have the power to have you killed?" And the martyr answered, "Yes, but I have the power of letting myself be killed."*

*Anyway, it is terribly crowded in Westerbork, as when too many drowning people cling to the last bit of **flotsam** after a ship has sunk. People would rather spend the winter behind barbed wire in Holland's poorest province than be dragged away to unknown parts and unknown destinies deep within Europe, from where only a few indistinct sounds have come back to the rest of us. But the quota must be filled; so must the train, which comes to fetch its load with mathematical regularity. You cannot keep everyone back as being **indispensable** to the camp, or too sick for transport, although you try it with a great many. You sometimes think it would be simpler to put yourself on transport than have to witness the fear and despair of the thousands upon thousands of men, women, children, infants, invalids, the feebleminded, the sick, and the aged who pass through our helping hands in an almost uninterrupted flow.*

Ambiguous: Capable of being understood in two different ways.

Provinces: Outlying areas.

Rucksack: Knapsack.

Accord: Voluntary impulse to act.

Martyr: Someone who chooses to suffer death rather than give up religious beliefs and practices.

Flotsam: Floating wreckage after a ship has sunk.

Indispensable: Absolutely necessary; essential.

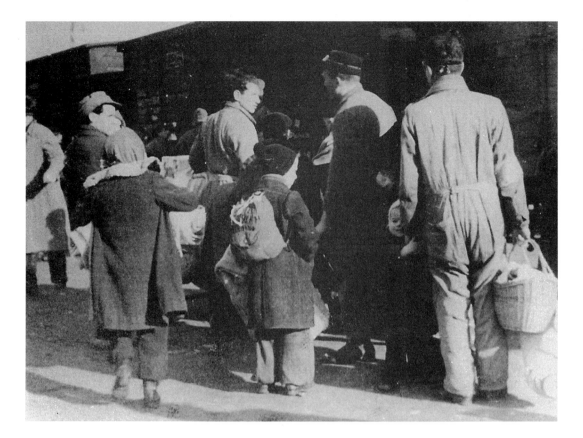

My fountain pen cannot form words strong enough to convey even the remotest picture of these transports. From the outside the impression is of bleak monotony, yet every transport is different and has its own atmosphere.

*When the first transport passed through our hands, there was a moment when I thought I would never again laugh and be happy, that I had changed suddenly into another, older person cut off from all former friends. But on walking through the crowded camp, I realized again that where there are people, there is life. Life in all its thousands of **nuances**—"with a smile and a tear," to put it in popular terms.*

It made a great difference whether people arrived prepared, with well-filled rucksacks, or had been suddenly dragged out of their houses or swept up from the streets. In the end we saw only the last.

Members of the Jewish police, or "Ordedienst," supervise the deportation of Jews from the Westerbork transit camp.

Nuances: Delicately varied aspects or qualities.

*After the first of the police roundups, when people arrived in slippers and underclothes, the whole of Westerbork, in a single horrified and heroic gesture, stripped to the skin. And we have tried, with the close cooperation of people on the outside, to make sure that those who leave are equipped as well as possible. But if we remember all those who went to face the winter in Eastern Europe without any clothes, if we remember the single thin blanket that was sometimes all we were able to **dole** out in the night, a few hours before departure....*

*The slum-dwellers arrived from the cities, displaying their poverty and neglect in the bare **barracks**. Aghast, many of us asked ourselves: what sort of democracy did we really have?*

The people from Rotterdam were in a class by themselves, hardened by the bombing raids. "We don't frighten easily anymore," you often heard them say. "If we survived all that, we'll survive this, too." And a few days later they marched singing to the train. But it was midsummer then, and there were no old people yet, or invalids on stretchers bringing up the rear....

*The Jews from Heerlen and Maastricht and thereabouts came telling stories that **reverberated** with the great send-off the province of Limburg had given them. One felt that morally they could live on it for a long time. "The Catholics have promised to pray for us, and they're better at that than we are!" said one of them.*

*People came with all their **rivalries**. The Jews from Haarlem said somewhat loftily and acidly: "Those Amsterdammers have a grim sense of humor."*

*There were children who would not accept a sandwich before their parents had had one. There was a remarkable day when the Jewish Catholics or Catholic Jews—whichever you want to call them—arrived, nuns and priests wearing the yellow star on their **habits**. I remember two young **novices**, twins, with identical*

Dole: Distribution of goods.

Barracks: An extremely plain structure that provides temporary housing.

Reverberated: Resounded; echoed.

Rivalries: Feelings of a competitive nature.

Habits: Distinctive dress or costume worn by members of a religious order.

Novices: Beginners in a religious order who have not yet taken final vows of devotion.

*beautiful, dark ghetto faces and **serene**, childish eyes peering out from under their skullcaps. They said with mild surprise that they had been fetched at half past four from morning mass, and that they had eaten red cabbage in Amersfoort.*

There was a priest, still fairly young, who had not left his monastery for fifteen years. He was out in the "world" for the first time, and I stood next to him for a while, following his eyes as they wandered peacefully around the barracks where the newcomers were being received.

The others—shaven, beaten, maltreated—who poured in along with the Catholics that day stumbled about the wooden hut with movements that were still unsteady and stretched out their hands toward the bread, of which there was not enough.

A young Jew stood very still next to us. His jacket was much too loose, but a grin broke through his stubbly black beard when he said, "They tried to smash the wall of the prison with my head, but my head was harder than the wall!"

Among all the shaved heads, it was strange to see the white-turbaned women who had just been treated in the delousing barracks, and who went about now looking distressed and humiliated.

*Children dozed off on the dusty plank floor; others played tag among the adults. Two little ones floundered helplessly around the heavy body of a woman lying unconscious in a corner. They didn't understand why their mother just lay there without answering them. A grey-haired old gentleman, straight as an arrow and with a clear-cut, **aristocratic** profile, stared at the whole **infernal canvas** and repeated over and over to himself: "A terrible day! A terrible day!"*

*And among all this, the **unremitting** clatter of a **battery** of typewriters: the machine-gun fire of bureaucracy.*

Serene: Calm.

Aristocratic: Noble; superior.

Infernal: Hellish.

Canvas: Picture.

Unremitting: Persistent.

Battery: A number of similar items used together; a set.

Etty Hillesum (1914-1943)

Etty (Esther) Hillesum was born in Middelburg, Holland. When she was ten years old, Hillesum settled with her family in Deventer, a city in the eastern part of the country by the Ijssel River. Her father, Dr. Louis Hillesum, taught classical languages and served as headmaster in the town gymnasium, or academic high school. Her mother was Russian by birth, having fled to the Netherlands after one of the *pogroms* (organized violent attacks against Jews). Hillesum, along with her two brothers, Mischa and Jaap, were gifted with intelligence and creativity. She received a law degree and studied Slavonic languages and psychology. Mischa, a brilliant musician, became one of the most promising pianists in Europe. Jaap discovered several new vitamins at the age of 17 and went on to become a doctor.

Hillesum's parents were gassed at Auschwitz-Birkenau in September 1943. Etty died two months later; her brother Mischa perished in March 1944. Jaap Hillesum survived the Bergen-Belsen labor camp but died shortly after liberation while returning to Holland.

Heath: Open meadow.

Unwavering: Steady and unchanging.

Imperturbably: With unshakable calmness.

Vespers: An afternoon hour set aside for prayer.

*Through the many little windowpanes one can see other wooden barracks, barbed wire, and a blasted **heath**.*

*I looked at the priest who was now back in the world again. "And what do you think of the world now?' I asked. But his gaze remained **unwavering** and friendly above the brown habit, as if everything he saw was known, familiar from long ago. That same evening, a man later told me, he saw some priests walking one behind the other in the dusk between two dark barracks. They were saying their rosaries as **imperturbably** as if they had just finished **vespers** at the monastery. And isn't it true that one can pray anywhere, in a wooden barracks just as well as in a stone monastery, or indeed, anywhere on this earth where God, in these troubled times, feels like casting his likeness?*

10 July 1943

Maria, hello,

*Ten thousand have passed through this place, the clothed and the naked, the old and the young, the sick and the healthy— and I am left to live and work and stay cheerful. It will be my parents' turn to leave soon, if by some miracle not this week, then certainly one of the next. And I must learn to accept this as well. Mischa insists on going along with them, and it seems to me that he probably should; if he has to watch our parents leave this place, it will totally **unhinge** him. I shan't go, I just can't. It is easier to pray for someone from a distance than to see him suffer by your side. It is not fear of Poland that keeps me from going along with my parents, but fear of seeing them suffer. And that, too, is cowardice.*

This is something people refuse to admit to themselves: at a given point you can no longer <u>do,</u> but can only <u>be</u> and accept. And although that is something I learned a long time ago, I also know that one can only accept for oneself and not for others. And that's what is so desperately difficult for me here. Mother and Mischa still want to "do," to turn the whole world upside down, but I know we can't do anything about it. I have never been able to "do" anything; I can only let things take their course and if need be, suffer. This is where my strength lies, and it is great strength indeed. But for myself, not for others.

Mother and Father have definitely been turned down for **Barneveld***; we heard the news yesterday. They were also told to be ready to leave here on next Tuesday's transport. Mischa wanted to rush straight to the commandant and call him a murderer. We'll have to watch him carefully. Outwardly, Father appears very calm. But he would have gone to pieces in a matter of days in these vast barracks if I hadn't been able to have him taken to the hospital—*

Unhinge: Unsettle, disrupt, or make unstable.

Barneveld: A small town containing a castle where influential Jews were temporarily held or detained.

which he is gradually coming to find just as intolerable. He is really at his wits' end, though he tries not to show it. My prayers, too, aren't going quite right. I know: you can pray God to give people the strength to bear whatever comes. But I keep repeating the same prayer: "Lord, make it as short as possible." And as a result I am paralyzed. I would like to pack their cases with the best things I can lay my hands on, but I know perfectly well that they will be stripped of everything; about that we have been left no doubt. So why bother?

I have a good friend here. Last week he was told to keep himself in readiness for transport. When I went to see him, he stood straight as an arrow, face calm, rucksack packed beside his bed. We didn't mention his leaving, but he did read me various things he had written, and we talked a little philosophy. We didn't make things hard for each other with grief about having to say good-bye. We laughed and said we would see each other soon. We were both able to bear our lot. And that's what is so desperate about this place: most people are not able to bear their lot, and they load it onto the shoulders of others. And that burden is more likely to break one than one's own.

Yes, I feel perfectly able to bear my lot, but not that of my parents. This is the last letter I'll be allowed to write for a while. This afternoon our identity cards were taken away, and we became official camp inmates. So you'll have to have a little patience waiting for news of me.

Perhaps I will be able to smuggle a letter out now and then.

Have received your two letters.

'Bye, Maria—dear friend,

Etty

[postmarked 15 September 1943]

Christine,

Opening the Bible at random I find this: "The Lord is my high tower." I am sitting on my rucksack in the middle of a full freight car. Father, Mother, and Mischa are a few cars away. In the end, the departure came without warning. On sudden special orders from The Hague. We left the camp singing, Father and Mother firmly and calmly, Mischa, too. We shall be traveling for three days. Thank you for all your kindness and care. Friends left behind will still be writing to Amsterdam; perhaps you will hear something from them. Or from my last letter from camp.

Good-bye for now from the four of us.

Etty (Hillesum, pp. 243-360)

What happened next...

Etty Hillesum and her family arrived at Auschwitz-Birkenau from Westerbork on September 10, 1943. The Nazis gassed her mother and father the same day. The Red Cross reported Etty Hillesum's death on November 30, 1943, and her brother Mischa's death on March 31, 1944. After being sent to the Bergen-Belsen labor camp, Etty's brother Jaap survived the war but died shortly afterward, while returning to Holland.

While still at Westerbork, Hillesum sensed she would not return from Auschwitz and gave her diaries to a friend with instructions to pass them on to Dutch writer Klass Smelik. Hillesum wanted the diaries published after her death as a way to share with future generations all that she had witnessed. Smelik could not find a publisher and passed the diaries to his son. In 1980, the diaries were rediscovered and finally published. These diary entries, along with many letters written from Westerbork, encapsulate Hillesum's life from 1941 to her death in 1943.

Did you know...

- Trains left the Westerbork camp every Tuesday from July 1942 until September 1944. These trains consisted of ten to fifteen cattle or freight cars, which together held a thousand or more prisoners. The Nazi guards rode on two attached coach passenger cars.

- The writings of Hillesum can be viewed as the adult counterpart to the work of Anne Frank. Hillesum began her job with the Jewish Council at the same time Frank started her diary and went into hiding. In fact, for a while, Hillesum lived just a few miles away from the now famous annex in Amsterdam where the Franks stayed for two years.

- Hillesum's surviving diary consists of eight tattered notebooks—she took the last one with her on the train to Auschwitz-Birkenau. First published nearly 40 years after her death, her diaries have been translated into 12 languages and printed in 14 countries.

- The pre-war Jewish population of the Netherlands was 140,000. Historians estimate that 75 percent (or 105,000) of the Dutch Jews perished in the Holocaust.

For Further Reading

Adler, David. *We Remember the Holocaust.* New York: Henry Holt, 1989.

Hillesum, Etty. *Etty Hillesum: An Interrupted Life—The Diaries, 1941-1943 and Letters from Westerbork.* New York: Henry Holt, 1996.

I Never Saw Another Butterfly: Children's Drawings and Poems from Terezin Concentration Camp, 1942-1944. Edited by Hana Volavkova. New York: Schocken Books, 1978.

Egon "Gonda" Redlich

Excerpt from *The Terezin Diary of Gonda Redlich,* written from 1942-1944

Edited by Saul S. Friedman
Published in 1992

The Nazi (National Socialist) government of Germany (1933-1945) aimed to remove Jews not only from Germany, which actually had a small Jewish population, but from all of Europe. After 1939, the Nazis replaced their original emigration tactics with deportation (forced exit) measures, which consisted of physically displacing millions of Jews and other victims from their homes to designated ghettos (small sections of a city) or camps. Beginning in 1941, groups of Jews were deported into Eastern Europe in preparation for their physical extermination at death camps specially designed for mass murder. The Nazis used the code name the "Final Solution" to refer to their secret plan of annihilation, which ultimately led to the death of 6 million Jews.

To disguise their murderous intentions from the world, the Nazis funneled Jews through a series of ghettos, then channeled victims into the various death camps. In November 1941, the city of Theresienstadt in Czechoslovakia became a ghetto, or restricted area, for Jews. The Nazis originally planned to present Theresienstadt as a "model Jewish settlement." They used this location to house prominent Jewish artists and intellectuals and other Jews who warranted special merit, such as World War I veterans. But the hope that Theresienstadt would somehow be a refuge was dashed when major deportations to death camps began in January 1942.

Egon "Gonda" Redlich arrived in the ghetto in December 1941. Redlich, a Jewish Czech, had been working as an assistant school director in Prague. He taught Hebrew and Jewish history, coached soccer, counseled students, and was

Children in Theresienstadt.

active in the Zionist movement (which supported the establishment of a Jewish homeland in what is now known as Israel). Due to his reputation as an educator, he was appointed head of the Youth Welfare Department within the ghetto. In this role, Redlich oversaw the housing, care, and education of 15,000 children who passed through Theresienstadt. He began keeping a diary in January 1942 and started a second diary dedicated to his son, Dan, who was born in the ghetto March 16, 1944.

Things to Remember While Reading Redlich's Diary to His Son:

- Redlich's diary to his son gives a day-by-day account of his impressions of life in the ghetto amidst the fateful deportations to the East. As a Jewish official within the ghetto, Redlich received certain privileges; this made him feel guilty.

- While religious marriages did take place in the ghetto, they were not officially recognized by the Nazi government. For this reason, Redlich refers to his child as a *mamzer,* or bastard.

- Gestapo officials outlawed births within the ghetto. Redlich may have referred to this decree when he says that his son Dan was born twice: the first time meaning the mother's decision not to abort, and the second time referring to the actual birth. Redlich and his wife feared the prospect of their captors murdering their infant son.

- Redlich comments about the preparations for the visit of the International Red Cross in June 1944. The Nazis allowed the Red Cross to visit Theresienstadt only after they erected dummy stores, a cafe, a school, and flower gardens. Before the arrival of these visitors, deportations to death camps were accelerated to relieve overcrowding.

- The Nazis discovered that Jewish artists were painting realistic depictions of ghetto life. In July 1944, these artists were taken to a nearby fortress and tortured.

Diary of Dan

March 16, 1944

*This is the fate of our people. That in every generation a new **Pharaoh** arises and brings disaster—destruction to the Jews, fear and dread. Even in our generation a great enemy arose, hated and terrible, an even greater foe than Pharaoh in Egypt. The ancient pharaoh only wanted to kill male infants, but the new pharaoh did not even show compassion for the girls.*

It was forbidden for Jews to be born, for women to give birth. We were forced to hide your mother's pregnancy.

*Even Jews themselves asked us to slaughter you, the fruit of our womb, because the enemy threatened to **levy** punishment on the community for every Jewish birth in the ghetto.*

Pharaoh: A king of ancient Egypt.

Levy: Impose or sentence.

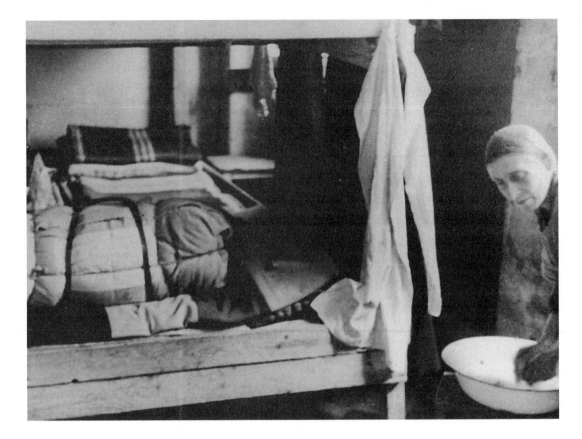

A woman cleans clothing in a Theresienstadt barracks.

Degradations: Insults; the act of wearing down or corrupting.

I hope that you will never have to encounter these **degradations** and insults, the weakness of a people on foreign soil, a people without a homeland.

I admit that your mother was stronger than I. Remember this, my son, and honor your mother, the heroine, among all women. Without her, you would not be alive today. You would not play or be happy. You would not cry or laugh. You would not drink or eat. You would return to the nothingness that was before your birth.

For the light of the world, twice you should give thanks to her. Twice she gave birth to you....

They say that in our generation miracles do not occur. They occur, my son, for by a miracle were you saved, along with her.

*Why did they cancel the order forbidding births when you and others were born? Do you know of the **plagues** that God sent upon Egypt? The last plague also came on our enemies. The wife of an enemy officer gave birth before her time to a stillborn child. Jewish doctors saved the woman. Our enemies felt for the **bereaved** mother and allowed your mother and other mothers to give birth.*

An occurrence or a miracle? I believe that a miracle occurred.

March 20, 1944.

*Your mother had no peace and quiet during her pregnancy. In the outer world, a war raged fiercely, the fourth and fifth year. Men killed each other, without pity or compassion. Our enemies declared that Jews are responsible for the war. A heavy burden **oppresses** us like a dark and heavy cloud. [One] lightning bolt, and we, a Jewish community among tens of thousands of Germans, would burn to ashes.*

You were born on a spring day. There was mud in the streets and the sun was reflected in puddles. Even your birth wasn't easy, as if you did not want to come out from the secure enclosure into this godforsaken world.

March 22, 1944.

*Every day, the Judenältester (head of the Jewish community and its spokesman **vis-a-vis** the Germans) informs the Dienststelle (the German office that supervises the ghetto) of births, number of deaths, and new incidents of dangerous and contagious diseases. After you were born, he [Eppstein] announced your name: Dan Peter Beck, along with thirty dead and another outbreak of typhus. You carried your mother's family name because our marriage was performed in the ghetto and such marriages were not legal according to the law of the land.*

Plagues: Disastrous evil thought to be punishment from God.

Bereaved: Deprived of a loved one by death.

Oppresses: Suppresses; crushes or burdens by abuse of power or authority.

Vis-a-vis: Face-to-face with; in relation to. This parenthetical explanation was added to Redlich's diary by editor Saul S. Friedman.

Sick prisoners lay on pallets in the women's camp at Theresienstadt.

Mamzer: Bastard.

Proletarian: Characteristic of the laboring class—the lowest social and economic class of a community.

Bedbugs: Wingless bloodsucking insects that infest dwellings.

*I must acknowledge that you are my son and I your father. Formally, you are a **mamzer**. Please note that the public formality never was and never will be crucial. What counts is what's inside, the real, inner feelings and not outward appearances, even if they seem important.*

April 13, 1944.

You are beginning to see, to see this world which is draping itself slowly in the green and warmth of spring. The world is casting off winter a little by little. The weather is still cold and there isn't enough coal.

*We live a **proletarian** life. We have a small kitchen where we live, sleep and eat. In the hospital, we found **bedbugs** on you.*

All the surroundings are proletarian. But even here, there are great social differences. We have a small kitchen and live with your mother. Most of the families do not live together, a husband with his wife. There are separate barracks for men and women. There isn't enough food for everyone. We have a lot of advantages. There is no **justification** for this. Sometimes I am ashamed. But for you, they are very important.

A child died from among those whom the Germans permitted to be born. Just think of a mother's sorrow, who by a miracle gained a child only to lose it. It is true that: "The Lord giveth and the Lord taketh away." A great truth—but truth doesn't **console**.

April 13, 1944 [continued].

A strong bond exists among women with the same fate, similar to people who have endured a common experience.... Out of ten women, three children have died. One woman still has not given birth, but will do so shortly.

The mothers go for walks together. They talk to each other, sharing concerns, whether their children are drinking, growing, etc.

[From] a conversation: one mother, a gardener, boasts: "I'm already giving spinach to my son." (The child is three months old.)

Another mother asks: "How much do you give him?"

The mother answers: "A little—but if he wants, he could have a few kilos."

The modesty is hilarious. It is legally impossible to get vegetables into the ghetto. Spinach is stolen, taken **surreptitiously** because if the spinach is handed over to our enemy, it isn't "stolen." "A thief of thieves is innocent...." The boastfulness is ridiculous.

Justification: Way of showing or proving that something is right or reasonable.

Console: Comfort.

Surreptitiously: Secretly.

Yesterday, you reached the weight of three kilos. Your mother was as happy as a small child. She wanted the doctor to come in order to announce the happy news. I went to the doctor and humbly requested that he visit us. Everyone thought it funny to call a doctor for a healthy child. But the mother—who understands a mother's soul? I went humbly because I was a little embarrassed. Your mother was proud—so very proud.

April 13, 1944 [continued].

Today we went out with you for the first time. We have a nice baby carriage, a product of the ghetto. Usually the craftsmanship in the ghetto is second-rate, but this baby carriage is very pretty. It was made by two young men, relatives of your mother. It's made of wood, light as a feather, with springs.

*Bright afternoons. In the city square, the Jewish orchestra played. A Jewish orchestra, as if a hard war full of blood was not being fought, a war of survival. Our enemies have new tactics—eyecatching, building a "**Potemkin Village.**" So the Jewish orchestra played in the ghetto when people were permitted to stroll. But the melody never blocked out the memory of the terrible sacrifice, the **pogroms**, the danger still ahead of us, the danger that only now has a new face.*

June 2, 1944.

One week: for you it means you have grown in weight a few grams. One week: seventy-five hundred Jews left the ghetto and went somewhere unknown, to greet an uncertain future. They went in order to make space. Now the [International Red Cross] Commission will come, inspect the city and express its opinion: everything is fine, the city is beautiful, full of children's houses, coffee houses, beautiful halls and gardens, Jews living in spacious quarters.

Potemkin Village: An impressive facade—meaning false appearance or front—designed to hide an undesirable fact or condition.

Pogroms: Organized acts of violence against Jews.

They ordered us to vacate the ground floor of these houses. The first floors won't be seen by members of the commission at all. In the houses they shall visit everything will be ready and prepared. There won't be any reason to object.

Our enemies are merciful, full of compassion. They will send the sick, the weak, orphans, old people eastward in boxcars. But they have commanded that we change a picture on a wall of a tiger with a small tiger in its mouth, lest it frighten small children. The orchestra is to perform only light music. They want us to be cheerful. They want to show that the Jewish city is happy. They are the merciful ones.

Yesterday, I was at the chicken house. There is a small chicken house. The fowl are raised for the Germans. For the first time in my life I saw a hen turkey, sitting with its young. It reminded me of your mother.

Your baby carriage disappeared. Maybe someone took it and will bring it back later.

Yes, after a few hours the "thief" returned the carriage.

June 23, 1944.

The first movement that you have made with your hands. You already play with your hands and feel everything around you. The first sounds are also heard from your mouth.

Meanwhile, many things have occurred in the great world. The invasion has started. [This is a reference to the 1944 Allied invasion of Normandy, France, a massive campaign led by American general Dwight D. Eisenhower that led to the liberation of Western Europe from German control.] German armies have retreated on all fronts, and here in the ghetto (it is forbidden to use "ghetto"), we play a big game. They built a Potemkin Village. The Red Cross Committee inspected it. They visited us and saw the wonderful children, houses, post office, hospitals, and nice schools. The ban on teaching has not been lifted, but we have schools.... It's enough if there is a sign "school" and magically, overnight, one appears. Jews are laughing, content with their fate.... Thus the committee has looked around and then they left.... The only question is: did they really believe what they were shown?

July 20, 1944.

Your eyes are as blue as heaven. This is no poetic exaggeration. Your eyes stand out the most. Everyone praises them.

Your mother fears that you will have long, drooping ears. Why? Don't ask. Every mother must have the most beautiful, the smartest, the healthiest child.

I wanted to give your mother a gift on her birthday: a picture of you. I asked an artist to draw your picture. Today they arrested the artist and took him to an unknown place. What was his crime? Along with others, he sketched realistic drawings of the ghetto (funerals, hospitals), drawings that served no purpose in the beautification of the city. These drawings were found in the possession of a collector.

October 6, 1944.

*... One of your games! I lift your body and you flutter with your legs like a fish on dry land. Afterwards, I bring my face to yours and you look at me with such surprise. Learn, my son, to read the face of a man, because everything is written in the **countenance** of a man: his wisdom and his **folly**, his anger and his calmness, his happiness and his sadness, his honesty and his falsehood—everything, everything.*

They are making a movie of the ghetto, a nice movie. They ordered the evacuation of two beautified youth homes. But before

Countenance: Face; look; expression.

Folly: Lack of good sense; foolishness.

Gonda Redlich (1916-1944)

Egon "Gonda" Redlich was born in Olmutz, Moravia. The youngest of five children, Redlich grew up in a working-class family. He witnessed the tumultuous years between the world wars when Czechoslovakia struggled to become an independent, democratic nation. The dream of freedom ended when Nazi Germany occupied the country in March 1939. Redlich did not have a strongly religious upbringing, but antisemitic incidents in school led him to join a local Zionist Youth movement. He abandoned his legal studies following the Nazi takeover and prepared to immigrate to Palestine. When deported to Theresienstadt, he led the Youth Welfare Department (*Jugendfursorge*) within the ghetto. The Nazis transported Redlich from Theresienstadt in October 1944 and executed him in Auschwitz.

*they did it, they filmed the "happy" children's houses. A movie on ghetto life which will show the happy life of the Jews, without worry, "with praises and celebrations." (Indeed, they filmed Jews dancing **parlor** dances.) They wanted to film you, in order to show a happy family. Luckily, it did not work out. This film would have been a nice reminder of your infancy in place of a photo. In spite of this, it was depressing and degrading. Even the kings of Egypt did not film the children they wanted to kill.*

We bought a new baby carriage for you. The seller was one of my clerks and wanted to bribe me by giving me the carriage free. We paid one kilo of sugar, one kilo of margarine, and two cans of sardines.

What is going to happen? Tomorrow, we travel, my son. We will travel on a transport like thousands before us. As usual, we did not register for the transport. They put us in without a reason. But never mind, my son, it is nothing. All of our family already left in

Parlor: A room for special functions.

Cunning: Crafty, clever, or sly.

Malice: Ill will; desire to cause pain or injury to another.

Prams: Baby carriages.

Redemption: Process of redeeming or saving; the act of freeing from the consequences of sin.

the last weeks. Your uncle went, your aunt, and also your beloved grandmother. Your grandmother who worked from morning to evening for you and us. Parting with her was especially difficult. We hope to see her there.

It seems they want to eliminate the ghetto and leave only the elderly and people of mixed origin. In our generation, the enemy is not only cruel but also full of **cunning** *and* **malice***. They promise [something] but do not fulfill their promise. They send small children, and their* **prams** *are left here. Separated families. On one transport a father goes. On another, a son. An on a third, the mother.*

Tomorrow we go, too, my son. Hopefully, the time of our **redemption** *is near. (Redlich, pp. 151-61)*

What happened next...

Shortly after the inspection by the International Red Cross in June 1944, the Nazis deported most of the residents of Theresienstadt to Auschwitz. In his entry from this time, Redlich refers to the Nazis filming conditions within the ghetto for propaganda purposes. The majority of the film "cast" was subsequently sent to Auschwitz for extermination. There is no evidence that the inspection of Theresienstadt by the Red Cross aided the masses of Jews in Nazi custody across Europe—in fact, some historians suggest deportations were accelerated due to their intervention.

Although the Nazis established Theresienstadt as a "model Jewish settlement," it eventually became the principal transit camp for Jews from Central Europe. Records show that 140,000 Jews were deported to Theresienstadt. Of these, 33,000 died in the ghetto and 88,000 were sent to extermination camps. A total of 19,000 survived the Holocaust. Of the 15,000 children who passed through Theresienstadt, a mere 100 survived.

Records indicate the Redlich family (Gonda Redlich, his wife, Gerta Beck, and their son, Dan) went directly to Auschwitz in October 1944 and were executed.

Did you know...

- The Nazis created currency (money) for Theresienstadt as part of their attempt to fool the world into believing that the ghetto existed as an autonomous Jewish community.

- The Nazis made a film about Theresienstadt as part of their propaganda campaign designed to deceive the world about the so-called "paradise ghetto." Twenty minutes of "Aktion Z" survived the war and are part of the Yad Vashem archive in Jerusalem.

- Gonda Redlich wrote his diary on sheets of office calendars and used a notebook for his *Diary of Dan.* In preparation for his own deportation, Redlich left the manuscripts behind at Theresienstadt hidden inside a woman's purse.

- Redlich's writings remained undiscovered until 1967, when workers clearing an attic found the documents and turned them over to the State Museum in Prague. The communist Czech government eventually gave copies to Theresienstadt survivors living in Israel.

For Further Reading

I Never Saw Another Butterfly: Children's Drawings and Poems from Terezin Concentration Camp, 1942-1944. Edited by Hana Volavkova. New York: Schocken Books, 1978.

Redlich, Gonda. *The Terezin Diary of Gonda Redlich.* Edited by Saul S. Friedman. Translated by Laurence Kutler. Lexington, Kentucky: University of Kentucky Press, 1992.

Primo Levi

Excerpt from *Survival in Auschwitz*

Translated by Stuart Woolf
First published in 1947; reprinted in 1958

To successfully conduct their plan for the annihilation of European Jews, German Nazis built a series of camps expressly designed for mass murder. The "final solution" to the "Jewish question" required transporting millions of European Jews by train to "extermination" camps, or death camps, located in German-occupied Poland. The largest of these camps, Auschwitz-Birkenau, was situated 30 miles west of Crakow, Poland, near the border of Czechoslovakia. Auschwitz first opened in 1940 as a concentration camp, where prisoners were brutally tortured and used as a source of labor for the war effort. A year later, the Nazis added a larger section called Birkenau, which eventually housed the gas chambers and crematoriums (places for burning corpses) used in the killing operations. The inscription over the main gate of the camp read *Arbeit macht frei,* or "Work leads to freedom." However, most people who arrived at Auschwitz-Birkenau did not survive.

History tells us that as the trains pulled up to the railway platform at the camp, the people inside the boxcars were quickly forced to form two lines. Officers of the Nazi police force (the SS) organized the *Selektion,* or selection, to determine which prisoners would go immediately to the gas chambers and which would be assigned to forced labor. Only about 10 percent of the most able-bodied prisoners were selected for work. Women with small children, children under 15, the elderly, and those who appeared ill or disabled were usually killed the same day they arrived. Believing that they were going to be disinfected for lice, the prisoners entered what looked like large shower rooms. In fact, the

shower rooms were specially equipped gas chambers designed to kill up to 24,000 people a day. Poisonous gas released into the air-tight rooms killed the victims within 15 to 30 minutes. Prisoners assigned to the work crew known as the *Sonderkommando* had the gruesome task of loading bodies from the gas chambers into the crematoria. The corpses of victims were burned either in crematoria or on wooden pyres.

The path for one Auschwitz prisoner, Primo Levi, began in the mountains of northern Italy. At the age of 24, this young Jewish man abandoned his university studies to fight fascism. (Fascism is a political philosophy that places nation and race above the individual. Fascist governments are run by a single, dictatorial leader and are characterized by extreme social and economic restrictions.) After his arrest in December 1943, he was deported to Auschwitz in February 1944. However, Levi's destiny would be different from millions of other Jews: he became one of the very fortunate few who lived to tell the story of his experiences of the death camp.

Hungarian Jewish women await selection on the arrival ramp at Auschwitz.

Things to Remember While Reading *Survival in Auschwitz*:

- Those men and women selected for work in the camps were forced to have their heads shaved and to trade in their personal belongings and clothes for a striped prison uniform. Next they were tattooed with a registration number and then sent to "quarantine" to await work assignment.

- Selection into the labor force usually only postponed death. Prisoners faced a daily fight for survival against starvation, contagious disease, exposure, and the violence of guards. If an inmate escaped from a work site, the remaining laborers often faced execution.

- Levi attributes his survival to luck and "entering the camp in good health and knowing German." Another element of Levi's fate involved fortunate timing: he arrived at Auschwitz in 1944 after the Germans decided to lengthen the average life span of prisoners in order to increase their labor supply. Due to the dates of his arrival and liberation, Levi was also spared the sufferings of a full winter season at Auschwitz.

Survival in Auschwitz

Haftling [prisoner]: I have learnt that I am Haftling. My number is 174517; we have been baptized, we will carry the tattoo on our left arm until we die.

The operation was slightly painful and extraordinarily rapid: they placed us all in a row, and one by one, according to the alphabetical order of our names, we filed past a skilful [skillful] official, armed with a sort of pointed tool with a very short needle. It seems that this is the real, true initiation: only by 'showing one's number' can one get bread and soup. Several days passed, and not a few ***cuffs*** *and punches, before we became used to showing our number promptly enough not to disorder the daily operation of food-distri-*

Cuffs: Strikes or hits with an open hand.

bution: weeks and months were needed to learn its sound in the German language. And for many days, while the habits of freedom still led me to look for the time on my wristwatch, my new name ironically appeared instead, a number tattooed in bluish characters under the skin.

*Only much later, and slowly, a few of us learnt something of the **funereal** science of the numbers of Auschwitz, which **epitomize** the stages of destruction of European Judaism. To the old hands of the camp, the numbers told everything: the period of entry into the camp, the **convoy** of which one formed a part, and consequently the nationality. Everyone will treat with respect the numbers from 30,000 to 80,000: there are only a few hundred left and they represented the few survivals from the Polish ghettos. It is as well to watch out in commercial dealings with a 116,000 or a*

Female Auschwitz inmates sort through a pile of shoes.

Funereal: Suggestive of a funeral.

Epitomize: To serve as the typical or ideal example of.

Convoy: Group moved together.

*117,000: they now number only about forty, but they represent the Greeks of Salonica, so take care they do not pull the wool over your eyes. As for the high numbers they carry an essentially comic air about them, like the words 'freshman' or '**conscript**' in ordinary life. The typical high number is a **corpulent**, **docile** and stupid fellow: he can be convinced that leather shoes are distributed at the infirmary to all those with delicate feet, and can be persuaded to run there and leave his bowl of soup 'in your custody'; you can sell him a spoon for three rations of bread; you can send him to the most ferocious of the **Kapos** to ask him (as happened to me!) if it is true that his is the Kartoffelschalenkommando, the 'Potato Peeling Command,' and if one can be enrolled in it.*

*In fact, the whole process of introduction to what was for us a new order took place in a **grotesque** and sarcastic manner. When the tattooing operation was finished, they shut us in a vacant hut. The bunks are made, but we are severely forbidden to touch or sit on them: so we wander around aimlessly for half the day in the limited space available, still tormented by the parching thirst of the journey. Then the door opens and a boy in a striped suit comes in, with a fairly civilized air, small, thin and blond. He speaks French and we **throng** around him with a flood of questions which till now we had asked each other in vain.*

*But he does not speak willingly; no one here speaks willingly. We are new, we have nothing and we know nothing; why waste time on us? He reluctantly explains to us that all the others are out at work and will come back in the evening. He has come out of the infirmary this morning and is **exempt** from work for today. I asked him (with an **ingenuousness** that only a few days later already seemed incredible to me) if at least they would give us back our toothbrushes. He did not laugh, but with his face animated by fierce **contempt**, he threw at me 'Vous n'êtes pas à la maison.' And it is this refrain that we hear repeated by everyone: you are not at home, this is not a **sanatorium**, the only exit is by*

Conscript: A draftee or someone enrolled by force.

Corpulent: Excessively fat.

Docile: Submissive and easy to teach.

Kapos: Prisoners selected by the Nazis to oversee other prisoners in work groups.

Grotesque: Unnatural; bizarre.

Throng: A crowd of people packed closely together.

Exempt: Excused; freed from duty.

Ingenuousness: Innocence; in a childlike way.

Contempt: The act of looking down on another.

Sanatorium: A place for rest, treatment, or recovery.

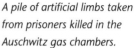

A pile of artificial limbs taken from prisoners killed in the Auschwitz gas chambers.

way of the Chimney. (What did it mean? Soon we were all to learn what it meant.)

And it was in fact so. Driven by thirst, I eyed a fine icicle outside the window, within hand's reach. I opened the window and broke off the icicle but at once a large, heavy guard prowling outside brutally snatched it away from me. 'Warum?' [Why?] I asked him in my poor German. 'Hier ist kein warum' (there is no why here), he replied, pushing me inside with a shove.

The explanation is **repugnant** but simple: in this place everything is forbidden, not for hidden reasons, but because the camp has been created for that purpose. If one wants to live one must learn this quickly and well:

'No Sacred Face will help thee here! it's not

Repugnant: Hostile; repulsive.

A **Serchio** bathing-party ...'

Hour after hour, this first long day of **limbo** draws to its end. While the sun sets in a **tumult** of fierce, blood-red clouds, they finally make us come out of the hut. Will they give us something to drink? No, they place us in line again, they lead us to a huge square which takes up the centre [center] of the camp and they arrange us **meticulously** in squads. Then nothing happens for another hour: it seems that we are waiting for someone.

A band begins to play, next to the entrance of the camp: it plays <u>Rosamunda,</u> the well known sentimental song, and this seems so strange to us that we look **sniggering** at each other; we feel a shadow of relief, perhaps all these ceremonies are nothing but a **colossal farce** in **Teutonic** taste. But the band, on finishing <u>Rosamunda,</u> continues to play other marches, one after the other, and suddenly the squads of our comrades appear, returning from work. They walk in columns of five with a strange, unnatural hard gait, like stiff puppets made of jointless bones; but they walk **scrupulously** in time to the band.

They also arrange themselves like us in the huge square, according to a precise order; when the last squad has returned, they count and recount us for over an hour. Long checks are made which all seem to go to a man dressed in stripes, who accounts for them to a group of **SS** men in full battle dress.

Finally (it is dark by now, but the camp is brightly lit by headlamps and reflectors) one hears the shout 'Absperre!' at which all the squads break up in a confused and turbulent movement. They no longer walk stiffly and erectly as before: each one drags himself along with obvious effort. I see that all of them carry in their hand or attached to their belt a steel bowl as large as a basin.

We new arrivals also wander among the crowd, searching for a voice, a friendly face or a guide. Against the wooden wall of a hut

Serchio: A river flowing from the Tuscany region of Italy to the Mediterranean Sea.

Limbo: A place of confinement; a state of uncertainty.

Tumult: Commotion; disorderly agitation or irregular action.

Meticulously: With extreme care.

Sniggering: Snickering or laughing under one's breath.

Colossal farce: Big joke.

Teutonic: Germanic.

Scrupulously: Exactly and properly.

SS: Nazi political police who also ran the concentration camps.

holocaust

two boys are seated on the ground: they seem very young, sixteen years old at the outside, both with their face and hands dirty with soot. One of the two, as we are passing by, calls me and asks me in German some questions which I do not understand; then he asks where we come from. 'Italien,' I reply; I want to ask him many things, but my German vocabulary is very limited.

'Are you a Jew?' I asked him.

'Yes, a Polish Jew.'

*'How long have you been in the **Lager**?'*

'Three years,' and he lifts up three fingers. He must have been a child when he entered, I think with horror; on the other hand this means that at least some manage to live here.

'What is your work?'

'Schlosser,' he replies. I do not understand. 'Eisen, Feuer' (iron, fire), he insists, and makes a play with his hands of someone beating with a hammer on an anvil. So he is an ironsmith.

'Ich Chemiker,' [I am a chemist] I state; and he nods earnestly with his head, 'Chemiker gut.' But all this has to do with the distant future: what torments me at the moment is my thirst.

'Drink water. We no water,' I tell him.

He looks at me with a serious face, almost severe, and states clearly: 'Do not drink water, comrade,' and then other words that I do not understand.

'Warum?'

*'Geschwollen,' he replies **cryptically**. I shake my head, I have not understood. 'Swollen,' he makes me understand, blowing out his cheeks and sketching with his hands a monstrous **tumefaction***

Lager: Camp.

Cryptically: Secretly or with a hidden meaning.

Tumefaction: The processes of swelling.

Primo Levi (1919-1987)

Primo Levi was born in Turin, Italy, to a long-established Jewish family. He was a chemistry student when anti-Jewish racial laws were introduced in 1938. Despite growing discrimination, Levi completed his doctorate in 1943. When the Italian government of Benito Mussolini fell and Germany took over northern Italy, Levi joined the antifascist resistance. He was arrested by fascist militia in December 1943 and deported to Auschwitz in February 1944.

Following liberation, Levi traveled throughout Eastern Europe for nine months. After returning to his ancestral home in Turin, he established himself as an industrial chemist and raised a family. Haunted by his camp experiences, he wrote *Survival in Auschwitz* in 1947. In his next book, *The Reawakening,* Levy describes his colorful adventures and warm encounters with people he met during his travels following liberation.

For most of his life, Levi worked as a chemist and factory manager while writing his books. He retired in 1977 to devote all of his time to writing. Without leaving behind any explanation, Levi committed suicide in 1987.

of the face and belly. *'Warten bis heute Abend.' 'Wait until this evening,' I translate word by word.*

Then he says: 'Ich Schlome. Du?' I tell him my name, and he asks me: 'Where [is] your mother?'

'In Italy.' Schlome is amazed: a Jew in Italy? 'Yes,' I explain as best I can, 'hidden, no one knows, run away, does not speak, no one sees her.' He has understood: he now gets up, approaches me and timidly embraces me. The adventure is over, and I feel filled with a **serene** *sadness that is almost joy. I have never seen Schlome since, but I have not forgotten his serious and gentle face of a child, which welcomed me on the threshold of the house of the dead....*

Serene: Calm.

Such will be our life. Every day, according to the established rhythm, Ausrücken and Einrücken, go out and come in; work, sleep and eat; fall ill, get better or die....

And for how long? But the old ones laugh at this question: they recognize the new arrivals by this question. They laugh and they do not reply. For months and years, the problem of the remote future has grown pale to them and has lost all intensity in face of the far more urgent and concrete problem of the near future: how much one will eat today, if it will snow, if there will be coal to unload.

If we were logical, we would **resign ourselves** *to the evidence that our fate is beyond knowledge, that every* **conjecture** *is* **arbitrary** *and* **demonstrably devoid of foundation**. *But men are rarely logical when their own fate is at stake; on every occasion, they prefer the extreme positions. According to our character, some of us are immediately convinced that all is lost, that one cannot live here, that the end is near and sure; others are convinced that however hard the present life may be, salvation is probable and not far off, and if we have faith and strength, we will see our houses and our dear ones again. The two classes of pessimists and optimists are not so clearly defined, however, not because there are many* **agnostics**, *but because the majority, without memory or* **coherence**, *drift between the two extremes according to the moment and the mood of the person they happen to meet.*

Here I am, then, on the bottom. One learns quickly enough to wipe out the past and the future when one is forced to. A **fortnight** *after my arrival I already had the prescribed hunger, that chronic hunger unknown to free men, which makes one dream at night, and settles in all the limbs of one's body. I have already learnt not to let myself be robbed, and in fact if I find a spoon lying around, a piece of string, a button which I can acquire without danger of punishment, I pocket them and consider them mine by full right. On the back of my feet I already have those numb sores that will not heal.*

Resign ourselves: Accept as inevitable; give up.

Conjecture: Assumption based on incomplete evidence.

Arbitrary: Random; not based on sense or necessity.

Demonstrably devoid of foundation: Apparently or obviously without basis.

Agnostics: People who believe there is no proof of God's existence but do not deny such a possibility.

Coherence: With clarity, understanding, or consistency.

Fortnight: Two weeks.

Levi

Under SS guard, Auschwitz-Birkenau prisoners unload the property of deported Jews.

I push wagons, I work with a shovel, I turn rotten in the rain, I shiver in the wind; already my own body is no longer mine: my belly is swollen, my limbs **emaciated**, my face is thick in the morning, hollow in the evening; some of us have yellow skin, others grey. When we do not meet for a few days we hardly recognize each other.

We Italians had decided to meet every Sunday evening in a corner of the Lager, but we stopped it at once, because it was too sad to count our numbers and find fewer each time, and to see each other ever more deformed and more **squalid**. And it was so tiring to walk those few steps and then, meeting each other, to remember and to think. It was better not to think. (Levi, pp. 27-37)

Emaciated: Extremely thin due to starvation.

Squalid: A dirty and repulsive appearance.

What happened next...

During his ten months as a prisoner in Auschwitz, Levi was fortunate to be given a labor assignment as a chemist at a nearby rubber factory. He also received extra food from an Italian civilian who worked at the camp. This helped sustain him until the liberation of Auschwitz by the Soviet army on January 27, 1945.

Just before the Soviet liberation, Levi fell ill and was placed in the infirmary. His hospitalization saved his life by preventing him from joining other prisoners on the mass camp evacuation or "death march" ordered by Nazi officials.

Before World War II, about 57,000 Jews lived in Italy—over 10,000 were refugees who had fled Germany and Austria. After the German occupation began in September 1943, thousands of Jews were sent to Italian prisons and concentration camps. More than 8,000 Italian Jews were deported to extermination camps. Levi was one of the very few who survived.

Did you know...

- Under strict supervision by SS guards, a group of prison laborers known as "Kanada" gathered the belongings of recently arrived deportees to the camps. They stored the stolen property in specially built warehouses to be shipped to Germany in support of the war effort. Canada represented wealth to the prisoners, so they adopted its name.

- Historians estimate that 2 million prisoners, mostly Jews, died in the gas chambers at Auschwitz-Birkenau. When the Soviet army liberated the camp in January 1945, they found 7,650 prisoners alive and warehouses crammed with the property stolen from the victims. The storage buildings contained 350,000 men's suits, 837,000 outfits for women, plus 7.7 tons of human hair packed in paper bags for shipping.

- Levi's ancestors settled in the Piedmont region of Italy in 1500. In an interview with author Philip Roth in 1986, Levi discussed his "rootedness." He spent only two years away from Turin and lived his entire life in the same apartment where he was born.

- Levi enjoyed both writing and his career as a chemist and manager at a local paint factory. He felt that working at the factory kept him "in touch with the world of real things."

For Further Reading

Levi, Primo. *Survival in Auschwitz*. Translated by Stuart Woolf. New York: Simon & Schuster, 1996.

Sender, Ruth Minsky. *The Cage*. New York: Macmillan, 1986. Reprinted, Bantam Books, 1988.

Elisabeth Kusserow

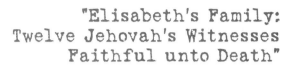

"Elisabeth's Family:
Twelve Jehovah's Witnesses
Faithful unto Death"

From The Other Victims
Written by Ina R. Friedman
Published in 1990

The racialist doctrine that propelled the Nazis (National Socialists) of Germany to murder 6 million European Jews targeted other victims as well. According to Nazi racialist beliefs, German people belonged to a superior "Aryan" race, which was destined to rule the world. With brutal violence, the Nazis attempted to eliminate ethnic or social groups that they felt threatened the purity of German blood. While the racialists considered Jews to be the main enemy of the Aryan race, they also persecuted other supposedly dangerous groups.

Nazi leader Adolf Hitler labeled members of a small Christian denomination, Jehovah's Witnesses, a "degenerate race." Despite being German descendants, Jehovah's Witnesses were considered "enemies of the state." They differed from other Christians by incorporating the teachings of the Bible into their daily lives. Their fundamental beliefs included recognizing only Jehovah God as the supreme sovereign and remaining politically neutral. The Witnesses also believed God would resurrect those who had proved faithful to him until death.

Their religious beliefs put Jehovah's Witnesses at odds with the Nazis. In the fervently nationalist environment of Germany at the time, Jehovah's Witnesses refused political affiliation. (Nationalism is the extreme—in this case, fanatical—devotion to one's country.) They refused to salute the swastika flag of the Nazi state since their beliefs prohibited them from showing obedience to any political authority. They also refused to raise their arms in the "Heil Hitler" salute. By law, this Nazi greeting, meaning "Hail Hitler," took the place of most ordinary greetings used throughout the day, such as "good day." In addition, the beliefs of Jehovah's Witnesses prohibited them from serving in the military—a position the Nazis considered traitorous (constituting treason, or betrayal of one's country). According to the teachings of the Bible, Jehovah's Witnesses believed they must "love thy neighbor as thyself" and only engage in the battle between good and evil on Judgment Day.

Shortly after Hitler rose to power, the Nazis began their persecution of Jehovah's Witnesses. As early as 1933, Witnesses were banned from practicing their faith. They were prohibited from assembling in their churches (called Kingdom Halls). In time, the Nazis sent some Witnesses to concentration camps. Others lost their jobs, civil rights, and welfare benefits.

Like many Jehovah's Witnesses, the Kusserow family practiced the teachings of the Bible. Franz and Hilda Kusserow and their 11 children lived on a farm in Paderborn, where they studied the Bible, took turns with chores, and played musical instruments. By continuing to practice their religion, they incurred the wrath and hatred of Nazi Germans. Excerpted below is an account given by Elisabeth, one of the Kusserow children who survived persecution.

Things to Remember While Reading "Elisabeth's Family":

- Elisabeth Kusserow refers to herself and family members as belonging to the International Bible Students Association. This denomination officially changed its name to Jehovah's Witnesses in 1931.

- The Nazis outlawed the distribution or possession of religious literature, yet the children continued in their mission of faith. Due to his religious practices, their father lost his pension benefits, even though he was a veteran of World War I.

- Jehovah's Witnesses always had the option to end their own persecution by simply renouncing their beliefs. They could free themselves from prisons and concentration camps if they signed government papers. Few chose that option.

Elisabeth's Family:
Twelve Jehovah's Witnesses
Faithful unto Death

*"Quick, Elisabeth," Annemarie shouted, "the **Gestapo**!" In Paderborn, very few people besides the Gestapo had cars. The clouds of dust raised by a car coming down the road signaled danger.*

*Before the Mercedes stopped, I scooped up the **Watchtower** pamphlets and put them in my knapsack. Magdalena stuffed the books into hers. We ran outside and hid the literature behind the bushes. At eight, I knew to walk over to the coops and feed the chickens. Magdalena, who was nine, picked up a bottle to feed the baby lamb.*

We were Jehovah's Witnesses. Our parents, Franz and Hilda Kusserow, had taught their eleven children to hide the books and pamphlets of the International Society of Bible Students if anyone spotted the men from the Gestapo coming toward the house. Anyone found with literature from our Watchtower Society could be arrested.

What a happy family we were before Hitler. Our parents had been sent by the Watchtower Society from Bochum, Germany, to Paderborn to set up a congregation of Jehovah's Witnesses. The house sat on three acres of land. Father organized our daily chores. One week the boys took care of the chickens and ducks and lamb. That week, the girls worked in the garden. Then the following week we switched chores. When the apple and pear trees were ripe, everyone helped to pick the fruit.

But it wasn't all work. Before we went to school in the morning, and in the evening, we sat around the table talking about the Bible and what the passages meant. Mother had graduated from teachers' school, and Father made time for her to teach us music and painting. The house was filled with musical instruments: five violins, a piano, a reed organ, two accordions, a guitar, and several

Gestapo: Secret police force of the Nazi party.

Watchtower: Religious booklet published and distributed by Jehovah's Witnesses.

flutes. What joyful music we made as we played from the book <u>*Hymns to Jehovah's Praise*</u>*....*

In 1936, the Nazis tried to get Jehovah's Witnesses to **renounce** *their faith. When the Gestapo knocked on our door, one of them waved a piece of paper in Father's face and shouted, "Franz Kusserow, you must sign this document promising never to have anything to do with the International Society of Bible Students. If you don't, you will be sent to prison."*

The whole family stood, dumbfounded. Promise not to be Jehovah's Witnesses? Hitler was truly Satan.

Father read aloud the first paragraph. "'I have recognized that the International Society of Bible Students spreads a false doctrine and pursues goals entirely **hostile to the state under the cover of** *religious activity.'" Father shook his head. "This is ridiculous, I can't sign."*

The S.S. man, who was about the same age as my oldest brother, became angry. "Stubborn fool!"

I was shocked; no one ever talked to Father that way. He was one of the most respected people in Paderborn.

The S.S. man turned to Mother. "And you? If you don't, your children will be without parents."

Mother removed her apron and placed it over the chair. "No, I cannot sign. Annemarie" —Mother turned to my oldest sister— "take care of the children."

The agent shoved my parents outside and into the car.

Paul-Gerhard, who was five, began to cry. Hans-Werner, who was six, put his arms around his little brother. Fifi, our dachshund, began to growl. I bent down to calm her and to hide my tears.

Renounce: To refuse to follow or obey any further.

Hostile to the state: Opposing the Nazi-run government.

Under the cover of: Using as an excuse.

After a few days the Nazis released Mother from prison. They kept Father. Why was it a crime to be a Jehovah's Witness? Mother couldn't understand why they released her, because she still refused to sign the paper. Mother and my oldest brother, Wilhelm, made sure we followed Father's schedule and always did our chores. But how we missed Father and his talks about the Bible! What a joyful reunion we had when he was released a year later. All thirteen of us took up our instruments, and the house resounded with hymns of praise....

As the years passed, the situation in school became more and more painful. Every day, the teacher **reprimanded** *me for not saluting the Nazi flag. The big black* **swastika** *on the red banner flew over the schoolhouse and hung on a pole in every classroom. My stomach churned as I tried to think of how I could avoid saluting it or saying "Heil Hitler." My parents had taught me to salute only Jehovah God. To salute a flag or a person was the same as worshiping* **idols**. *I wouldn't sing the horrible Nazi songs, either. I kept my lips together.*

The teacher always watched me. "So, Elisabeth, you do not want to join in praise of our leader. Come to the front of the classroom." She turned to the others. "Children, Elisabeth thinks it is all right to insult our leader. Tell us why, Elisabeth."

"Acts 4:12 of the New Testament says, 'There is no salvation in anyone else except Jesus Christ.'"

"Imagine, Elisabeth Kusserow believes in that ridiculous New Testament."

The children laughed. I couldn't understand why. All of them went to church. On the way home from school, they pushed me and threw my books to the ground. It got worse when Hans-Werner and then Paul-Gerhard were old enough to go to school. Now I had to worry about the children tormenting them.

Reprimanded: Scolded severely.

Swastika: A Greek cross with bent arms representing good luck or well-being. The symbol was adopted by the Nazi party and has since taken on a negative meaning.

Idols: False gods.

Sachsenhausen prisoners wearing identification triangles. Jehovah's Witnesses wore purple triangles; political prisoners wore red; "asocials" wore black; homosexuals wore pink; habitual prisoners wore green; and Jews wore yellow.

Our troubles grew. It wasn't just the terror of going to school. The Nazis cut off Father's pension from World War I because he still refused to say "Heil Hitler." It was hard doing without the money, even though my older brothers and sisters had jobs. We planted more vegetables and canned as much as we could. In 1938, the Gestapo arrested Father for a second time. What could be wrong in obeying Jehovah God?

In the spring of 1939, the principal came into my class. "Elisabeth, since you refuse to salute our flag and say 'Heil Hitler,' it is obvious that your parents are neglecting your spiritual and moral development. I have taken it upon myself to obtain a court order to remove you and your two younger brothers from your home. The three of you will be sent to a place where you will get proper instruction." He pulled me into his office. Paul-Gerhard, who was then eight, and Hans-Werner, who was nine, stood there trembling.

At thirteen, the words made no sense to me. "Our parents raised us according to the teachings of Jehovah God," I protested.

"Quiet! This policeman will take you to your new home."

I was so upset, I hadn't noticed the policeman standing next to the window.

"Please, please, let me call my mother." I begged. "She'll be frantic when we don't come home."

"**Traitors** are not to know what happens to their children."

For several months Mother tried to find out where we were. She went to the police, called orphanages, hospitals, and prisons. Finally, she reached the clerk at the reform school in Dorsten who admitted we were there. Secretly, Mother sent us letters. "Always know that we love you. Be **steadfast** in your faith to Jehovah God. One day we will be together in heaven or on earth."

The director of the reform school couldn't understand why we were there. "You are the best behaved children I have ever seen. It's ridiculous to have you here with these **delinquents**." He sent a letter to Mother, "Your children will be arriving in Paderborn on Friday at two P.M."

As we started to climb the steps of the train, two men stopped us. "The director was guilty of **misconduct**. You are coming with us." They drove us to Nettelstadt, a Nazi training school.

"Don't cry," I told the boys. "Jehovah God will one day rule the earth. We will see our family, either here or in heaven." I didn't feel as brave as I sounded.

Traitors: People who are disloyal to their country and attempt to overthrow the government.

Steadfast: Firm in belief; faithful; immovable.

Delinquents: People who behave in an unacceptable way; violators of duty or law.

Misconduct: Improper behavior; intentional wrongdoing.

At the training school, the teachers became furious when we still refused to salute the flag or say "Heil Hitler." In punishment, the three of us were sent to different places. I kept worrying about Paul-Gerhard and Hans-Werner. They were just little boys.

For six years I remained in the custody of the Nazis, praying that all of my family would survive the war....

One sunny spring morning, I was awakened by songbirds. I ran downstairs. The doors were unlocked. The matron had fled. The war was over! There was nothing to stop me from going home! I said a prayer of thanksgiving and ran to the railway station. The station was jammed with people trying to board the trains. Somehow I squeezed onto the platform between the cars. As the train chugged into the station at Paderborn, I began to have fears. What would I find? Had the boys been forced to go into the army? Was the house still standing?

Would my family recognize me? I had left an awkward teenager. Now I was nineteen. The train stopped. Slowly, I climbed down the steps onto the station platform. I looked at the men and women and children searching the faces of those stepping off the train.

"Elisabeth," three voices shouted.

"Praise Jehovah God," I said aloud as Hans-Werner and my sisters Waltraud and Hildegard ran toward me.

"We've been meeting every train," Hildegard said, her voice breaking, "praying some of us would be on it." She hugged me so hard, I thought my bones would break.

I had so many questions, I didn't know where to begin. Hans-Werner looked so much like [our older brother] Siegfried [who had died in an accident at the age of 21], my heart ached. We walked hand in hand toward the house.

I could scarcely recognize my sisters. Waltraud had been in prison for two years. Hildegard was so thin she looked older than Mother had looked when I last saw her. Hildegard had been at the Ravensbruck concentration camp with Mother and Annemarie.

"Somehow we were separated when we were ordered to march out of the camp," Hildegard said. "I don't know where they are...."

"Tell me everything that happened while I was away. For six years, I've had no news."

Hildegard and Waltraud began to cry. Hans-Werner brushed his tears away with his sleeve. "It was terrible," Hildegard said. "In 1940, Wilhelm was shot for refusing to serve in the army. Mother asked the authorities to permit Father to attend the funeral. By some miracle, he was released. Even in our sadness, we couldn't help noticing how thin and worn he looked. It was such a comfort to have him, if only for the hour of the funeral.

Waltraud nodded. "It was a beautiful funeral. Karl-Heinz read from the Scriptures. But when the Gestapo shouted 'Heil Hitler' at the end of the service, Karl-Heinz refused to return the salute. The Gestapo beat Karl-Heinz and left him on the ground. A few weeks later, they went to the factory where he was working and took him away. We've heard nothing since then...."

"Everyone else was taken away, because we would not renounce our faith. We don't know if the others are dead or alive, except for Wolfgang."

I looked from one face to another.

"When he refused to serve in the army, he was beheaded. It happened on March 28, 1942," Waltraud said softly.

"He was only twenty years old." I couldn't stop trembling.

Hildegard held me in her arms. "Come into the garden, Elisabeth. Mother hid Wilhelm's and Wolfgang's letters so whoever came back would have them. They have been a great comfort to us."

In the garden where I had once played with the baby lamb, I read aloud Wilhelm's letter. "My dear parents and brothers and sisters, ... You know already how much you mean to me.... I have been faithful until the death as it is stated in the scripture.... It is true that it is difficult to follow this course.... But we must still love God above all as our leader Jesus Christ taught. When we stand steadfastly for him, he will reward us...." I put the letter down and began to sob. Wilhelm was only twenty-six.

Among Wolfgang's letters, I found a copy of the defense he had given for refusing to serve in the army. "I was brought up as one of Jehovah's Witnesses according to God's Word contained in the Holy Scriptures.... The greatest and most holy law he gave mankind is, 'You shall love God above all else and your neighbor as yourself....'

"We are living in a time ... that has been predicted in the Bible. People today are unbelievers; they do not respect the Bible.... They ridicule Jehovah's name and say He is a God of the Jews and persecute those who keep God's laws and apply them.

"If Jehovah's Witnesses refuse military service for the reasons above, because God's laws forbid it, they are sentenced to death by the military court, only because they remain faithful to Jehovah and obey Him first....

"For it is better to suffer because you are doing good, if the will of God wishes it, than because you are being evil."

I hugged the letter to my chest. My brothers had left us a great treasure. (Kusserow in Friedman, pp. 49-57)

What happened next...

The Nazis scattered members of the Kusserow family across Germany during the war. Two of the Kusserow sons were executed for failing to serve in the German army. After the war, Elisabeth and her brother Hans-Gerhard returned home safely from state-run reform schools. Their father, Franz Kusserow, came back from prison with a broken leg and in poor health. Another brother, Karl-Heinz, spent the war in Dachau, where he contracted tuberculosis (a debilitating disease of the lungs). Although he did make it home, he died a year later from his illness. Elisabeth's mother and her sisters Annemarie and Magdalena also returned from their imprisonment shortly after the war.

Nazi brutality only strengthened the faith of the Jehovah's Witnesses. While succeeding in breaking the will of millions of people across Europe, Nazi terror could not crack the resolve of thousands of Jehovah's Witnesses. Of the 25,000 Witnesses in Germany, very few renounced their faith to earn freedom. (Those who did were acting in the interest of their children—they felt it was the only way to keep them from being raised in state-run Nazi homes.) The Nazis imprisoned up to 10,000 Jehovah's Witnesses, many in concentration camps. After followers of Judaism, Jehovah's Witnesses were the most persecuted of religious groups. However, unlike the Jews, the Witnesses were never targeted for systematic murder.

Did you know...

- Heinrich Himmler, chief of the Nazi SS, or political police, used Jehovah's Witnesses as an example of unshakable faith. He stated that when all SS officers possessed that same depth of conviction in National Socialism, Nazism would be permanently secure.

- Because Witnesses did not attempt to escape or resist guards in prison, they were often selected as domestic servants by Nazi camp officials and officers.

- All inmates held in concentration camps wore an identifying patch sewn to their prison uniforms. Color-coded triangles indicated the category or type of prisoner. Jehovah's Witnesses wore purple triangles; political prisoners wore red; "asocials" wore black;

homosexuals wore pink; habitual prisoners wore green; and Jews wore yellow.

- According to estimates, today there are nearly 5 million Jehovah's Witnesses worldwide in nearly 70,000 congregations from 229 countries.

For Further Reading

Bachrach, Susan D. *Tell Them We Remember.* Boston: Little, Brown, and Company, 1994.

Friedman, Ina R. *The Other Victims.* Boston: Houghton Mifflin, 1990.

Rogasky, Barbara. *Smoke and Ashes: The Story of the Holocaust.* New York: Holiday House, 1988.

Hirsch Grunstein

Excerpt from
Hiding to Survive

Written by Maxine Rosenberg
Published in 1994

During the Nazi (National Socialist) reign, the fate of European Jews depended greatly on each conquered country's wartime relationship with Germany. Wherever German rule was total and uncontested, or unchallenged, the Jews of that nation faced almost certain annihilation (complete destruction). About 90 percent of the Jews living in Germany, Austria, Poland, the Baltic counties (Lithuania, Latvia, and Estonia) and the Protectorate of Bohemia and Moravia perished in the Holocaust. Better odds for survival existed for those Jews living in countries that had remained neutral before German invasion and occupation. In the spring of 1940, German armies invaded several neutral countries in Europe—Norway, Denmark, Belgium, Luxembourg, and the Netherlands—which all quickly capitulated (or fell) to Nazi control. Each of these countries was eventually forced to implement anti-Jewish measures.

German armies attacked Belgium in May 1940. The Nazi government quickly incorporated several districts into the Reich (pronounced RIKE; German word for "empire") and placed the majority of Belgium under military rule. Six months after occupation began, the Nazi regime issued the first anti-Jewish decrees (orders or laws), which barred certain Jewish religious practices, defined Jews according to German racialist standards, and excluded them from positions in civil service (government management), education, law, and the media. Other decrees required Jews to register themselves with the authorities and to surrender their assets (wealth and belongings) and businesses in a process called "Aryanization."

In the fall of 1941, the Nazis began the practice of isolating the Jews from other Belgians. Jews were required to live in certain cities and abide by nightly curfews. In the city of Antwerp, they were prohibited from using public parks or walking on the streets. Eventually, laws expelled Jewish children from public schools, instituted forced labor, and required all Jews to wear Star of David arm bands (symbolizing Judaism). In the summer of 1942, the Nazis began deporting Jews from Belgium to the Auschwitz-Birkenau death camp via transit camps.

At the time of the German invasion, 90,000 Jews lived in Belgium, most of them refugees or immigrants. When the Nazis first occupied Belgium, some 25,000 Jews fled to France. With the help of sympathetic non-Jewish Belgians and the organized underground resistance, about 20,000 Jews went into hiding and were safeguarded from their persecutors.

Such remarkable kindness and courage helped save the Grunstein family. They immigrated to Belgium from Poland in 1930. About the time the deportations began, Hirsch and Salomon Grunstein and their parents went into hiding. Hirsch and Salomon were sent to live in a small village with a couple they did not know. Over the next two years, these strangers became more like family as they risked their lives to protect the two brothers.

Things to Remember While Reading about Hirsch Grunstein:

- Those who helped the Jews placed themselves in great danger. Both of the people who helped Grunstein—Adrienne and Gaston—faced punishment and even death if they were caught.

- Grunstein went into hiding in 1942 when he was 14 years old. For two years he lived with Adrienne and Gaston, staying inside their house by day to hide from villagers. Since his younger brother, Salomon, could pass as a non-Jew, he went to school and played with neighborhood children.

- To help them assimilate, the brothers changed their names. Hirsch became "Henri" and Salomon became "Sylvain."

Hiding to Survive

For the first two years of my life I lived in Poland. Then my family moved to Antwerp, Belgium, where my father was in the diamond business. Although I went to a state high school and was called "Henri" there, my family was very religious. We didn't *travel or turn on lights on the Sabbath, and I always kept my head covered.*

As I was growing up, my parents talked about why we had left Poland. They said it was dangerous for us there, because the police did not protect the Jews. Yet my parents didn't seem to mind that in Belgium there were signs saying JEWS DON'T APPLY HERE FOR APARTMENTS. They felt this country was safe. Then in 1940 the Germans invaded. I was twelve at the time, and my brother Salomon was six and a half.

Within two years Jews weren't allowed on the street, and there was a rumor that Jews were being sent back to their country of origin. When my mother heard this, she cried, "Go back to Poland? We might as well throw ourselves into the river."

*That's when she and my father decided to hide my brother and me. She spoke to a friend whose two young sons were already with the Van Dammes, a **Gentile** couple in a small village. The couple's daughter, Alice, had made the arrangements and had now convinced her brother, Gaston, and his wife, Adrienne, to hide Jewish children too.*

Gaston and Adrienne were in their twenties and were hoping to get very young children. When Adrienne came with Alice to meet us, she was disappointed to see how old we were. Yet she and Gaston decided to take us in anyhow, thinking the war would be over soon and our stay would be short.

Meanwhile my father was saying that maybe our family should escape to Switzerland. He told Adrienne that if we came to live with her, we'd arrive unannounced on a Saturday, the day Belgians dressed up and visited one another.

By the end of the week my father had contacted my former schoolteacher, René Govaerts, who was helping to hide Jews. He

Gentile: A non-Jewish person.

asked René to take us to Adrienne and Gaston's house on the Friday night of Rosh Hashanah, the Jewish New Year, when we'd ordinarily never travel. My father said that if we were going to **play Aryan**, we might as well do it all the way. He even told my brother and me not to cover our heads anymore. And he changed our last name to "Govaerts" to sound Gentile, while Salomon became "Sylvain," and I kept "Henri."

My father packed one tiny suitcase for both of us so we wouldn't attract attention. In mine he put a little prayer book and the Book of Psalms. "If Mama and I don't survive, I want you to teach your brother about Judaism," he said. He also made me memorize the address of my uncle in America in case I needed to get in touch with him after the war....

At ten the next morning we arrived at Adrienne's house and surprised her as she was busily scrubbing her patio. Later Gaston came home and was happy to see us. He and Adrienne gave us their room with the big bed, while they moved into a smaller one. They wanted us to be comfortable and did whatever they could to cheer us up, even staging wrestling matches on the kitchen floor. But Salomon and I were very sad. We missed our parents.

From the beginning I felt responsible for reminding Salomon he was a Jew and insisted that he pray every day. But he wanted to play with the village kids, while I read books and took long walks. Soon he was speaking the local **Flemish dialect** and wearing wooden shoes and peasant clothing like a native.

Two weeks after we arrived, my parents suddenly appeared. They were going to be staying close by, with Adrienne's parents. At first I was thrilled to have them near, but then I realized this wasn't a good arrangement. Because they had heavy Polish accents, they couldn't move about freely, so visiting them was like seeing people in jail. Also, Salomon and I were running to Adrienne's parents' house too often, and Adrienne was afraid the villagers might

Play Aryan: Act like a German; engage in non-Jewish activities, in this case, traveling on a holy day.

Flemish: A Germanic language spoken in Belgium.

Dialect: A regional variety of a language.

become suspicious. So my parents went to live with her sister in another town.

By the middle of October, it was obvious the war was not ending quickly. As city kids supposedly on a short vacation, Salomon and I should have been returning home, especially since the local children my age were already in school or taking up a trade. When I asked Gaston if I could help him and his father in their blacksmith shop, he said he didn't want me around the glowing hot irons.

Meanwhile he and Adrienne had already told the villagers that Salomon was staying with them longer because he was sickly and needed fresh country air. But they couldn't think of an excuse for my being there. So they said I should stay indoors and keep out of sight.

Now that Salomon and I were going to be around for a while, Adrienne and Gaston reclaimed their bedroom. Since I had to be inside, they let me use it during the day because it was large and had a window. If I stood in the shadows, I could watch the people on the street.

Other than that there wasn't much for me to do. After I said my morning prayers, read the newspaper, and ate the meals that Adrienne brought up for me, I was very bored. I knew that all my Gentile friends in Antwerp had started their third year of Latin and algebra and thought maybe I should teach myself those subjects. When Govaerts came to visit Adrienne and Gaston (they had become friends), I asked him to bring me some textbooks. But as soon as I took one look at the books, I put them aside for another day, thinking I had plenty of time to study....

In the late spring, it was even harder for me. Through the open bedroom window I sometimes heard music and saw people going to the cafes or for a walk. I had just turned fifteen, and I too

wanted to be free to come and go. Instead I was in my own private prison. Other than the cat, there was no one to keep me company. Sometimes Salomon came up, but he was five and a half years younger than I, and we didn't share the same interests.

Each day I became more and more furious. I'd read the ritual prayers, wanting to hear about a God who would sock it to the Nazis, but that wasn't the kind I was finding. Although I knew that there were periods in history when Jews suffered, I wondered, Why is this happening to me? Sometimes I'd remember Bible passages with the phrase "because of your sins" and think maybe I was being punished for having torn paper on the Sabbath. For spite, I'd rip up paper to see what might occur.

*Then one day I opened the Hebrew Book of Psalms that my father had slipped into my suitcase. I wasn't even sure what I was looking for. Suddenly I came upon phrases like "**smite** the enemy" and "shatter them to pieces." The words startled me. They had been written thousands of years ago, and yet they seemed to be directed at the Germans. For the first time in months, I was excited. I felt a connection in time and space to the Jewish people.*

I couldn't wait to read more of the Psalms and made them my reward for the day. I'd rush through my morning prayers, do my exercise, and read the newspaper, building up energy toward the Psalms. The words were so gripping, I felt as though I was being transported to another world....

Around this time Gaston gave me a book titled <u>Automobile Course,</u> written by an engineer. As a blacksmith, Gaston knew that the days of the horse and wagon were numbered, and he thought I would be interested in what the future might bring. Although the book was very thin, it carefully detailed how a car worked, starting with the very first raw explosion within the engine to the car's being thrust into motion. I was fascinated. Then and there in my isolated room I decided to become an engineer and an inventor....

Smite: To attack or strike suddenly or sharply.

Occasionally on a holiday or a Sunday Adrienne and Gaston told people that I had come for a short visit, having arrived from the city on the night train....

On some of these "visits," Adrienne took Salomon and me to see our parents. Although I was happy being with them, the get-togethers were always sad. Instead of the four of us sitting down to dinner like a real family, I felt more like a guest who had to leave at a certain hour.

Meanwhile Salomon had learned how to move among the villagers without arousing the slightest suspicion. Whenever he got into a fight with another child, he was the first to throw the insult, "You Jew!"

One time he was on the road when the priest came by, leading a procession through the village. Salomon saw the people go down on one knee and cross themselves, and he did the same. Later he came home all excited and proudly told Adrienne what had happened. From my room upstairs I overheard Adrienne say, "You did just fine...."

*One day in April of 1944 they captured **a courier from the underground** and found him with a list of Jewish children being hidden. From the list, the Germans learned about the two young boys who were staying with Gaston's parents and came to get them. Gaston, who had been in the house, ran for the fields under a hail of bullets.*

The Germans then came looking for him at our house. When Adrienne said she didn't know where he was, they arrested her and me. Salomon, who had been watching all this from the street, hid in the field until dark, and then he went to Adrienne's mother's house.

The Germans took all of us on the list to a temporary shelter for children until we could be deported. They didn't know that the

A courier from the underground: A messenger from a secret group or operation designed to aid and protect the Jews.

Hirsch Grunstein (c. 1928—)

Hirsch Grunstein immigrated to the United States in 1958 and is an engineer who works in data communications. His story, included in Maxine Rosenberg's *Hiding to Survive*, documents the plight of Jews in Poland and Belgium during Hitler's reign. Hirsch and his brother, Salomon, apparently made a lasting impression on the couple who helped them to hide during World War II. When Adrienne and Gaston had a son, they gave him Salomon's war name, "Sylvain."

Following the death of Grunstein's parents, his rescuers told him: "As long as we are alive, you'll have another home." Both brothers, along with their families, remained close to Adrienne and Gaston. In 1993 the Grunsteins helped the pair celebrate their joint eightieth birthday. Le Consistorie Central Israelite de Belgique awarded Adrienne, Gaston, and Gaston's sister Alice with a medal and certificate on behalf of the entire Jewish-Belgian community.

Belgian underground was helping us there, making sure we had enough food while they planned for our escape. Oddly, at the shelter I felt more free than at Adrienne and Gaston's house. At least I was with Jewish kids my age. Still, I was petrified that at any moment the German police would surround the place and take us away.

Four months later, just two days before the Germans were to deport us, the Belgian underground got us out of the shelter and brought us to a little village. Soon after, Belgium was liberated, and within a few days my parents found me. We returned to Antwerp and waited to hear news about Adrienne. The day she was let out of the concentration camp, I went to visit her. (Grunstein in Rosenberg, pp. 95-103)

What happened next...

As testimony to the strength of the resistance effort and the compassion of non-Jewish citizens, about 25,000 Jews in Belgium managed to live through the war. The Grunsteins were among 8,000 Polish Jews who survived. Many Jews died from hunger, disease, exhaustion, or random violence before being deported to extermination camps. About 40,000 of the Jews living in Belgium perished: this figure represents 60 percent of the nation's Jewish population. Memorials honoring the slain Jews of Belgium were unveiled at Anderlecht in 1970 and at Yad Vashem in Jerusalem in 1987. Memorial marches take place annually to the Dossin transit camp at Mechelen, the place where thousands of Jews departed for the extermination camps. Yad Vashem has awarded the Righteous Among the Nations medal to dozens of non-Jewish Belgians for helping to save Jews during the war.

Did you know...

- Between 10,000 to 50,000 children throughout Europe were hidden from the Nazis during the war. More precise estimates are impossible because of the absence of records.

- The Jews of Belgium were active in the underground resistance movement, including the Red Orchestra spy ring. This pro-Soviet espionage network managed to penetrate important military and civilian offices in the German capital of Berlin.

- In April of 1943, armed Jewish resisters intercepted a deportation train carrying Jews from a transit camp in Belgium to the Auschwitz death camp. This operation is the only recorded instance of an armed attack against a train taking Jews to their death.

For Further Reading

Kuper, Jack. *Child of the Holocaust.* New York: Doubleday, 1967. Reprinted, New American Library, 1987.

Reiss, Johanna. *The Upstairs Room.* New York: Crowell, 1972. Reprinted, Harper & Row, 1990.

Rosenberg, Maxine B. *Hiding to Survive: Stories of Jewish Children Rescued from the Holocaust.* New York: Clarion Books, 1994.

index

Bold type indicates main documents and speaker profiles
Italic type indicates volume numbers
Illustrations are marked by (ill.)

H

Haferkamp, Frau Wilhelmine *1:* 4-5, **62-72**
Hannah Senesh: Her Life & Diary 2: 259-71
Heine, Heinrich *1:* 44-45
Hemingway, Ernest *1:* 34
Heroic Heart: The Diary and Letters of Kim Malthe-Bruun, 1941-1945
    2: **272-86**
Hess, Rudolph *2:* 414, 425
Heydrich, Reinhard *1:* 75-76, 95-96, 105, 167; *2:* 332
The Hiding Place 2: 256, 289
Hiding to Survive 1: **243-52**
Hillesum, Etty *1:* 159, **192-204**
Himmler, Heinrich *1:* 163, 167, 241; *2:* 255, 260-61, 385, 393, 424, 438
Hitler, Adolf *1:* 2, **19-32**, 20 (ill.), 27 (ill.), 61, 94, 192; *2:* 253, 384-95
Hitler Youth (Hitler Jugend) *1:* 5, 66; *2:* 315, 388
Holocaust (definition) *1:* 155
Horst Wessel song *1:* 41
Höss, Rudolph *1:* 157, **160-75**, 170 (ill.)
Hotel Royal *1:* 79 (ill.), 81

I

Inside the Third Reich 2: 350, **384-95**
International Bible Students Association *1:* 232
International Conference on Refugees *1:* 79 (ill.), 81
The International Jew 1: 16, 17
International Military Tribunal *2:* 350-51, 394, 395
International Red Cross *1:* 203, 207, 216; *2:* 319, 396, 438
An Interrupted Life—The Diaries, 1941-1943 and Letters
    from Westerbork 1: 159, **192-204**

J

Jackson, Robert H. *2:* 351, **411-25**
Jehovah's Witnesses *1:* 144, 159, 231-42; *2:* 353
Jewish Council (Joodsche Raad) *1:* 123-24, 130, 194
Jewish migration *1:* 74, 80-81
Jewish police (Ordedienst) *1:* 197 (ill.)
"Jewish Question in Occupied Territory" *1:* 95–96
Jewish Residential Quarter (Judischer Wohnbezirk) *1:* 106
Judenrat *1:* 97, 102 (ill.), 108, 123

K

Kanada *1:* 229
Kaplan, Chaim A. *1:* 76, **93-106**
Kapo *1:* 171
Keitel, Wilhelm *5:* 414, 419 (ill.)
Keller, Helen *1:* 34
Keneally, Thomas *2:* 332, 346
Kibbutz *2:* 260, 264
Kindergeld *1:* 62, 71
Kinderreiche (definition) *1:* 64
King Christian X of Denmark *2:* 272
"The Knife" 2: **396-410**